12⁵⁰

Imperial San Francisco

Imperial San Francisco

Politics and Planning in an American City, 1897–1906

Judd Kahn

UNIVERSITY OF NEBRASKA PRESS • LINCOLN AND LONDON

The publication of this book was assisted by a grant from The Andrew W. Mellon Foundation.

Copyright © 1979 by the University of Nebraska Press
All rights reserved

Manufactured in the United States of America

Library of Congress Cataloging in Publication Data

Kahn, Judd, 1940–
 Imperial San Francisco

 Includes bibliographical references and index.
 1. San Francisco—City planning—History. 2. San Francisco—Politics and government. 3. City planning—California—Case studies. I. Title.
HT168.S2K34   309.2'52'0979461   79-9096
ISBN 0-8032-2702-7

For my mother and father
Miriam and Abraham Kahn

Contents

List of Illustrations ix
List of Tables and Graphs x
Acknowledgments xi
Introduction 1
1. **Metropolitan Ups and Downs**
   San Francisco in the Nineteenth Century 5
2. **Conflict and Conciliation**
   Labor, Business, and Politics in San
     Francisco, 1897–1906 29
3. **A New San Francisco**
   James Duval Phelan and the City Beautiful 57
4. **An Image of Order**
   The Burnham Plan for San Francisco 80
5. **The Ideal and the Real**
   "Civicism" and Shady Politics 103
6. **Relief and Rehabilitation**
   The Power of Ideology 128
7. **Urban Phoenix**
   Broader Lines and Wider Streets 154
8. **The Defeat of Planning**
   Politics and Property Rights 177
Conclusion: Planning and Politics
   The Search for Authority 210
Appendix: Tables 1–10 217
Notes 227
Index 257

Illustrations

All following page 146

1. Daniel Hudson Burnham
2. The Burnham Plan
3. Downtown, March 1906
4. East down Geary Street
5. Nob Hill
6. View from Nob Hill
7. Refugee tent camp
8. Relief cottages
9. James Duval Phelan
10. Abraham Ruef
11. Panorama, 1906
12. Kearny Street
13. Rebuilding on Kearny Street
14. Eugene E. Schmitz
15. Edward T Devine

Maps
1. The Extent of the Fire   131
2. Street Changes Proposed by the Citizens' Committee   174

Tables
1. Population of San Francisco, 1848–1900   6
2. Earnings and Income of the United Railroads of San Francisco   113
3. Persons Carried from San Francisco, April 1906   136
4. Applicants and Grants for Rehabilitation   144

Graphs
1. Population of San Francisco Compared to that of California and the Pacific Coast, 1852–1900   8
2. Population of San Francisco Compared to that of Other Western Cities   9
3. Manufacturing in San Francisco Compared to that of California and the Pacific Coast, 1860–1900   10
4. Foreign Commerce in San Francisco Compared to that of the Pacific Coast, 1860–1901   11

Acknowledgments

Over the years I worked on this book, many friends and colleagues have aided me with suggestions and encouragement. I thank them all, but list only some: Gunther Barth, Michael Frisch, Barry Gruenberg, Henry Mayer, Russell Murphy, Michael Rogin, Lee Sigal, and Hayden White. The University of California, Berkeley, supported me with fellowships for two years, and Wesleyan University has been generous with sabbatical and research funds. Librarians at the Bancroft Library, Berkeley, the California Historical Society, the San Francisco Public Library, the California State Library, the Art Institute of Chicago, Yale University Library, and Olin Library, Wesleyan University, were all accommodating. Alice Pomper typed more than two versions of the manuscript. Michael Griffith located illustrations for me, and Rogene Gillmor drew lovely graphs. Coppélia and Gabriel Kahn have been dear companions.

Imperial San Francisco

Introduction

A powerful earthquake and the raging fires it unleashed destroyed most of San Francisco in April 1906. Pious observers around the country labeled the disaster a divine judgment on an American Sodom. Those San Franciscans who saw God's hand at work claimed the destruction was not punishment but a blessing in disguise. Half a century of spectacular but chaotic growth had left the city with a spatial structure that seemed to impede further progress. The streets were too narrow and often too steep, they did not take advantage of the magnificent natural site, and they left sections of the city isolated from one another. The fire—San Franciscans preferred to ignore the earthquake—gave the natives the chance to start afresh. They could rebuild San Francisco along "broader lines," make it modern, beautiful, and efficient.

They felt fortunate, perhaps even blessed, to have in hand a master plan for the city that Daniel Hudson Burnham had recently completed. Burnham, who had directed the Columbian Exposition in Chicago in 1893, was a dominant figure in the youthful city planning movement, and his San Francisco work represented his most comprehensive urban design to date. He intended the plan to serve "for all time to come," expecting that fifty years would be needed to realize his recommendations. But with the central area of the old city virtually levelled, the way seemed clear for a new San

Francisco to arise immediately from the ashes. The seal of the city, adopted in the 1850s, prefigured the episode; at its center, wings spread, stood the Phoenix.

This story of destruction and renewal did not work out the way it was supposed to. The Burnham plan did not reshape San Francisco after the earthquake and fire. Planning as envisioned by Burnham and his supporters had almost no bearing on the rebuilding of the city. Reconstruction was the work of persons and firms pursuing their own interests, without regard for Burnham's noble design. The lines of the new San Francisco were drawn by the marketplace, not the planner.

My purpose in this book is to interpret what may be called the city planning persuasion as it emerged in San Francisco around 1900. I argue that planning in its City Beautiful phase was more than aesthetic distaste for the ugliness of the turn-of-the-century city. Decades of explosive urban growth had created a novel environment in great American cities. Planners sought to reshape the social and political, as well as the physical structures that had developed. The advocates of city planning believed that these elements were interrelated. They hoped that by reordering the physical form of the city, they could improve the social and political features as well.

In San Francisco the drive for city planning was given special urgency by the fear that the city might be losing its position as the metropolis of the Pacific Coast. From the gold rush until about 1880, San Francisco stood unchallenged as the leading, and virtually the only, city in the area. Then Los Angeles, Portland, and Seattle began to expand, while San Francisco's own growth rate slowed. By 1900, its regional dominance had been waning for two decades. Some leading citizens believed that this trend could be reversed and the city's premier position secured by a program to make San Francisco physically more beautiful, politically more efficient, and socially more orderly. To realize these goals they turned to planning and to Daniel Burnham. His work embodied the social and aesthetic ideals of his sponsors.

I have chosen the term *imperial* to characterize the city planning enterprise in San Francisco and, by extension, in the country at large. The description is not my invention; previous writers have linked the architecture and planning of turn-of-the-century America with the growth of trusts and an expansionist foreign policy.[1] In the case of San Francisco, *imperial* had more specific meanings. First, city merchants saw San Francisco as the capital of a developing American commercial empire in the Pacific. Second, both the planners and their sponsors took as their models the great imperial cities of Europe: the Athens of Pericles, the Rome of the Caesars, the Paris of Napoleon III and Baron Haussmann. The architecture itself and the layout of streets, parks, and other open spaces were intended to inspire awe in an unruly public, to encourage identification with the glories of a state that stood enshrined in enormous public buildings. Finally, in the American context, planning on this scale meant that the hurly-burly of urban politics must somehow give way to a unitary authority capable of imposing its vision of the ideal city on an individualistic, diverse, and contentious society. Here again, the example of the cities of empire spoke with force to the proponents of planning.

The appeal was tempting but specious. American city governments were notoriously weak, inefficient, and corrupt, with San Francisco no better than the mean. Formal institutions of government had been overwhelmed by the brute social facts of urbanization. They bent under the strains of enlarged and overlapping boundaries, inexperienced and heterogeneous populations, and novel and expanded responsibilities. Americans' ingrained distrust of government in general and cities in particular made the situation even more intractable, as state legislatures, under the domination of rural interests, refused to grant adequate authority to municipalities. To fill this gap, pragmatic Americans created the urban political machine, an innovative organization whose prime accomplishment was to centralize enough power through informal means to allow city governments to function. Basically the machine worked as a complex system of exchange, with the leader of the organization, the "boss," serving as chief broker. He negotiated the myriad individual rewards that tied people to the machine: patronage for party workers; contracts and licenses for businessmen; welfare, services, and recognition for voters. Though not all these incentives were tangible, money was more than ever the mother's milk of politics. Principles, ideologies, and other abstract bases of loyalty were pallid by comparison. People turned to politics to benefit themselves. Many bosses were among the leading beneficiaries, exacting a sometimes exhorbitant price for their services.

Respectable citizens frequently attacked bosses and machines as perverters of American democracy, alien influences who depended on an ignorant immigrant vote to sustain themselves in office. Yet there was something distinctively American about a social institution utilizing exchange to satisfy individual desires. If the machine violated the canons of morality, it was not because it ignored the common good—Who, other than editorialists, paid any attention to that?—but because its market operated in an imperfect and therefore grossly inefficient fashion. The search for some alternative to machine politics, if it were to be more than an indulgent fantasy, would have to lead to a system equally solicitous of private needs, especially property.

Because the imperial approach to urban planning and politics failed this test, it came to very little. It was brought low both by the strengths of its opponents and the ambivalence of its friends, who could not resolve their conflicting attitudes toward politics, authority, and private rights. My own judgment is that San Francisco was better off without the Burnham plan and the organization of society that it implied.

Still, it is important to credit the advocates of planning with addressing an issue that continues to challenge American society: How, or indeed should, the nation's cities be restored? That cities today are the victims of chronic social catastrophe, rather than earthquake and fire, only makes a solution more difficult. We are still striving to find a way of organizing urban space that will increase the well-being of the people who live in cities, or at least not lessen it. After seventy years, this remains the central task of city planning, even though both cities and the planning profession have changed drastically. Cities are one kind of human community, and while there is no complete agreement on how they differ from other types, probably the least controversial distinction is that cities are bigger and more dense. This simple ecological fact has an important consequence, described by Charles Tilly:

> The concentration of people and their activities in big, busy, complicated centers made most people vulnerable to the decisions of many other people, some of them far away. As collective creations, cities impose collective risks and collective responsibilities.[2]

An enduring question for American society in general and American cities in particular is how, while maintaining private property, political liberty, and democracy, these collective responsibilities are to be met.

1
Metropolitan Ups and Downs

San Francisco in the Nineteenth Century

At the time of the American conquest of California in 1846, the future city of San Francisco was a tiny hamlet separated by two-thirds of a continent from the inhabited parts of the nation. By 1900 it ranked ninth in population among American cities and was the largest west of St. Louis. It had more people than Los Angeles, Portland, and Seattle, its three Pacific Coast rivals, combined. It was by far the greatest manufacturing center in the region, it handled the lion's share of foreign commerce, and it dominated finance. In slightly more than fifty years, the hamlet had become a metropolis of international stature. Chicago grew much faster, of course, and there were other cities that kept pace with San Francisco. Still, in an era that equated growth with a city's well-being, San Francisco was an undeniable success. That it had emerged so suddenly and so far away from any other major city made its history more thrilling.

A close look at the city's growth to 1900, especially when compared to that of other cities in the area and the Pacific Coast section as a whole, discloses a distinct pattern. From the discovery of gold in 1848 until about 1880, San Francisco expanded faster than the region; afterwards it fell behind. Before 1880 San Francisco outpaced other western cities; afterwards they began to catch up. When James Bryce visited the Pacific Coast in the 1880s, he observed that:

San Francisco dwarfs the other cities and is a commercial and intellectual centre, and source of influence for the surrounding regions, more powerful over them than is any Eastern city of its neighborhood. It is a New York which has got no Boston on one side of it, and no shrewd and orderly rural population on the other, to keep it in order.[1]

Twenty years later, San Francisco was still the largest city in the region, but no one regarded it as the only one.

The questions this chapter addresses concern the pattern of urban growth on the Pacific Coast. Why was San Francisco able to expand from hamlet to metropolis so quickly? And why did it grow faster than other cities until 1880, but then more slowly? The answers are spun from two strands, one drawn from the history of San Francisco, the other from theories of urbanization found in economics, geography, and other social sciences. The strands lead from comparatively firm evidence on demography and economic activity into murkier areas of social structure and the abilities of government. The chapter concludes by arguing that the declining position of San Francisco relative to other West Coast cities began to worry some influential San Franciscans, and that attempts to reform the city's government, improve its economic position, and reshape its physical and social structure can be understood against this background.

Table 1
Population of San Francisco, 1848–1900

	Population	Percent Increase
1848	1,000	
1850	30,000	
1852	34,776	
1860	56,802	89% [1850–1860]
1870	149,473	163 [1860–1870]
1880	233,959	57 [1870–1880]
1890	298,997	28 [1880–1890]
1900	342,782	15 [1890–1900]

SOURCE: The estimates for 1848 and 1850 come from Roger W. Lotchin, *San Francisco, 1846–1856: From Hamlet to City* (New York: Oxford University Press, 1974), pp. 8, 37. For more complete figures and other sources, see Appendix, Table 1.

The Dimensions of Growth

City building was a heroic adventure in nineteenth-century America, but the triumphs are recorded more appropriately in numbers than verse. Before accounting for the form of city growth on the West Coast, let me present figures that measure some of the dimensions.

In the pre-gold-rush days of 1848, there were about 1,000 people in San Francisco. Two years later, the population stood near 30,000; the number is approximate because the federal census returns were burned. The California census of 1852 put the figure at almost 35,000, and by 1860 it had jumped to 57,000. Table 1 summarizes San Francisco's population growth to 1900. The population of New York City reached 150,000 sometime between 1820 and 1830, or two centuries after the Dutch settled Manhattan. San Francisco equalled that size in twenty-five years.

For the first two or three decades after the gold rush, San Francisco grew more rapidly than the rest of the West Coast. In 1880, 27 percent of all Californians lived in San Francisco, up from 15 percent in 1852. By 1900, however, the city's share of the state's population had fallen to 23 percent. A similar pattern prevails when the population of the city is compared to the combined populations of California, Oregon, and Washington: increasing concentration in the city until 1880; dispersion thereafter.

Another revealing comparison is between San Francisco and other cities in the region. As Bryce observed, San Francisco dwarfed its nearest rivals. It was four times as large as Sacramento in 1860, nine times as big in 1870. Oakland, as much a suburb as a rival, took second place in 1880 by trebling its population in the 1870s. San Francisco was still more than six times its size. In 1890, Los Angeles emerged as San Francisco's chief competitor. With 50,000 people, it was only slightly larger than Oakland, Portland, and Seattle, but it had grown by 350 percent since 1880, despite the collapse in 1888 of a land boom. Its population doubled in the next decade, and in 1900 it reached 100,000, compared to the 343,000 in San Francisco. Portland and Seattle were also bursting at the seams. None of these cities was as yet the equal of San Francisco, but the five of them combined finally exceeded it in population. Urbanization had ceased to be a solo performance.

San Francisco's supremacy on the West Coast was even more complete in manufacturing than in population, but the pattern of

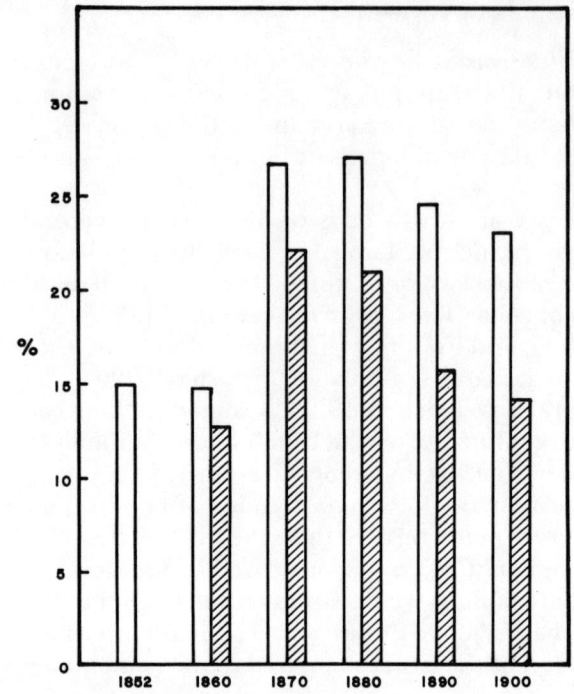

Population of San Francisco as percentage of population of California

Population of San Francisco as percentage of population of California, Oregon, and Washington

SOURCE: See Appendix, Table 2.

change was the same: increasing concentration in San Francisco until 1880, then diffusion. Though slow in starting, first Portland in the 1880s, then Seattle and Los Angeles in the 1890s developed into industrial centers. They were still small by comparison; in 1900, each had a manufacturing base about one-fifth as large as San Francisco's. In 1880, at the height of its industrial preeminence, San Francisco manufacturing was more than twenty times as large as that of its nearest competitor.

Trade flourished in San Francisco before there was any manufacturing to speak of. In 1850–1851, the city already stood fourth among American ports in total foreign commerce measured by

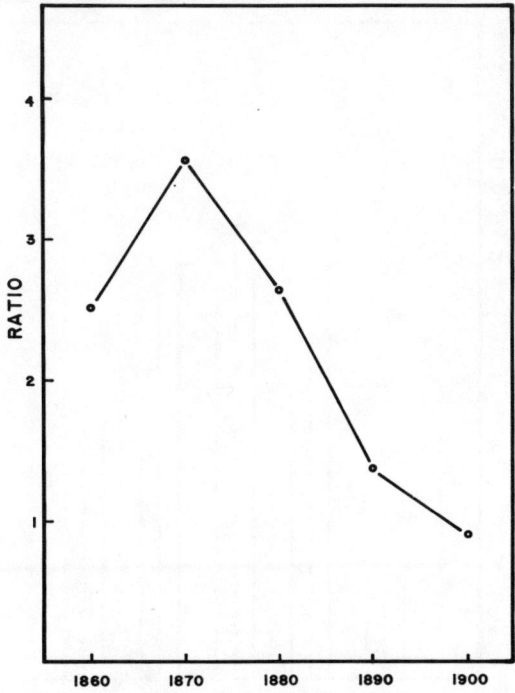

Ratio of population of San Francisco to combined population of Los Angeles, Oakland, Sacramento, Portland, and Seattle

SOURCE: See Appendix, Table 1.

weight, behind New York, Boston, and New Orleans.[2] Because San Francisco virtually monopolized the foreign trade of the Pacific Coast for twenty years, we can hardly expect to see its share expand. In 1870, for example, more than 97 percent of the region's foreign commerce passed through the port of San Francisco. Then the city began to lose some ground, slowly until 1890, rapidly thereafter. It retained a larger share of imports than exports, though neither increased much after 1890. In 1901, not an exceptionally poor year, San Francisco's foreign trade had fallen more than 20 percent below its level of 1890. Meanwhile, the port of Seattle flourished. It accounted for nearly a fifth of the region's total foreign commerce in 1900 and a fourth of its exports.

These data describe the sudden emergence of San Francisco

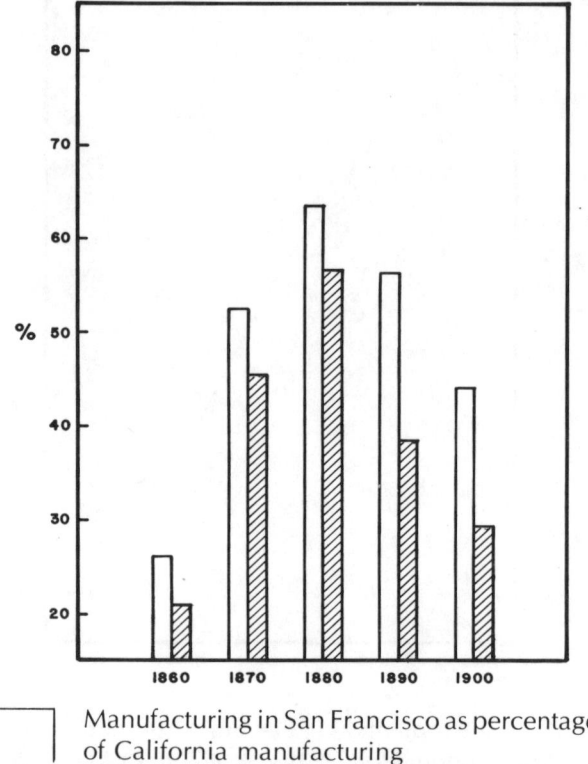

Manufacturing in San Francisco as percentage of California manufacturing

Manufacturing in San Francisco as percentage of Pacific Coast manufacturing

SOURCE: See Appendix, Table 3.

into a regional metropolis, and they show that its preeminence increased for about thirty years and then began to wane. They trace the rise of potential rivals like Los Angeles and Seattle. They are revealing, but we should not regard them as very precise. Even if the collection and processing of the information had been free from error—an impossibility—the problem of changing boundaries would still remain. Some cities, like Los Angeles, gobbled up suburbs in the nineteenth century. What the census records as an influx of people may actually have been an expansion of the city limits. Nonetheless, we can have confidence that the quantitative evidence catches at least the basic outlines of the growth of cities in the West.

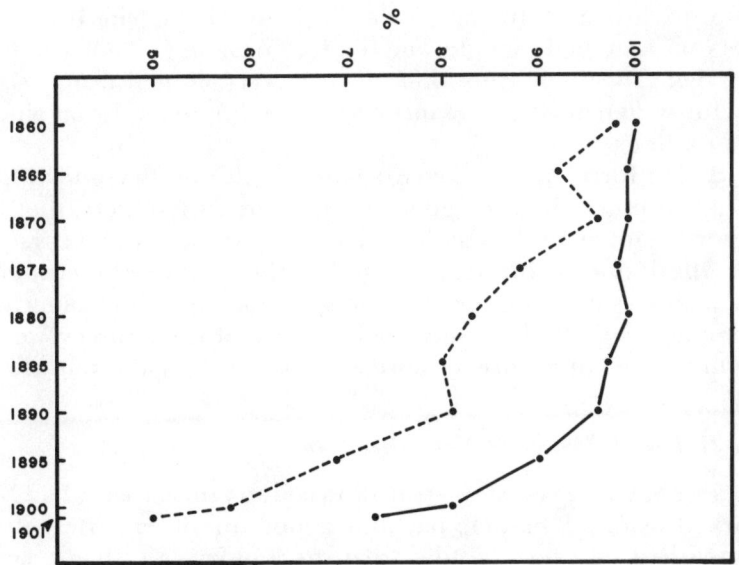

San Francisco foreign commerce as percentage of Pacific Coast foreign commerce: imports ———; exports — — — —

SOURCE: See Appendix, Table 5.

What the data do not provide, of course, is an understanding of why things happened the way they did. For that we must look to the history of San Francisco and the region, and to what we know about urbanization in general.

Instant City: 1848–1880

The gold rush built San Francisco. News of James Marshall's discovery at Coloma on the American River spread slowly at first, but in less than a year, gold fever infected the nation; "from Maine to Texas there was one universal frenzy. It occupied the thoughts of all; it disturbed business; it prevented marriages; it broke up families; it was the hope of those who could go, and the despair of those who could not."[3] Most people stayed put, but there were enough hopeful ones to constitute a massive and sudden migration. The population of California swelled from fewer than 15,000 in 1848, exclusive of Indians, to more than 220,000 in 1852. Not everyone searched for gold, and few found enough of it to compensate them for their pains. Still, the discovery of gold transformed California and made San Francisco, as "warehouse for the diggings," an instant city.[4]

Other forces also worked to shape the city's history, and though less picturesque than the gold rush and the forty-niners, they are important for an understanding of its growth. Four influences stand out: the historical context; the geographic setting; the economic foundations; and the locational dispositions of wholesaling and manufacturing. By following the operation of these forces, we can begin to see San Francisco more as a city and less as a miracle.

The Historical Context: A Network of Cities

Because San Francisco was born into a country that already had New York, Boston, Philadelphia, and a host of other cities, it accomplished in a few decades what these older cities had taken a century or more to achieve. In its early years, at least until 1870, San Francisco served as a trading center linking a frontier region to more economically advanced places. It handled both exports of raw materials and imports of finished products. This same function had been played by Atlantic Coast cities in the seventeenth and eighteenth centuries and by interior river ports in the first half of the nineteenth. In all these cases, long-distance trade between cities was an essential ingredient of growth. A network of transportation and trade routes emerged, organized by firms within the major centers. Both firms and host cities competed with one another for business. The rapid and uneven growth of American cities in the first half of the nineteenth century owed as much to the positions that different towns carved out within this urban commercial network as to the more immediate relationship between a city and the hinterland whose resources it tapped.[5]

Trade between San Francisco and distant ports sprouted quickly in the two years after the American conquest of California. When forty-niners started to flow into California, the city's commerce doubled and redoubled. Its harbor overflowed with ships that carried new kinds of cargo but plied many of the established routes. In the early 1850s, city and state even had to import necessities like food and building materials. Gold was the principal export. Though this specific exchange did not last very long, the links between San Francisco and the other ports in the network were durable. They were sustained by the banks, shipping and transport companies, and other institutions of trade that had forged important connections with firms located in the other cities.[6]

San Francisco drew from these cities people already skilled in the ways of city life. A high proportion of early migrants to California and the West arrived with urban experience and an urban outlook. They helped to fashion the character of San Francisco in its early years, its politics, culture, economy, and society. John S. Hittell, one of the city's more articulate boosters, might complain about the evil consequences of a spoils system "under the lead of men who received the highest education in political corruption before they left New York."[7] On balance, though, it seems likely that San Francisco profited by being able to import a range of urban expertise, a whole culture for city living, from centers in the East.[8]

The Geographic Setting: Land and Sea

Since more than half a continent separated the mining frontier of the Far West from populated regions, settlers could not seep into the area across a broad front. They had to make an arduous journey, either over the plains, mountains, and deserts, or by sea via Panama or around the Horn. Though more people followed the overland routes, many came by ship, as did most of the imported goods. The port was a great funnel for supplies. As the neck of that funnel, San Francisco became a great entrepot, where goods moving inland were distributed, and exported resources collected. The cities of the Atlantic seaboard had served similar functions two centuries earlier, but there had been a number of them. On the Pacific slope, settlement in the interior was more concentrated. Also San Francisco Bay had natural advantages over any other port in the area as a harbor for ocean-going vessels and a gateway into the interior by way of the Sacramento and San Joaquin rivers.[9]

A comparison of the Pacific Coast with the Old Northwest region underscores the importance of geography. In the Old Northwest, the Ohio River was the main artery of commerce. It nourished three towns into important cities: Pittsburgh, Cincinnati, and Louisville. Overland trade, though slow and costly, provided some alternative to the river, as did canals and the Great Lakes. So the early history of urbanization in the Old Northwest was a tale not of one city, but of many.[10]

Economic Foundations: City and Country

Urbanization in the nineteenth century is often equated with industrialization. In fact, until around 1870, the growth of America's largest cities owed more to commerce than to manufacturing. San Francisco was no exception. Because of the extraordinary value of its gold exports, California could import goods and even services that would have been produced locally had not striking it rich in placer mining seemed more attractive. Consequently, a remarkable volume of trade moved through the port while San Francisco was still a relatively small city on the fringes of a sparsely settled interior. Wealth from the mines furnished enough capital to sustain the kind of specialized business community on which commercial cities depend. Wharves and warehouses, banks and insurance companies, law offices and printing firms quickly appeared, transforming San Francisco from a primitive colonial outpost into a major center of trade.[11]

In 1852, some 100,000 miners pulled about $80 million in gold from the streams and out of the ground. Then wealth from the mines began to fall off. Having grown so rapidly on a narrow foundation, San Francisco was vulnerable to a depression. Promoters in the city tried to hasten the development of the interior so that San Francisco might continue to flourish. These efforts did not pay immediate dividends, and the city suffered during economic contractions. But the state's economy was beginning to diversify as wheat and wool growing, horticulture, and timber mining came to supplement the search for precious metals.[12] San Francisco probably lost some long-distance trade when local products were substituted for imports, but overall it gained as the area grew in size and complexity. It became a metropolis, the place where "administrative, financial, legal, educational, recreational, medical, . . . governmental" and other specialized services are provided in regions that are large enough to demand them.[13]

The city's economic supremacy was also enhanced because a large share of the West's wealth-producing assets were owned by people who lived in San Francisco. Some had made fortunes in the city itself and then invested in the hinterlands. Others had struck it rich in the interior and then moved to the metropolis. Where else was a western millionaire to live? These nabobs stimulated the local economy by a high—one should probably say extravagant—level of consumption. Their presence also helped to ensure the ascendancy of San Francisco's commercial and financial institutions against potential realignments of trade, which changes such as the building of railroads might encourage.[14]

Locational Dispositions: Wholesaling and Manufacturing

Even before the discovery of gold, San Francisco had been the largest settlement on the bay. It offered more services and information to traders than any other town. Far-sighted promoters had changed its name from Yerba Buena in January 1846, so that it might attract settlers and merchants who knew of Mission San Francisco and San Francisco Bay. This early lead helped it become the commercial center of the gold rush and continued to influence the structure of urbanization long after the last forty-niner had disembarked for the diggings. Wholesaling and later manufacturing took root in an urban environment found only in San Francisco. Growth became self-generating, a "circular and cumulative process," and San Francisco built its relatively minor initial advantage over other towns into a durable and substantial one.[15]

As the city quickly became a major international port, it attracted more wholesale merchants and fostered the expansion of firms already in the city. The locational needs of wholesalers differ from those of retailers. Retailers have to be close to their customers; as population spreads out, retailers follow. Wholesalers tend to cluster where there are established transportation and communication routes. Shipping and insurance companies, banks, law offices, exchanges, commercial newspapers, and other services necessary for wholesale merchants develop in these centers of trade. The range of services available only in a large commercial city draws new firms as forcefully as do the physical facilities. Even if a second city could duplicate the warehouses and wharves it would still be at a disadvantage until it could also offer these services. So long as wholesaling plays a leading role in the economic development of a region, the city with a head start as a wholesale center will tend to maintain and even extend its original lead.[16]

There are no neat data to show if San Francisco did maintain or increase this early lead in wholesaling after 1850. Occupational statistics from the census of 1900 do indicate the continued importance of wholesaling in the city. Ninth in population, San Francisco held sixth place in the number of wholesale merchants and dealers. Its two closest West Coast competitors were Portland, which ranked twenty-eighth, and Los Angeles, thirtieth. In San Francisco there were 2.3 wholesalers for every thousand inhabitants; Portland had 1.9, Los Angeles 1.5.[17]

Manufacturing only became a potent stimulant of urban growth in the years after 1860. For the East Coast and the Midwest, industry supplanted trade as the most important city-building activity, spurring expansion in established commercial metropolises and creating new factory cities. But the Far West was sparsely populated and distant from major markets for both consumer and producer goods. It lacked an adequate coal supply. Higher returns on investments were still available in commerce. Manufacturing did expand, especially in California, but modestly. Western industry mostly served the region, where it was protected from eastern competition by high transportation costs.[18]

The manufacturing that did develop was highly concentrated in San Francisco. Like the trading centers on the Atlantic Coast, San Francisco built industry onto a flourishing commercial base. These cities all had capital to invest and populations large enough to provide both a labor force and a market for local products. Shipbuilding and its related crafts were closely tied to the commercial activities of these cities, as was the processing of raw materials passing through the ports. Established transportation networks could carry the products to distant markets. As in wholesaling, an early lead in manufacturing gave these cities an initial advantage from which they outdistanced competitors.[19]

Because they produced for a smaller market, manufacturing plants in San Francisco were probably not as efficient as those in eastern cities. But remoteness offered some compensations. High transportation costs that kept San Francisco goods from competing in the East made eastern merchandise more expensive in the West. Also, the limited western market was not large enough to call forth a second industrial center, duplicating the specialized services and other advantages for manufacturers already available in San Francisco.[20] Compared to Pittsburgh or Cincinnati, San Francisco was not a major manufacturing center. Compared to other cities on the Pacific Coast, it was an American Manchester.

Two facts highlight the regional character of industry in San Francisco. The first is the racial division of the labor force. The coming of the transcontinental railroads reduced transportation costs, and eastern goods entered the previously protected markets. Manufacturers facing this competition had to cut costs to survive. They turned to Chinese laborers, whom they could hire for less than Caucasians. White workers protested, and they succeeded in pressuring employers to adopt a white-only policy in industries where goods from the outside were not a threat, such as construction or building and repairing vessels in the coastal trade. But in national market industries like cigar-making, the Chinese took both the skilled and unskilled jobs.[21]

The second fact is the kinds of goods turned out in the city. Some firms made mining equipment and agricultural machinery suited to the special conditions of California, and others canned and preserved the produce of the region. Printing and publishing was one of the largest industries in the city, natural for a commercial metropolis, as was brewing what the census called "liquors, malt," normally a local enterprise. San Francisco's industrial profile differed from that of other metropolises in that only a small share of the workers manufactured "intermediate goods," meaning goods that are sold to other industries rather than to the ultimate consumer. The city was too far from the "manufacturing belt" of the nation to make this type of exchange economical. On the other hand, it was close to an extraordinarily rich hinterland, and its manufacturing specializations reflected its position as regional metropolis.[22]

A concatenation of forces created a city on the shores of San Francisco Bay where previously there had been only a village. The thousands of adventurers drawn west by the magnetism of gold depended on the outside world for wants of all sorts. The natural features of the land and the prior existence of trading routes combined to make San Francisco the supply center for the miners, as cities in the East and abroad exchanged manufactured goods for the gold and other riches of the West. San Francisco's initial lead over other settlements made it the most attractive profitable site for commercial and industrial enterprise, so that its early advantage was compounded. For thirty years after the American conquest of California, San Francisco lengthened the gap between itself and any rival.

About 1880, San Francisco's increasing dominance came to an end. Towns such as Los Angeles, Portland, and Seattle grew into cities that numbered their populations in tens of thousands, and the structure of urbanization on the West Coast began to change. It shifted away from what geographers called a "primate city" form, with one very large city and a number of much smaller centers, and toward one shaped more like a pyramid, the metropolis resting atop several cities of medium size, below which sit a larger number of smaller cities and so on down to the more numerous towns and villages. Why the change? What happened to overcome or undermine the influences that had made western urbanization so concentrated? What hastened the growth of other cities? What slowed San Francisco down?

Primus Inter Pares: 1880–1890

One reason the other cities in the area started to catch up with San Francisco after 1880 is simply the development of the Pacific Coast region. Population in the three states jumped from slightly more than 1 million in 1880 to almost 2.5 million by 1900. Washington alone, which only achieved statehood in 1889, had more than half a million people in 1900. The economy became larger and more complex. Transcontinental railroads now reached all the major cities. New crops were developed and planted on thousands of acres of previously uncultivated land. Industrial mining extracted gold, silver, copper, and even some coal in diggings far removed from the Mother Lode country. All this activity spurred the growth of the smaller cities. So did a series of speculative manias in urban real estate, which stretched from Los Angeles to Seattle. The railroad builders in particular stood to gain from the rise of the new cities, where they profited from the sale of land made more valuable by the presence of the roads.[23] There were simply more reasons for cities of decent size to exist in the years after 1880 than before, and the "primate city" form of urbanization gave way as "the number and complexity of the forces affecting urban structure" increased.[24]

Developments internal to San Francisco also explain the changed shape of urbanization. The advantages that had concentrated wholesaling and manufacturing in San Francisco before 1880—easier access to credit, a larger supply of labor, a bigger local market, more developed transportation facilities, better legal advice, more information, greater possibilities for complementary exchanges among firms, and a number of other services, some free, some for sale—began to wane about 1880. Some of the other cities were becoming large enough to duplicate the physical facilities and intangible services formerly available only in San Francisco. Also, the process of self-generating growth, of bigness begetting bigness, now began to be undercut by its very success. The costs that a large city can impose on its residents now confronted the benefits. Negative aspects of urban life started to catch up to the positive ones. While for a time San Francisco collected premiums on its head start, it now began to pay a penalty for taking the lead.

What costs are involved? There are a number of economic disadvantages—one can call them diseconomies—generally associated with large urban environments. Crowding is an obvious one; it stems from density as well as size. It means traffic congestion, higher rents charged for prime city space, and pollution. There are technological ways of dealing with these problems: mass transit systems and even wider streets to reduce congestion; high-rise buildings to increase the supply of urban space; sewer lines and incinerators to dispose of refuse. All of them, however, are expensive, and paying for these improvements can undermine some of the advantages of proximity. So can not paying for them.

Another diseconomy, for employers at least, is the higher cost of labor in cities where powerful unions have taken root. Unions may demand higher wages or impose rules restricting output and preventing innovations that would increase productivity. Since the degree of unionization varies from city to city, among industries, and historically, it is a mistake to identify high labor costs with an urban environment per se. On the other hand, it does seem reasonable to expect that labor organizations will be stronger in cities where manufacturing and other industries have long been in operation than in smaller and newer centers. If manufacturers locate elsewhere to escape higher labor costs, there is another force that may hinder the self-generating process of growth.[25]

A third diseconomy stems from the difficulties of running a large city. The costs of many of the services municipal governments provide, such as fire and police protection, sanitation, road maintenance, education, welfare, public health, may rise faster than the population, making a big city a more expensive per capita operation than a small one.[26] Besides the purely economic questions, there is the managerial strain imposed by a large city. Good management is a scarce resource, as many business firms have painfully discovered. A city may also grow to a point at which it cannot efficiently deliver important public services because the administrative mechanisms cannot cope with the complexities associated with cities of great size. It takes a lot more skill to run large cities than small ones. The difficulty is not merely administrative; it is political and social as well. A large city is more apt to have many groups claiming a share of public authority, making it tougher to fashion any coherent policy. And the problem becomes more vexing where there are cultural as well as social and economic divisions within the city, when the populace is not unified by commonly held values. Unless a city can overcome these obstacles, it may find itself losing ground to smaller, simpler, and more cohesive rivals.[27]

These reflections hardly constitute a precise model to forecast the growth and stagnation of cities, but they do identify some of the reasons why cities do not expand indefinitely. They portray city development as a dialectical process, a contest between benefits and costs as influenced by technology and social organization. They also provide a theoretical context in which to place some of the impediments to growth that confronted San Francisco in the last part of the nineteenth century.

Land

The existence of legal boundaries means that cities have limited amounts of land, although a city can extend those limits by annexing surrounding areas. Many American cities have been able to grow by gobbling up their suburbs.[28] San Francisco could not. The city's last expansion took place in 1856, when the city and county were consolidated and the current southern boundary was fixed.[29] At that time, there was plenty of empty space within the 42-square-mile area, so the boundaries were hardly constricting. But from the start the city had a shortage of usable and accessible land. The forty or so hills scattered about created spectacular vistas, but they also held up traffic and limited the number of sites suitable for commerce, industry, and even inexpensive homes. At first, the city was able to add to its supply of level land by filling in parts of the bay and flattening some of the hills. In the late 1860s, for example, the demand for more land and better access motivated some enterprising San Franciscans to tear down Rincon Hill, site of the city's first elite neighborhood in South Park.[30] These projects were expensive and could not proceed indefinitely. The state took control of the waterfront in 1863 and ended the practice of indiscriminate and often speculative land fill.

Intense competition for the scarce resource of flat land sorted out the contestants. Commercial and industrial users came to dominate the waterfront area, and working class residents gradually moved away to the west and south.[31] Homes became separated from places of work, and commuters had to resort to various forms of mass transit. The cable car, an ingenious device well suited to mounting the city's steep hills, was a local invention. But cable cars were less than ideal for moving large numbers of people over flat terrain, and their use elsewhere was confined to the downtown areas of a dozen or so large cities. When electric trolley cars were introduced after 1888, they proved so superior to cable cars that they were quickly and universally adopted; by 1902 they accounted for 97 percent of the track mileage in urban transit.[32]

Without the trolley, supplemented in a few places by subways, American cities in the period after 1880 might have grown much more slowly. Crowding residence and workplace together was a mortal danger, and the rising cost of accessible land in the central city deterred entrepreneurs selecting a plant location. Mass transportation multiplied the amount of usable land by solving the "journey-to-work dilemma," making outlying areas available for residential and, on a lesser scale, industrial purposes. It also altered the form of city development from the traditional pattern, with a highly concentrated central city, to the modern "metropolitan," or city and suburban, shape.[33]

The process of dispersion may have begun earlier in San Francisco than in other American cities of similar size. The bay served as a highway for the movement of people and goods. The streetcar accelerated this outward movement, and it altered the nature of the relationship between the core city and the periphery. In its "Venetian phase," San Francisco had stood at the center of a unified area, the hub of the wheel and the only commercial node. As the streetcar suburbs grew, especially in the East Bay, they spawned their own jobs, services, and neighborhoods, and relied less on San Francisco. Oakland, which has always had an ambiguous relationship with San Francisco, became less a dependent and more a rival.[34] Between 1880 and 1900, the population of the "commuter district" of the Bay Area, including places as far away as San Jose, more than doubled. It equalled 29 percent of the city's population in 1880, and 44 percent in 1900.[35]

Within San Francisco, the transportation system modernized more slowly than in the East Bay. Owners of cable car lines used political influence, mainly bribing supervisors and state legislators, to delay the conversion of horse car lines into trolleys. Trolleys did come into increasing use after 1893, yet despite considerable electrification and the consolidation of the most important lines into a single company, the system in San Francisco remained disorganized and inefficient. Cable cars continued to run on the heavily used Market Street line until after the earthquake and fire in 1906. Passengers on electric trolleys had to transfer at Market to the smaller and slower cable cars to complete their journey. Almost all the service in the city was still concentrated in the downtown area, leaving other districts, including huge tracts in the western and southern portions of the city, isolated and sparsely populated. People chose home sites across the bay or down the peninsula, where they had better access to places of employment within San Francisco. In other parts of the Bay Area and in other American cities, the streetcar lines were often ventures of real estate speculators, less concerned with the profitability of the roads than with the increased land values that the roads brought. For some reason, perhaps because of the terrain and the need for several tunnels, this speculative inducement to streetcar building did not seem to operate in San Francisco. Only after 1912, when the city began its own career as a street railway developer, did people begin to settle these outlying areas in large numbers.[36] The costs of central city crowding may have weighed more heavily on San Francisco than on other large American cities that made better use of the streetcar.

Labor

The first unions appeared in San Francisco so soon after the gold rush that, a historian commented, "one is tempted to believe that the craftsmen met each other on the way to California and agreed to unite."[37] For the next fifty years, the fortunes of labor organizations in the city fluctuated with the business cycle, waxing during prosperous times, waning in depressions. But unionism was always more potent in San Francisco than elsewhere on the Pacific Coast. Manufacturers in the city who had to compete with goods produced elsewhere by non-union labor felt so handicapped that they even tried to encourage labor organizations in Los Angeles to lessen the differential.[38] Unions may have improved the lives of workers fortunate enough to belong, but it is hard to see how they could have helped the city attract new businesses or expand existing ones in the face of competition from less unionized rivals.

Government

Government can influence the quality of the urban environment. In some respects a city resembles a large firm, with the officials playing the role of managers. Both sets of officers are charged with keeping a complex organization operating efficiently, the managers to make a profit, the officials to provide an environment in which private firms may operate profitably. They have to oversee the "set of local public services that must be integrated or co-ordinated to preserve the efficiency of the city, seen now as a huge factory with its streets, power lines, and pipes as the assembly lines, and its complex of legal, financial, and technical services as a magnified version of the 'front office.'"[39] Good management makes some firms more profitable than others. Likewise, some cities benefit by selecting capable officials who can reduce the effects of urban diseconomies.

Over the years, American cities have appeared less able than large corporations to promote efficiency, both because efficiency is only one goal among many which must be served, and because inefficient firms disappear while inefficient cities merely stagnate. Yet the gap between the firm and the city seems to have been especially wide during the second half of the nineteenth century. It was during these years that a number of manufacturing and distributing firms, responding to the challenges and opportunities of national markets, developed new techniques of organization that allowed them to integrate vertically, extending their operations all the way from raw material to wholesale distribution.[40] In the same period, city governments were condemned as the most conspicuous failures in the American experiment with democracy. Because of what James Bryce called their "extravagance, corruption and mismanagement," they produced grossly inadequate services at vastly inflated costs. The complaint of Bryce, echoed by many American contemporaries, was directed not merely at the immorality of these governments and their subversion of democratic principles, but at their glaring inefficiency. Dominated by "city bosses" and "political machines," these governments allowed a few well-placed politicians and some of their business allies to line their pockets at public expense, while the ordinary citizens suffered from high taxes and the problems created by unmanaged urban growth.[41]

Scholars have challenged this grim opinion, which was held by most reformers, by portraying the bosses and machines as adaptive responses to the great difficulties presented by rapid urban expansion. A number of problems confronted the political leaders: the fragmentation of formal governmental authority; the unmet welfare needs of new urban residents, particularly the recent immigrants unfamiliar with American political traditions; the legitimate and illegitimate demands of business trying to survive in novel environments; and the strains that city building on an unprecedented scale imposed on frail governmental structures. Bosses and machines may have supplied as much governmental coordination and as much humane concern for those suffering most severely as was possible under these conditions. Moralistic critics, especially the "good government" interests concerned primarily about low tax rates, appreciated neither the reasons for the emergence of these institutions nor the magnitude of their achievements. "The organizations . . . helped incorporate new groups into American society and aided them up the social ladder," claims one student of machine politics. Though corrupt and inefficient, the machines "*did* manage urban growth at a time when other instrumentalities for governing the city were inadequate." The payoffs of "Thanksgiving Day turkeys and buckets of coal," may have helped to siphon off discontent, keeping American politics relatively peaceful.[42]

Nevertheless, neither the positive effects of machine rule nor the absence of alternative methods of political coordination means that machines were economically efficient when measured against some absolute standard, or when compared with the management of the new vertically integrated corporations. Progressive reformers struggled to introduce "business-like," meaning bureaucratic, methods into urban administration, both to achieve social welfare aims and to improve the operating efficiency of the municipalities.[43] Moreover, some bosses were less rapacious and more benign than others, so that a general explanation and defense of the boss and the machine do not prove their positive worth in any particular locale.

San Francisco had a boss in the 1880s; indeed, it had several. The most powerful and notorious was Christopher Augustine Buckley, the "Blind White Devil," whose career as Democratic leader spanned the decade. Resurrecting a moribund Democratic party, he managed by 1882 to become its undisputed leader and the most powerful politician in the city. His reign lasted until 1890, when disclosures of his corruption and the active opposition of a reform group ended his career in disgrace, though not in jail. Buckley's success depended on his political skill, lack of principle, and the apparent need for some masterful political organizer. The city was still beset with deep-seated and frequently violent conflicts, like the anti-Chinese riots, the Workingmen's party, and anti-monopoly crusades. Large corporations and rich individuals tried to grasp political as well as economic control. The city government, with restricted power and fragmented responsibility, could not produce either coordination or democratically based control. Thus, "the city grew in giant convulsions, leaving a wide gap between the ever-expanding economic organizations and the lagging agencies of government." The situation seemed to cry out for a city boss, "the man who could step into this breach and act as middleman between the economic and political institutions."[44]

In filling this role, Buckley brought a modicum of order and predictability to the politics of San Francisco. Those corporations needing franchises or other favors from the Board of Supervisors could go to Buckley and get what they wanted, provided they were not outbid. The costs, of course, were simply added to the bills these monopolies charged their customers. But the system was fragile. When Buckley raised his fees in 1889, the water company took him to court and helped bring him down. Though he had a reputation for generosity to the needy, Buckley apparently relied more on bribery, fraud, and the strong arms of his supporters to retain his control of the city political machinery. The portrait of the boss as Irish Robin Hood, winning the loyalty of the masses through his personal welfare work, paid for by those quasi-tax assessments he levied on the major corporations, seems too benign for Buckley. If without him the government of the city might have been chaotic to the point of anarchy, with him it was larcenous to the point of piracy.[45]

Society

In the ninteenth century, American cities grew by attracting enormous numbers of people who had been born elsewhere. San Francisco was a prime example of the importance of migration for urban growth. According to the censuses of 1870, 1880, and 1890, it had a higher percentage of foreign born residents than any other major American city. It exceeded even New York and Boston, the main East Coast ports of entry, and Chicago, Milwaukee, Detroit, and Cleveland in the industrial Midwest. Only a few Massachusetts mill towns, such as Fall River, Lowell, and Lawrence, had proportionally more foreign born. By 1900, San Francisco had dropped slightly behind New York, Chicago, and Boston, but it still stood near the top of the list, far ahead of the other Pacific Coast cities.

The migrants who flocked to San Francisco came from virtually everywhere. In 1900, Germans made up the largest group of foreign born, but there were substantial numbers of Irish, French, English, Canadians, Swedes, and Italians, and the largest concentration of Chinese in any American city. Seventy thousand people, 20 percent of the city's total population, had been born in the United States outside of California.[46] San Francisco was a city of newcomers, with none of the migrant streams dominant enough to impose its vision of society and culture on the rest.

The convergence of all these different folk in a place devoid of tradition and open to new influences gave San Francisco a cosmopolitanism rare for cities of its size. Beatrice Webb, the English Fabian, noted some of the social consequences of heterogeneity in a diary entry written in 1898. She found San Francisco to be:

> isolated from and unconcerned with any other part of America. It is out and away the most cosmopolitan city I have yet come across. It has no standards, no common customs; no common ideals of excellence, of intellect or manners—only one universal anarchy, each race living according to its own lights, or rather according to its own impulses, seeing that all alike are free from their own racial public opinion. To the person who wishes to live unto himself without any pressure of law, custom or public opinion, San Francisco must be a Haven. If he combines with this "individualism" a Bohemian liking for variety of costume, manners, morals and opinions, San Francisco must be a veritable paradise.[47]

She goes on to state that a Scottish merchant whom she met admitted some homesickness for "a moor with a blinding Scotch mist sweeping over me; but the shackled life of Glasgow, Edinburgh or London—I could na return to it."

This ethnic heterogeneity probably made San Francisco a more difficult city to govern. If it did not lead to the "one universal anarchy" that Beatrice Webb thought she saw, it did make it harder for political leaders to fashion and implement any coherent policy designed to keep the city competitive. Once again, the same forces that made rapid city growth possible, in this case foreign and domestic migration, could also work to slow the process once the city had reached a certain size.

By 1900, San Francisco was clearly in a declining position of dominance relative to a number of other places. Although it remained the largest city by a comfortable margin, its rate of increase was considerably slower than that of the three West Coast states and the chief cities within them. Perspectives on urbanization, drawn from several academic disciplines, help to account for this pattern of development.

The problem, though, was more than academic for certain San Franciscans in the period around 1900. They regarded expansion as a sign of health and necessary for prosperity, and they sought to reinvigorate the growth of the city so that it might retain its metropolitan status. The San Francisco Chamber of Commerce, for example, tried to increase American trade with Asia, especially with China. The Chamber saw San Francisco as the natural center of an American commercial empire in the Pacific. So it passed resolutions, sent memorials to the government, and dispatched a lobbyist to Washington to demonstrate support for a policy of commercial expansion in the Far East. The Washington representative assured the Chamber in 1904:

In the interest of American trade in the Pacific, in the interest of our Island possessions, and especially in the interest of Asiatic trade, the Government is duty bound to promote the use of San Francisco as the great American trade base of today. This city is financially and geographically the starting point for the greatest trade conquest of modern times.[48]

Reform of local government and politics, strategies for dealing with conflicts between organized labor and employers, and above all an extensive effort to improve the physical structure of the city, piecemeal as well as by an ambitious city plan, were motivated by the idea that San Francisco's metropolitan standing was at stake. The depression of the 1890s, which devastated the city's economy, underscored the precariousness of its position.

San Francisco was hardly unique in its attempts at promotion, reform, and planning. These years were an age of reform, and much of the reformers' energies were focused on urban problems. Explaining the San Francisco reform movements as a response to declining metropolitan status seems to ignore the national political context. Still, the form and content of the nationwide phenomenon known as progressivism were shaped by local needs and opportunities, with much variety from place to place. The importance of these local issues helps to explain the amorphous and even self-contradictory character of progressivism. The reformers and planners in San Francisco, then, may best be regarded as men who were part of a nationwide movement, who shared its general aims, outlook, and proposals, adapted them to the needs and possibilities of their particular city, and thereby became contributors to the ongoing "search for order"—and for growth.[49] The details of politics, reform, and especially planning in turn-of-the-century San Francisco provide the subject of the rest of this book.

2
Conflict and Conciliation

Labor, Business, and Politics in San Francisco, 1897–1906

In July 1901, the Brotherhood of Teamsters struck against the draying companies. The conflict lasted for two months. As it spread, it took on aspects of a general strike. It nearly crippled the local economy, and it was bloody. It exposed serious class divisions within the society and made obvious why employers feared unionism as a threat to the city's economic health. The strike also upset the existing political order by giving birth to a new political force, the Union Labor Party.

The party captured the mayor's office in 1901 and held it in the elections of 1903 and 1905. Under the brilliantly unscrupulous guidance of Abraham Ruef, the Union Labor Party actually managed to blunt the struggle between capital and labor. Placating both sides, it kept the city from being torn apart. But this political solution to social conflict was more poultice than cure, and it was corrupt at the core. By 1906, the administration could no longer protect itself against the numerous charges of malfeasance directed at it. Six months after the earthquake and fire had devastated the city, the Union Labor Party also lay in ruins. Its demise reopened the dangerous rift within the political and social fabric of San Francisco.

Since the 1870s, unionization in San Francisco had fluctuated with the business cycle. When the depression of the late 1870s gave way to a decade of prosperity, labor in San Francisco sought union recognition and sometimes even the closed shop, as well as conventional wages and hours. The unions held their ground during the depressed years 1883–1885, and began to grow vigorously with the return of prosperity after 1886. They continued to expand until the depression of 1893, despite growing opposition from merchants and manufacturers. The severity and length of those hard times, however, proved too much for most San Francisco unions. Faced with widespread unemployment, some unions simply disappeared, and nearly all lost members. The decline continued until conditions began to improve after the election of 1896.[1]

Two events that helped to end the nationwide depression were especially beneficial to San Francisco. The discovery of gold in the Klondike attracted miners to the city on their way to Alaska. Much of the gold they dug found its way back to San Francisco, where it helped to stimulate business. Afterwards, the development of Alaska led to durable commercial ties between the city and the territory. The war with Spain and the occupation of the Philippines also brought large sums into the city, this time from the federal treasury. To provision the troops, the government purchased supplies in San Francisco and shipped them to the Philippines. The army built special installations to carry out the operation. All this spending put money into circulation, created jobs, and primed the pump for the local economy.[2] To show its gratitude, the city erected a monument to Admiral Dewey in its most elegant downtown plaza.

The prosperity continued through 1905. Banking assets and transactions, real estate values, and building operations all grew.[3] Manufacturing activity also picked up, though here the gains were relatively more modest. Though it remained the leading industrial city on the coast, San Francisco accounted for less of California's industrial output in 1904 than it had in 1899.[4] Manufacturing in cities across the bay and in Southern California was growing more rapidly.[5] Also, new transcontinental railroads increased the inflow of eastern goods at the expense of local products.[6]

A reason frequently cited for the declining position of San Francisco's industry was that powerful unions drove up the cost of labor. However accurate the perception, unions did revive after 1896. Those that had survived the depression became larger and stronger, and new ones arose to take the place of those that had gone under. Unions in the building trades made the quickest and strongest recovery. They were followed by the organization of the previously unorganized, including even semiskilled and unskilled workers. After 1902, butchers, cooks and waiters, stablemen, street railway employees, retail clerks, laundry workers, teamsters, hod carriers, and laborers all unionized. The ninety unions in San Francisco in 1900 increased to 162 by 1902.[7]

San Francisco's reputation as a union town rested on the fact that organization penetrated beneath the traditional crafts to reach less skilled workers. Local conditions helped. Separated by almost 2,000 miles from Chicago and eastern industry, the city's isolation hindered employers trying to replace striking workers, especially the highly skilled. Unlike the situation in eastern cities, the influx of European immigrants did not depress the labor market. Most had come from Ireland, Britain, Germany, or Scandinavia, bringing both skills and trade union backgrounds with them. The small size of the local companies in the city also contributed to union strength. The unions were not, in most instances, forced to contend with giant corporations in command of vast resources.[8]

The strongest unions were those in the construction industry. Almost all construction workers were skilled craftsmen, difficult to replace especially in periods of rapid building, such as the one after 1897. The construction firms were generally small; before 1896 they suffered from an uncertain and highly competitive market. To reduce the perils of competition, the contractors turned to the unions.[9] In February 1896, some of the crafts formed the San Francisco Building Trades Council. From the start, it attempted to control the entire industry. The council, rather than the craft locals, issued working cards to building tradesmen, and its business agents saw to it that the rules of all crafts were enforced. Proportional representation, adopted in 1897, allowed the largest unions to dominate the council. The constitution permitted the officers to reject delegates selected by member unions and insist that others be chosen. After 1898, P. H. McCarthy of the Carpenters' ran the council as he saw fit.[10]

Tightly organized, the building trades unions dictated to the industry, winning high wages and good working conditions. Since construction was relatively immune from outside competition, contractors could pass on higher costs to the consumer. The Building Trades Council was even strong enough to insist that only lumber milled by union labor, or by workers operating under equal conditions, be used in local construction. Between mill owners and contractors, on one side, and the unions on the other, collusion rather than conflict led to profitable, monopolistic control.[11]

Similar agreements between unions and employer associations

were tried in some service occupations that were also free from outside competition. The Brotherhood of Teamsters and the Draymen's Association worked out an arrangement in 1900 intended for mutual benefit. The draymen had previously joined together to shut out nonmembers. Now they and the Brotherhood of Teamsters adopted rules stipulating that with certain exceptions, union men would work only for association members. The teamsters would not work for less than wages set forth in the agreement, and if a firm were expelled from the association, union teamsters would cease to drive for it. The brotherhood had the right to inquire into the causes for expulsion and to work for the firm until satisfied that the expulsion was justified. On its side, the association agreed to a closed shop and to boycott firms that did not obey the closed shop conditions. It also met union demands for shorter hours, overtime pay, and a sliding wage scale. Then the brotherhood learned, after signing a one-year contract in October 1900, that only 60 percent of the draymen in San Francisco were members of the association, rather than 80 percent as had been claimed. It realized that the draymen intended to use the teamsters to increase membership in the association. Despite some friction, there was no open break for several months.[12]

How strong then were San Francisco unions? In the building trades the answer is clear; the Building Trades Council, with the cooperation if not always the active support of employers, dominated the industry. But elsewhere, especially where products manufactured under non-union conditions with lower labor costs could compete, San Francisco unions were more or less dependent on the business cycle. They would grow in good times, when prosperous conditions created more jobs and employers found it more profitable to pay higher wages than to have production curtailed by strikes. But when prices leveled off, after 1903, so did union gains. There were more strikes as the resistance of employers against wage demands stiffened.[13]

In part, the strength of labor in San Francisco depended on the conservatism of the unions. Within the San Francisco Labor Council, the central body for unions other than those in the building trades, the more established locals had argued since 1900 for a policy of caution and gradualism and had tried to restrain the newly formed unions from too hasty action. The Building Trades Council, which stood aloof from the Labor Council and looked with scorn on the organizing efforts of less skilled workers, generally pursued a policy of conciliation, especially after employers accepted its dominance. The fact that many union officials were Irish Catholic, and that many sought political office, may have encouraged their conservative tendencies.[14] There were some militant socialists in San Francisco unions, but they were greatly outnumbered and produced no important leader. In 1903, factory workers in branch plants of eastern companies lost a series of conflicts against firms that, because of their greater resources, could afford to hold out.[15]

Despite its conservatism and vulnerability, the union movement in San Francisco was more advanced than in other West Coast cities and most metropolises in the nation. Employers and other local capitalists feared that a strong labor movement might hinder the economic growth of the city. If manufacturers paid higher wages to local workmen, could their products compete in an open market? If labor seemed so overpowering in San Francisco, might not investors look elsewhere to build their factories or purchase their real estate? Finally, the ability of unions to control working conditions had a moral as well as an economic aspect. The National Association of Manufacturers launched a campaign for the open shop in 1903, accusing San Francisco businessmen of cowardice in the face of union demands.[16] For some employers, ability to "run the shop" was as important as the cost of labor or the question of working conditions. They might be moved to undertake anti-union campaigns even when these conflicts meant loss of income, so long as the unions were hurt and their power reduced.

Business responded in various ways to the threat posed by the unions. Some sought to find an ingenious solution that would avoid industrial strife yet keep San Francisco prosperous; they aimed to replace conflict with cooperation. For example, members of the newly formed Commonwealth Club of California discussed possible arrangements that might ensure high wages to San Francisco workers yet allow San Francisco industries to compete with goods produced in open shop cities. A "good government" civic group, the club founders hoped that public-spirited men could use education and good will to improve the public welfare.[17] It turned quickly to the labor question. In a series of meetings from 1903 to 1905, it heard reports from some leading industrialists and merchants on the benefits of a contract payment plan that rewarded workers for increased productivity. According to these employers, more work was done, the workers earned more, everyone was happy. High wages could be compatible with low costs. Someone raised the objection that the contract system really paid the same wages for the same work done more quickly, and so profited the employers but not the workers. But club members were not deterred. They passed a resolution stating that "the most equitable and satisfactory method of recompensing labor is to contract with the employees as a whole for the amount allowed for labor in the estimate of cost."[18]

The noble intentions of the Commonwealth Club did not square with the realities of economic life. Many more employers, instead of working toward some cooperative arrangement, tried to handle the union movement by attacking it head on. In the 1890s, employer associations had organized to resist unionization and worker demands. To increase their strength, associations from several industries joined together in August 1891, to form the Board of Manufacturers and Employers. The board was active in support of firms and associations in conflict with unions; by 1894, it claimed to have defeated all but one of San Francisco's unions. No doubt the depression helped. With the destruction of many of the unions and the quiescence of most of the others, the board disbanded. But the precedent of a city-wide organization of employers' associations, united against unionization, helped to shape events in the next decade.[19]

By 1901, the labor movement was again healthy. Membership in the Labor Council grew from thirty-four unions in July 1900, to ninety a year later. In the first months of 1901 workers made important gains in laundries, meat markets, teaming, and other areas. Employers seemed willing to meet demands for shorter hours and better conditions. Yet the situation was not so rosy as it appeared. When cooks and waiters struck on May Day, they met stiff resistance from the newly formed Restaurant Keeper's Association, especially over the issue of a union shop. An agreement reached on May 1 between three craft unions and the Carriage Makers' Association was quickly repudiated by the association, and those small firms which settled with the unions were unable to obtain supplies. Bakery workers who went out in sympathy with the cooks and waiters found themselves confronting firms that stiffly resisted their demands. It turned out that these companies had been threatened with economic sanctions if they gave in. Similar situations prevailed in strikes called by the butchers and the metal polishers.[20]

Behind this change in attitude lay a secret body, the Employers' Association, formed in April 1901. Though only a small percentage of the city's employers were members, the association had solid financing from member firms. The aura of mystery surrounding it made its power seem even more awesome. The organization aimed to provide central direction and increased strength to employer groups in individual industries as they struggled with the unions. Its bylaws specified that strikes could be settled and demands granted only with the approval of the executive committee.[21] In many respects the association stood as a semisecret counterpart to the Labor Council and the Building Trades Council; it could both aid and discipline member organizations. It was the Employers' Association that successfully pressured restaurants, carriage makers, metal polishing firms, and bakeries into continued resistance to union shops.

By the beginning of summer 1901, an inevitable clash loomed between the Employers' Association and the labor movement. The association wanted a conflict to continue its spring victories. The unions, on the other hand, had lost some bitter strikes because of the intervention of the Employers' Association. They were fearful and uncertain about the extent of its power. Certainly a major victory over the association would improve a steadily worsening situation. So both sides accepted a showdown. It came in July, when a long simmering dispute between the Draymen's Association and the teamsters erupted into a large-scale strike.[22]

As the story of the strike has been told in detail elsewhere,[23] only the significant events and implications of the conflict need be related here. The Employers' Association pressured the draymen into breaking their understanding with the teamsters. In July 1901, a non-union firm, not a member of the association, subcontracted with a member company to haul baggage for a church convention. The arrangement clearly violated the 1900 agreement between the teamsters and the draymen, but the executive committee of the association insisted that teamsters haul the baggage. They refused and were fired, as were employees of other firms who also declined to touch the hot cargo. Though most of the member drayage firms did not initially approve of this policy of confrontation, they soon changed their position, apparently influenced by the Employers' Association. Each company ordered its drivers to haul the baggage; when the drivers refused, they were locked out. On July 25, the union began calling out all its members. It wanted to disrupt the economy enough to convince businessmen to halt the activities of the Employers' Association. Because of the importance of teaming in San Francisco, where the docks were some distance from the railroad terminals, and because it was the height of the season for perishable food, the walkout affected many people.

Attempts to reach a settlement were initiated by Mayor James D. Phelan and others, but failed because of the irreconcilable positions of the two sides. The union insisted that it have the right to organize, that the Employers' Association not discriminate against employers of only union men, nor against union members, and that all employees be reinstated. If these conditions were met, the union would order its members to obey all instructions of their employers. On its side the association would only promise to recommend that employers not discriminate against union men in filling vacancies. It demanded that union members promise not to engage in or support boycotts or sympathy strikes. Most important, the spokesman for the Employers' Association indicated that in the future, all differences between employers and workers must be settled without interference from union officials. While claiming that it did not oppose union organization, the association sought to make unionization toothless.

The draymen had replaced the strikers with discharged army teamsters returning from the Philippines and with other, less experienced drivers. When striking teamsters began to harass and attack the strikebreakers, the mayor ordered extra police to protect the wagons and drivers. Some rode on the wagons, and union men claimed the guards were helping to unload freight and otherwise assist the drivers. To the strikers, it seemed as if the city government were actually aiding their opponents. On the union side, the strike spread by the beginning of August to include members of the City Front Federation, the central body of off-shore and on-shore unions working in the port. The Teamster's Union was an affiliate of the federation. Because of the importance of the teamsters to the labor movement in the city, other unions knew it was imperative to defend the teamsters from this assault. A strike of the City Front Federation could cripple the economy of San Francisco immediately. In other bay ports, including Oakland, Crockett, and Port Costa, striking longshoremen and warehousemen tied up the shipment of California wheat at the height of the season. Though not a full-fledged general strike, the walkout began to inflict great damage on the local and even regional economy.

Yet it was not to be settled quickly. With stakes so high, neither side was ready to concede so long as it had remaining resources.

Further efforts at mediation during August and September failed; the contest became one of endurance. The Employers' Association and its allies sought to fill the vacated jobs with non-union men, including soldiers returning from Asia and college students from Stanford and Berkeley. Blacks were imported from the Midwest. By the third week in September, the number of strike-breakers had increased sufficiently so that the waterfront was again active. As a last effort, strikers became more violent against scabs and wagons. Skirmishes with police and private guards who had been deputized led finally to a pitched battle on September 28 between strikers and special policemen. Four days later, Governor Henry Gage finally brought the officers of the Draymen's Association and the Teamsters' Union together, and announced a settlement.

The unions were probably saved from total defeat by Gage's intervention. Having overestimated their control of the labor force, they had not been able totally to halt traffic and trade in the city. Their resources could not have carried them much further. Exact terms of the agreement were kept secret, but the settlement was in most respects a restoration of the *status quo ante*. Strikers were rehired by the employers, but strikebreakers were not discharged nor were union shop conditions reinstituted. Both sides lifted their boycotts. Employers claimed a complete and unconditional victory because the teamsters had lost their closed shop. In fact, however, the unions under attack were hardly destroyed, and the results of such a strenuous campaign on the part of the Employers' Association did not compensate for the tremendous cost. Having failed to root out unionism, the association found its constituency unwilling to undertake further offensives. Had the unions been seriously crippled, no doubt more employers would have continued to support the association. Instead, many chose to recognize the unions and entered into collective bargaining arrangements with them.[24] The association quickly withered away.

The next concerted anti-union drive was undertaken in 1904, when the Citizens' Alliance, a national open shop organization, attacked San Francisco labor. Executive Secretary Herbert George came to the city after triumphs in Colorado and in various California towns. Throughout the years 1904 and 1905, he sought to prod San Francisco employers into becoming more militantly antilabor. Despite new techniques and much publicity, the campaign fizzled. Unions were too securely established to be destroyed by an alliance that did not win enthusiastic support from local employers. George and his group were outsiders and could be portrayed as coming into San Francisco to upset peaceful labor-employer relations. Despite all its hopeful pronouncements, mostly directed to the East, about restoring civilization and law to the barbarous wilderness of San Francisco, the alliance failed in its aims.[25]

The open shop drives of 1901 and 1904–1905 did have significant political consequences. The strike of 1901 led directly to the formation of a new and unusual political organization, the Union Labor Party; the efforts of George and the alliance helped to strengthen the hold of that party on the city government.

The strike caught Mayor Phelan between hammer and anvil. Union men were angry with him because he had ordered policemen to guard the wagons and later allowed private detectives to be deputized and to carry guns. The Employers' Association was upset because he had refused to call out the militia. They also felt that the police courts were too lenient with arrested strikers.[26] Phelan tried to mediate the conflict but he failed. With the elections set for November 1901, there was little time for tempers to cool. Phelan's sudden fall from popularity created a political vacuum soon filled by a novel political organization.

The Union Labor Party was an amalgam of two ostensibly antagonistic movements, yoked together by the brilliant political imagination of Abraham Ruef. The son of Alsatian Jewish immigrants, a graduate of the University of California and Hastings Law College, Ruef had been actively involved in San Francisco politics since 1886, working first against, then with the various bosses who controlled the Republican political machine.[27] His early career revealed his ability to combine a moderate urge for reform with a sure understanding of the realities of power, which meant primarily the Southern Pacific Railroad and some public service corporations. He soon learned that the railroad directed not only the "regular" Republican machine but most of the independent, antiboss movements as well.[28] It also had ties with the minority Democratic party. Ruef developed the skills essential for this style of politics. He learned when to join the organization, when to oppose it, and how he might secure enough support to be a swing man during crucial disputes. He also became adept at gauging public opinion and appealing directly to the voters, a talent that took on added importance after the passage of a primary law in 1900. Under the law, which Ruef helped to draft, primaries became official elections rather than merely party devices. With the grosser tricks of political machines, such as ballot tampering, rendered impossible, insurgents now had a greater chance of winning control of nominating conventions. Bossism, though hardly eliminated, was perhaps democratized.[29]

Ruef moved quickly to take advantage of the new situation. Before the primary election of 1901, he organized the Republican Primary League, a volunteer group created to secure control of the local party for himself. It was to be large and broadly based, to include all classes of citizens who might now be taking a more active interest in politics. He also saw the necessity to organize it so "that one man could direct it and . . . be its legitimate power and control." As "a permanent organization" he hoped that eventually the Primary League "would be coextensive with the party itself." Ideally, almost every Republican in the city would be included, and "every element was to be represented—every religion and creed, labor, capital, merchants, practical politicians, professional men." Though it would appear truly representative and be strong enough to take on the railroad and the bosses, the league "must be constituted to work harmoniously under the leadership of one man. I wanted it so organized that it would follow along my lines."[30]

Ruef chose as directors men who were loyal to him and yet represented the diverse interests and cultural groupings of the city. He ran a strenuous and expensive campaign to elect his delegates for the local convention. Though his ticket won a majority of the votes, apportionment worked against him; the league elected fewer than half the delegates. The regular machine selected city auditor Asa Wells as Republican candidate for mayor. Ruef refused to support him, despite offers of patronage. He held his league together and waited for another opportunity.[31]

While Ruef was at work, labor unionists were trying to create a political instrument that might serve their needs better than Phelan's Democratic administration or the Republic opposition. In July, officials of some of the smaller unions began to push the idea of a union labor party. They called for a nominating convention. The older and stronger unions, initially cool to the idea, warmed somewhat as the Teamsters' strike spread, but ultimately kept aloof. Some key figures like P. H. McCarthy, who had held office under Phelan, strongly opposed the formation of the Union Labor Party. The Labor Council would not endorse it.[32]

If organized labor turned its back, Abraham Ruef and his Republican Primary League did not. Ruef later boasted that he had instantly seen the movement's potential, "that without strong outside influence it would never succeed, [but if] properly organized and handled, it might broaden from a purely local organization to one of State and even National importance." It might, in other words, be Ruef's road to power. He calculated that in a three-way race, the Union Labor Party, supported by the Republican Primary League, could elect a few candidates, perhaps even the mayor. He moved quickly to secure control of the Labor Party convention, using members of the Primary League who were also unionists. He chose Eugene E. Schmitz as his candidate for mayor. Schmitz was president of the Musicians' Union, a popular orchestra leader, Ruef's partner in some small business ventures, and a director of the Primary League. Aside from being controllable by Ruef, Schmitz's main assets were good looks, imposing stature, and German-Irish parentage. Ruef arranged that each candidate make a speech before the balloting. He wrote an address for Schmitz that easily captured the convention. "It was a repetition," Ruef modestly admitted, "of Bryan's speech on the 'Cross of Gold.' "[33]

Though a candidate of the Union Labor Party and a union president, Schmitz was not extreme on labor issues. Ruef felt Schmitz could win the votes of the "conservative element who are tired of all the industrial warfare." So he wrote a platform and an acceptance speech calculated to appeal to both capital and labor. Ruef shaped the whole campaign to present Schmitz as a moderate on labor questions, even if he had to be set apart from the rest of the Union Labor ticket. The scheme worked. Liquor interests, including dealers and saloon keepers, gave Schmitz "friendly help" without a formal endorsement. Grocery story owners also aided the campaign, spreading the word that Schmitz might win. Ruef had less luck with the major corporations and the press. The *San Francisco Call*, the *Chronicle*, and the *Bulletin* ridiculed Schmitz's candidacy. More significantly, William Herrin, legal counsel and political manager of the Southern Pacific Railroad,

> and all his organized forces, and those whom he could control, all the public service corporations and other big interests, all the large employers of labor, and the employers' association for the repression of labor demands, were centering their fire upon Schmitz and using all their weapons of political warfare.[34]

Though some union leaders like McCarthy opposed the idea of a labor party, the rank and file did not. Ruef had his men poll Building Trades Council members on job sites, and he found them overwhelmingly and openly in favor of Schmitz. Other union officials and organizations overcame an initial hostility and endorsed the ticket. Ruef attributed this fact to a "disaffection among the wage earners so deep that [they] hope for an amelioration from any change." In the Union Labor Party and in Schmitz's candidacy, workers saw the possibility of a friendlier city administration. Large corporations saw exactly the same thing. Only to this extent can the election be understood in class terms.[35]

Neither the Republicans nor the Democrats nominated strong candidates, and neither one established himself solidly as the best bet to defeat Schmitz. Ruef worked to keep them divided, planting false rumors where they would do the most good. On election eve he was confident of victory, having sounded out voters throughout the city. He claimed to have predicted Schmitz's total within 500 votes. Schmitz was elected along with three of eighteen Union Labor candidates for supervisor. He received 21,776 votes to 17,718 for Republican Asa Wells and 12,647 for Democrat Joseph Tobin.[36]

After the election, Schmitz took pains to deny that his triumph had been a victory of labor over capital. He said it was not the result of class politics but of the desire on the part of all the people for better government. Though he would not aid aggressive antilabor interests that sought to oppress wage earners by destroying the unions, he promised to protect legitimate investments on the grounds that capital and labor were mutually dependent. He endorsed the portions of the new city charter that called for municipal ownership of the public utilities. Otherwise, he said, the owners of the utilities would always be tempted to bribe public officials. He did state that he would not have allowed policemen to guide wagons during the teamsters' strike, but he promised to run the city on business principles. "I am going to give the taxpayers," he emphasized, "a conservative administration, and no one need fear that unfavorable conditions in the city government will frighten capital from investing. . . . Both employee and employer shall be treated alike."[37] Who could ask for more?

The first Schmitz administration was undistinguished and unobjectionable. Ruef worked to solidify his base of support in San Francisco. His goal was no less than a United States Senate seat for himself and the presidency for Schmitz. He knew that as a purely labor organization, the Union Labor Party could not carry him that far. He wanted to control the Democratic and Republican parties in the city and move out from there. The new city charter had given the mayor's office a good deal of patronage, including the selection of department commissioners. The appointments were supposed to be nonpartisan, and Ruef utilized this provision to justify the choice of non-Labor Party members and to "avoid the cry of a strictly class administration." The mayor could "recognize the help he had received outside the ranks of labor unions and select among the available supporters those comparatively best fitted by training and experience for the places." Ruef also decided that whenever possible a Protestant, a Catholic, and a Jew should be represented on each commission. The essential criterion for an appointee was that he had supported Schmitz in the last election. Ruef's machine would extend beyond the Union Labor Party and the Republican Primary League. If Schmitz's election had a basis in class antagonism, Ruef intended to use Schmitz's administration to mitigate that conflict.[38]

The first major strike after Schmitz took office gave Ruef and Schmitz an opportunity to act as reconcilers. In July 1901, Richard Cornelius started to organize the motormen, conductors, and gripmen of the San Francisco street railways. Every previous time the carmen had tried to unionize they had been badly defeated. Now, because of the hostility of the company, they worked in secret, but their activities were discovered and Cornelius and other leaders were fired. In November, the Market Street Railway and most other lines were sold to an eastern syndicate headed by Patrick Calhoun, a railway capitalist and grandson of John C. Calhoun. The syndicate merged the lines into the United Railroads Company of San Francisco. It retained as manager E. P. Vining, who had discharged Cornelius. The union was small; it represented less than a majority of the workers. When Vining continued in 1902 to fire suspected members, however, some called for a strike. Leaders of the Labor Council tried to delay action, fearful of violence. In April, Mayor Schmitz attempted to bring Vining and Cornelius together. The company refused to negotiate, and on April 19 the union went out, drawing with it many nonmembers until more than 2,000 men were on strike.[39]

Although the United Railroads was a large corporation, well backed by eastern financiers, the strike put it in a difficult position. The owners had paid an already inflated price for the lines they bought, and then issued $20 million in watered stock. To pay dividends, especially on the common stock that they kept for themselves, required a great increase in earnings and a corresponding decrease in expenses. A strike of employees for union recognition, better conditions, and higher wages threatened the syndicate's plans.[40] So there were strong reasons for continuing the firm anti-union policy of manager Vining. But the corporation was also a newcomer in America's most unionized city. It soon learned that the public sympathized with the men; rather than cross picket lines, people found other means of transportation. The newspapers endorsed the walkout. Mayor Schmitz refused to put police on streetcars that the company wanted to run with imported strikebreakers. He also would not allow privately hired armed guards to carry weapons. Yet to allow the strike to drag on would mean certain bloodshed, an increase in class antagonism, and the early political demise of Schmitz and Ruef.

Ruef decided to settle the issue. He called on his friend Tirey L. Ford, who was serving simultaneously as state attorney general and general counsel for the United Railroads. Ford arranged a meeting with United Railroads's president Arthur Holland. Holland arrived firmly convinced that mediation was hopeless, that the demands of the union and of the company were irreconcilable. After some heated discussion, Ruef suggested only "two or three slight verbal changes" in the proposals that "without material change of result, and without sacrifice of principle on either side changed the sense so that those [demands] of both sides seemed to be met." Holland rushed away to consult his directors and returned to say that the changes were approved. Schmitz promised to use his influence on the strikers, and they agreed to the amendments that evening.[41]

The compromise settlement was a political triumph for Schmitz and Ruef. They had indeed managed to reconcile capital and labor, much as their campaign had promised. Those who feared that Schmitz's election would mean a "class government" for the city could only be pleased with what the mayor had accomplished. Even the United Railroads was, for the time at least, content. To show its good faith, the company fired manager Vining.[42]

Electoral realities and Ruef's ambition quickly moderated whatever radicalism may have existed in the creation of a labor party. In state politics Ruef was still a Republican. In the years after 1902 he used his control of Republican convention delegates and much of the San Francisco electorate to select and aid Republican candidates for state office. In the 1902 gubernatorial race, Ruef and Schmitz campaigned for Republican George Pardee, despite the candidate's anti-union past.[43] Other favors for William Herrin and the railroad interests strengthened Ruef's influence in the party. His increasing control of the San Francisco legislators in Sacramento gave him additional leverage and independence. Ruef was becoming a power in the state, and there was little likelihood that, so long as he remained in charge, the policies of the Schmitz administration would jeopardize his position.

Some public service corporations believed they needed more direct influence to safeguard their interests. Shortly after the election in 1901, Theodore V. Halsey, representative of the Pacific States Telephone Company, came to Ruef and offered to retain him as an attorney for the company. In less than guarded terms, Halsey made it clear that the company wanted Ruef's political services. He would not have to try any court cases. "I may call on you," Ruef reported Halsey to have said, "from time to time for advice in matters of municipal law." In exchange for such advice, Ruef would receive $250 a month cash from the corporation. He accepted, and the sum was later raised to $500 a month. Tirey Ford of the United Railroads followed Halsey into Ruef's office and retained the little boss for $500 a month. Again, no appearance in court would be required. Though nothing was made explicit, Ruef "had no misunderstanding of what was meant by the employment." His well-known status as the mayor's advisor had drawn the corporations to him, and because he held no official position it was easy for them to employ him and avoid any charge of bribery. On his part Ruef could rationalize accepting the money, especially since nothing explicit was asked in return. Yet, as he later admitted, the position was morally untenable; "if occasion arose, I could not, as the paid attorney of the company, act in its strongest interest and at the same time fairly serve the city in whose interest I was a volunteer." In the early days of the Schmitz administration, however, Ruef did not reason so finely, nor did Mayor Schmitz, who was informed of all the transactions and raised no objections.[44]

The first challenge to Ruef's rising political star came from the labor movement itself. In his first term in office, Schmitz had appointed only two men who could be classified as union people rather than labor politicians. Leaders of some of the larger unions, awakened to the possibility of power by the election of Schmitz, formed a club within the Union Labor Party in order to drive out Ruef and the politicians. Ruef retreated temporarily, and a bona fide labor faction won control of the Union Labor Party in the 1902 primaries. But he managed effectively to regain his hold the following year, in part by winning the support of William Randolph Hearst and the *San Francisco Examiner*, and by establishing Schmitz as a national figure in labor politics. His ticket easily defeated the opposition in the 1903 primaries. The county convention then agreed to open the party to people who were not members of trade unions. The new provision allowed those who had received patronage or favor from Schmitz to join the party, thus ensuring Ruef's continuing control. Opening the membership made it possible to extend the party beyond San Francisco, whereas a strictly trade union organization would be confined to the city. Also, the party could run its own candidates for those city offices that demanded professional skills.

These changes weakened the ties that had existed between the unions and the party. In the mayoralty election of 1903, Ruef tried unsuccessfully to get Schmitz nominated on the Republican ticket. Then he worked, as in 1901, to make sure that anti-Schmitz voters would not unite behind either of the mayor's two opponents. He succeeded; the anti-Ruef Union Labor Central Club endorsed the Democrat Franklin K. Lane, but the leaders of the Building Trades Council supported Republican Henry J. Crocker. In spite of their efforts, Schmitz was reelected, along with only one Union Labor Party supervisor.[45]

Despite Schmitz's initial moderation as a labor candidate, Ruef's political ambitions, the changes within the Union Labor Party, and even the money Ruef accepted from the public service corporations, Ruef complained that the Union Labor Party could not fully win the confidence, much less the open support, of important economic interests in the city or the state. He attributed the failure to a deep-seated national prejudice that regarded soldiers, patricians, businessmen, lawyers, even intellectuals as fit for emulation and public trust, but which saw labor leaders and workingmen as tied exclusively to narrow class interests. "A strange commentary on our general intelligence," Ruef remarked,

is the belief that a labor man is not as fit or able to hold an ordinary public office as one from any other element of the people. As a matter of fact, the modern wage worker is comparatively better informed and has more thorough understanding of the vital current issues of the day—of economic, social and industrial policies and principles than the large bodies of the people from whom the criticism springs. Yet the selection to a municipal commissionership of a Samuel Gompers, a John Mitchell or a Eugene Debs, who have handled the largest affairs, would have been proclaimed not only a mistake, but an action against the best interest of the public. They would have been branded as incompetent and unfit.[46]

There were other, less ideological considerations. Ruef claimed that the position of the Union Labor Party on public ownership of utilities was incompatible with the promise to protect private investments in those areas. Eventually, the party must move toward public ownership. The privately owned public service corporations realized as much and worked to discredit the Schmitz administration. They feared not only municipal ownership in the city but also that success of a labor party in San Francisco might serve as a model and rallying point for labor politics elsewhere across the nation.

The movement for municipal ownership in San Francisco did not originate with the Union Labor Party; it had been written into a city charter drafted by "respectable" citizens appointed by Democrat James D. Phelan, one of the largest landowners and bankers in the city. Elsewhere in the country, the impetus for public ownership came as much from such middle-class reformers as Tom Johnson in Cleveland as it did from labor or socialist sources.[47] Yet Ruef was justified in recognizing that creditable operation of municipal utilities, particularly by an ostensible labor government, might ultimately jeopardize privately owned utilities throughout the nation. He felt that capitalists sought to undermine the financial credit of the city in order to weaken the administration and prevent it from accomplishing any large-scale ventures.[48]

San Francisco had the lowest per capita bonded debt of any major city in the country. In 1903, the voters authorized over $17 million of bonds, mostly for new sewers, street improvements, schools, and other municipal buildings. Slightly more than $13 million was intended for playgrounds, for Mission Park, and for an extension to Golden Gate Park.[49] The city charter prevented selling the bonds below par, and the 3½ percent interest did not make them an attractive investment. When bids were asked in 1904, there were very few takers. Ruef interpreted this rejection as a financiers' boycott of San Francisco because of its labor administration. Newspaper critics of Schmitz and Ruef contended that it was the smell of corruption and graft in city hall that drove investors away, that no one would put up money to be handled by Schmitz and his appointees on the Board of Public Works. Were the interest rate better, said a financier, the money would have been available, but an ordinary return did not justify taking chances with dishonest city commissions. James D. Phelan managed to place some $2 million of the bonds, those designated for purchase of land for park extensions and a library site. This money would be spent by the Democratic controlled Board of Supervisors and not fall into Union Labor hands.⁵⁰

Ruef later argued, correctly, that since the bonds themselves were legal, investors did not have to concern themselves with how the money would be spent. The entire resources of the city and its prospects of future growth stood behind the issue, and charges that the money would be foolishly spent, wasted, or used for additional graft were immaterial. Under normal circumstances, he wrote,

the foreign [outside] investor would . . . care for these arguments about as much as a national bank would care what became of its $20 bank note in the hands of a patron who exchanged a $20 gold piece for it; or a merchant what became of a dozen eggs after he had been paid for them. They might never be made into omelettes, or fried; they might be lost, stolen, or thrown away.⁵¹

In his view, it was not fear for the safety of their money, nor even the relatively low interest rate, but a concerted policy on the part of local and national financial leaders that kept the bonds from being sold and prevented the Union Labor administration from demonstrating its abilities. Attempts to sell the bonds in small lots to laboring people failed; bonds were less liquid and paid no more than money in savings banks. Aside from those placed by Phelan, the only bonds sold were bought by property owners who wanted a particular improvement made, which the sale of the bonds would finance. They were willing to take a loss and resell the bonds at a discount.⁵²

For years San Franciscans had been reluctant to finance needed municipal improvements. The inability of the Union Labor Party to sell the bonds was not unusual and probably did little harm to Ruef and Schmitz's political prospects. But Herbert George and the Citizens' Alliance were a more serious threat. After George failed to disrupt existing collective bargaining arrangements and to establish open shop conditions, he began in 1905 to attack the Union Labor Party as a class administration. He also called for more law and order, claiming that the police would not protect the members of his organization.⁵³ Fortunately for Schmitz and Ruef, George's actions were much too extreme for San Francisco. In politics as in industrial relations, he alienated more people than he attracted. His campaign against the Union Labor Party proved to be one of Ruef's strongest political assets.

The real challenge in 1905 came not from George but from the established political parties. Ruef again tried to get Schmitz the Republican nomination, in addition to the Union Labor endorsement. He hoped to certify Schmitz as a Republican so that he might run for governor the following year. Ruef almost succeeded, but at the last moment Herrin and other Republican powers, including the *Chronicle* and the *Call*, moved to oppose Schmitz. Herrin told Ruef that "the people I represent won't stand for this Union Labor recognition. They are not ready for it yet." Rather than force the issue and drive dissenting Republicans to the Democratic nominee—and perhaps tarnish Schmitz's image with union laborites—Ruef backed off. The Republican convention nominated John S. Partridge, a colorless young lawyer in the city attorney's office. Ordinarily Partridge would have been no threat, but in 1905 Schmitz's opponents united for the first time. The Democrats followed the Republicans and nominated Partridge.[54] The two parties also made joint nominations for all other elective offices. The election became a contest between the Union Labor Party and the united Democrats and Republicans, now called Fusionists.

Schmitz had new support in this campaign. The *Examiner* backed him enthusiastically, and P. H. McCarthy of the Building Trades Council finally endorsed him. Ruef wanted a Union Labor slate with the widest appeal. The prospects of election, however, appeared so bleak that he could not induce men of stature to run. He had to settle for a ticket made up of small businessmen, relatively unknown union leaders and members, incumbent office holders denied renomination by their own parties, and the few officials who had been elected in 1903 by the Union Labor Party. The list of candidates for supervisor was put together only two days before the election. The slate, though far from illustrious, did have a city-wide appeal; they were selected on the basis of residence, previous party affiliation, occupation, fraternal society memberships, and labor union ties.[55]

The Union Labor Party candidates had three principal assets in their favor. First was Ruef's remarkable ability as a campaign organizer, his imagination in devising new ways to reach the voters, and his determination to go all out, both in effort and expense. Second, in his two terms, Schmitz had done many favors for important people in the city, and the commissioners he had appointed had done more. Ruef had seen to it that opponents of Schmitz were treated especially well; ordinances were enforced with leniency and discretion. This "liberal" policy, though it aroused criticism and accusations of graft, had won friends for Schmitz, in addition to those bound by patronage. Third, and most important, the activity of the Citizens' Alliance allowed Ruef to make the campaign a pro-labor crusade. Some members of the Citizens' Alliance were vocally behind Partridge and the Fusionists. Ruef turned their support, as union leader Walter Macarthur said, into a brush with which to tar the whole Fusionist effort.[56] The campaign against Schmitz and the Union Labor Party was made to appear as an assault on organized labor in San Francisco. Union leaders had little choice but to endorse Schmitz.

On their side, the Fusionists attacked Schmitz as a grafter. Some charges against the mayor and Ruef had been appearing recurrently in the *San Francisco Bulletin* since 1902. They included accusations of favoritism in granting contracts and liquor licenses, of protecting gambling and prostitution, and of circumventing civil service provisions in some appointments. *Bulletin* editor Fremont Older, long convinced of Ruef's dishonesty, repeatedly filled the front-page news columns with stories of corruption. Older's was a voice crying in the urban wilderness. He had no solid proof for any of the charges. The other newspapers did not corroborate his accusations, and Ruef was able to castigate his motives as a personal vendetta.[57] Nevertheless, the Fusionists made much of the accusations. In a speech delivered three days before the election, Francis J. Heney, speaking for the Fusionists, said he knew personally of Ruef's corruption and promised, if called upon by the people, to send him to the penitentiary. Since Heney had already won fame as a public prosecutor in Oregon land fraud cases, the promise carried some weight.[58]

The campaign then pitted the unified forces of the Republicans and Democrats, endorsed by the Citizens' Alliance, against the Union Labor Party. The party ran on the record of the mayor. It also relied on the patronage and favors dispensed over two terms. It accused the Fusionists of being part of an antilabor movement. The strategy worked exceptionally well. Schmitz won reelection by a large majority, and the entire Union Labor slate triumphed with him. The rest of the ticket was doubtlessly aided by the use of voting machines for the first time, which made it more difficult to split the ticket. It appeared that labor had soundly defeated those who would destroy it, that the victory was a triumph for the working class.[59] But a close look at the returns weakens a strictly class interpretation. Schmitz ran ahead of Partridge in all but four election districts. He received majorities in the affluent Western Addition as well as in the labor strongholds south of Market Street. A San Francisco magazine, no friend of Schmitz's or organized labor's, admitted that:

> it is quite clear that he enjoyed the confidence and respect of citizens of all classes; he derived much strength from the labor unions, and he drew a big vote from the mercantile center; the denizens of the tenderloin turned the crank for Schmitz and so did many of our most eminent citizens who pay dues in the Pacific Union and Concordia Clubs.[60]

Compared with 1903, Schmitz's vote in 1905 increased in both labor and nonlabor assembly districts, hardly a surprise since he now had only one major opponent. But it is significant that he picked up about as much strength in those districts he had not carried in 1903 as in those he had. His city-wide percentage jumped from 43.5 percent in 1903 to 56.6 percent in 1905, an increase of thirteen points. In only two districts was his gain less than 10 percent, and he still carried both of these in 1905. He won less than 40 percent of the vote in only one district, and there he improved from 21.5 percent in 1903 to 33.8 percent in 1905.[61] His base of support remained in the strong labor wards, but at least the nonlabor areas lessened their opposition to him. The overwhelming triumph of the Union Labor Party destroyed the myth that only the competition between the two major parties kept Schmitz in office. It ended all hopes the Citizens' Alliance may have harbored about defeating labor in labor's stronghold.

Most of the eighteen supervisors elected with Schmitz were novices in public office. Their sharpest perception of the duties and privileges of a supervisor was the notion that the position paid a good deal more than the official salary. Even before the inauguration, Ruef found them fighting over committee appointments. They all wanted posts on the committees that dealt with private businesses through contracts or regulation, obviously the strategic locations in which cooperative lawmakers would receive favors from thankful businessmen. Believing the charges of bribery and corruption that had been leveled for years at previous boards, most of the new supervisors delighted that their turns had come. Ruef was less bothered by their dishonesty than their greed, independence, and carelessness. Public discovery would put an end to his political prospects and his lucrative retainer fees. With difficulty he convinced the new supervisors not to solicit bribes directly but to be content with money they would receive occasionally from James Gallagher, Ruef's leader on the board. Ruef was confident the funds would be forthcoming from large interests whose affairs could be affected by the Board of Supervisors. They would pay Ruef "attorney's fees," and he would pass half the sum to Gallagher, who would divide it, without discussion, among the supervisors. The supervisors would be told in closed caucuses how to vote on crucial matters. Ruef hoped the arrangement would keep the supervisors in line by paying them for their votes and still protect them from discovery.[62]

Ruef later claimed that after giving half of the fees to Gallagher, he split the remainder evenly with Schmitz. And Schmitz was receiving more than money. After his third victory, elements of the city's high society adopted the elegant mayor as their own. Having been snubbed and ridiculed for four years, he was suddenly invited to join the "fashionable skating club."[63] Though he declined the honor, his contacts with men of society and wealth increased. Schmitz had been courted before 1906, especially by William J. Dingee, a *nouveau* millionaire who wined, dined, and introduced him to New York society.[64] But only after the 1905 election did society in San Francisco recognize the mayor. Schmitz was evidently a charming man, but there were other motives behind the adulation he now received. According to "Autolycus," an astute, pseudonymous commentator on the San Francisco social and political scene, Schmitz's large margin of victory made people of influence aware of the importance of a man who "up to that time they [had] regarded . . . as a pestiferous accident likely to be wiped out of existence by the next turn of the political wheel." Schmitz and the Union Labor Board of Supervisors had the power to grant new public utility franchises. Showering him with attention could certainly not hurt prospective investors. A friendly city government could charge less than the franchises were actually worth; it could even grant them for nothing. After watching this process for several months, "Autolycus" remarked that although he did not believe the mayor had been in on rumored payoffs, he was certain that Schmitz was "vulnerable to the social attacks."[65]

The best example of the ability of men of society to get favors from Schmitz is the case of the Ocean Shore Railway. J. Downey Harvey, nephew of society leader Eleanor Martin and a member of the "High Irish Push," had paid some court to Schmitz before the election, but now his affection and attention really warmed.[66] Harvey and other local financiers were building an interurban railroad along the coast to the resort city of Santa Cruz, eighty miles south of San Francisco. The plans called for a terminal in the city at Twelfth and Market streets, and the company wanted a franchise from the city to operate an overhead trolley between that point and the county line. Application had been made to the previous Board of Supervisors and had received preliminary approval. Before the new board took office, Mayor Schmitz informed them and Ruef of his promise to see that the application be granted. He argued that the new road would bring business to the city and create employment for a large number of workers. Provisions in the new charter stipulated that a percentage of the receipts of any franchise must be paid to the city and the franchise be limited to twenty-five years. But Schmitz said these would not apply because this franchise would be used in connection with a previous grant that ran for fifty years.

The supervisors were upset. There was public opposition to trolleys with overhead wires, and it might be politically damaging to issue such a franchise. The terms made the franchise look like an incredible gift. The promoters of the corporation were not friends of the Labor Party and had opposed Schmitz in the last election. Most disappointing, there would be no payoff. Ruef also was unhappy about the proposal, but Schmitz remained adamant. "We will put that franchise through or there will be war," he told Ruef. To maintain solidarity, Ruef worked hard on the supervisors, and they came through after being assured that no one was making any money on the deal. No one, that is, except the Ocean Shore Railroad Company, which in a prospectus for the sale of bonds valued the franchise at $2 million.[67] J. Downey Harvey and William J. Dingee, who also was interested in the road, had managed to capitalize their friendship with Schmitz at considerably more than its value on the open market.

Ruef soon arranged other deals, based on monetary rather than social considerations. He took money from fight promoters, the gas company, real estate developers, and two competing telephone companies. He passed part of it to the mayor and the supervisors. Preliminary negotiations with the United Railroads were begun that would culminate, after the earthquake and fire of April, in a $200,000 payoff to Ruef. Dwarfing all the other ventures, the Bay Cities Water Company offered Ruef $1 million to help it sell its water rights to the city for $10.5 million.[68] These conspiracies, with several others, are the known or alleged cases of bribery and graft that riddled the third Schmitz administration. They came to light because criminal proceedings were instituted in October 1906, against Ruef, Schmitz, the Board of Supervisors, and those who had paid

Ruef the spurious attorney's fees. But long before the prosecution began, James D. Phelan unmasked the Schmitz administration in a brief fable:

> Once upon a time there was an election and the good merchants of the community were very much alarmed lest the success of the candidate would mean anarchy, but their fears were allayed when they saw the standard of the administration unfurled, and what they had believed to be the red flag of anarchy turned out to be the red flag of the auctioneer—everything was for sale![69]

Looked at moralistically, Ruef's actions and those of his associates were reprehensible. He did more than wink at vice; he and the mayor were in the business themselves.[70] After the election of 1905 gave Ruef control of the supervisors, he undertook an almost systematic sale of franchise privileges and rate regulations. The deals earned practically no revenue for the city nor savings for the citizens; they merely lined the pockets of public officials. When all this corruption came to light, it brought shame to what was supposedly a labor union government, reinforcing the commonly held idea that workingmen were not fit to hold public office. Yet a purely moralistic treatment of Ruef and the Union Labor Party is inadequate. It substitutes indignation for explanation, and it fails to see the functional relationship between machine politics and American urban life.

The most convincing general explanation for the persistence of bosses and machines is that they perform a number of important and desired services for which there are no legally or morally sanctioned instruments. Through favors and patronage they can serve the welfare and employment needs of groups that are ignored by official agencies, if such exist, or excluded from approved channels of social mobility. They can grease the wheels of bureaucracies in their dealings with private businesses, and they can use the regulatory powers of government to reduce competition and increase profits for friends of the administration. They can tolerate illegal activities for which there is still great demand. Acting as brokers between conflicting interests, they win enough political support, thanks to all the favors they dole out, to control the city government. Thus they can supply some direction to government handicapped by constitutional arrangements that disperse authority and make effective leadership highly improbable.[71]

Ruef, Schmitz, and the Union Labor Party fit comfortably within this general model. They did their favors for both legitimate and illegitimate businesses. They recognized the political claims of the various ethnic groups through appointments and nominations. They certainly provided avenues of social mobility for minor union leaders and union members by electing a number of them to the Board of Supervisors in 1905, though here the consequences were a travesty of the "rags-to-riches" motif.

The greatest achievement of Ruef and his associates was not the nickel-and-dime favors and signs of approval upon which political machines are customarily built. Open class warfare threatened San Francisco in these years. Two antilabor offensives challenged the powerful union movement. The Union Labor Party arose and Schmitz won election in 1901 because of a long, bloody, and costly strike. Yet in the years from 1902 to 1906, there was relative harmony in industrial relations. The unions recovered from the strike of 1901, helped to elect Schmitz, and made important gains in the next few years. Most employers, on their side, did not feel threatened enough to join the Citizens' Alliance crusade. Although there was some fatal violence in at least two strikes during these years, it did not compare with the teamsters' strike in 1901 or the carmen's against the United Railroads in 1907. Schmitz was partially responsible for the relative absence of bloodshed. By refusing police protection to strikebreakers, he discouraged employers from undertaking any pitched battles with labor.[72] Conversely, when called upon to mediate in labor disputes, he counseled moderation to the unions and would not support extreme demands. What Schmitz gave the unions primarily was his presence as the "visible symbol of labor's strength."[73] Having the symbol, they were less insistent on demanding the reality. Put another way, the political power of labor manifested in the election and reelections of Schmitz was a partial substitute for economic power; it served as a restraint both on capital and labor.

Ruef's ambition and his grasp of political reality helped to minimize whatever radical potential may have existed in the movement of labor into politics. As he recognized, the party's position on public utilities—advocating municipal ownership while promising to protect private investment—was ultimately untenable. In the short run, however, it worked very well. Socialism in principle and capitalism in action made few very unhappy. Opponents of the Union Labor Party claimed that capital was reluctant to enter San Francisco so long as the unions were in power. But in fact outside capital had never invested heavily in the city, and it was during

Schmitz's administrations that Eastern financiers completed acquisition of the city transit lines, moved to build a competing telephone system, and finished railroad lines that would center in San Francisco. More significant, from 1901 to 1906 local investors had enough confidence in the economic future of the city to drive up the price of real estate and to undertake expensive projects, such as the Fairmont and St. Francis hotels, large new office buildings, and major residential subdivisions. Local financiers did not abandon the city to invest their money.

That the bond issue of 1903 went begging detracts only slightly from this argument. The city had practically no tradition of financing public improvements through municipal bonds, the interest rate was low, and the $17 million not a significant figure when compared to the private investments and real estate purchases that were undertaken. Certainly it is too much to claim that the Union Labor Party was responsible for the prosperity of these years. Rather the point is that in spite of dire predictions, the city became neither a wasteland nor a hotbed of revolution. Ruef, Schmitz, and the Labor Party benefited the local economy by maintaining relative peace between capital and labor.

The corruption also served purposes beyond enriching Ruef, the dishonest supervisors, and other officials. The sale or gift of franchises meant that the city was being defrauded of revenue it should legally have had. It also meant that some improvements were made, railroads built, residential subdivisions developed. It may be too extreme to argue that these projects would not have been undertaken or completed without resort to bribery or the peddling of social respectability. But the United Railroads was already overcapitalized and might not have been able to afford the legal price for the right to convert its cable lines into overhead trolley lines. After the conversion, bonds of the company rose $25 in two days because of the expected decrease in operating expenses. The Ocean Shore Railroad had run out of money; after it got its franchise rights for nothing, it was able to issue new bonds and complete construction. Similarly, the Home Telephone Company paid very little for its franchise. The company had agreed with Ruef before the fire to pay $100,000. Since it donated $75,000 to the relief fund, the franchise went for $25,000. A competing company claimed it would have been willing to pay $1 million for the privilege.[74]

If nothing else, the bribery expedited these undertakings, not only by reducing costs for the corporations but also by ensuring approval from the supervisors. From 1901 to 1906, with a supposedly honest Democratic majority controlling the board, not a single franchise had been granted.[75] Bribery, in other words, was instrumental in attracting capital to invest in improvements and persuading elected officials to approve them.

The Union Labor Party, then, was a response to the social and economic divisions of San Francisco, especially the violent discord between capital and labor. It offered a political solution to the social problem, satisfying enough diverse groups with tangible and symbolic rewards to stay in office. The electoral victory of 1905 was testimony to Ruef's genius as a political broker. Perhaps Ruef could have worked his magic for many more years, taking his cut discretely, had he not been cursed with a Board of Supervisors whose greed was matched only by their inexperience. As it turned out, the politics of brokerage through corruption, at least on the grand scale toward which Ruef was heading, proved short-lived. In October 1906, the district attorney announced that the entire city administration was under investigation for graft. The tortuous prosecution that followed reopened all the divisions that had plagued San Francisco.

3
A New San Francisco

James Duval Phelan and the City Beautiful

Even before Abraham Ruef and Eugene Schmitz rode the Union Labor Party to electoral triumph and personal fortune, James Duval Phelan had begun to work out an idealized picture of what the city might become. Phelan's vision of a "new San Francisco" contrasted starkly with the corrupt politics and social cleavages that threatened to tear the city apart. Yet Phelan was no outsider to the local political scene. He had served as mayor from 1897 to 1901 and stayed active after he was forced out of office by the teamsters' strike of 1901 that gave Ruef his opportunity. Throughout these turbulent years, he fashioned a program for municipal rejuvenation through civic art and political reform. Drawing upon the idioms of the City Beautiful movement, especially the Columbian Exposition at Chicago in 1893, Phelan sought to inspire other San Franciscans with prospects of a new city, a place in which physical beauty fostered social harmony, and both ensured continued prosperity and growth.

Spokesmen for the City Beautiful argued that civic art could play a civilizing role. Magnificent public buildings, artistically arranged and elegantly adorned, would induce an awesome respect among the poor and foreign-born who crowded into the nation's cities. The City Beautiful aesthetic tended to glorify the state, and critics rightly perceived an imperial theme running through its imagery. Phelan's vision of a new San Francisco, drawing inspiration from Periclean Athens and Napoleonic Paris, and looking forward toward American commercial supremacy in the Pacific, shared this imperial idea. It was his vision of an alternative future for the city, and he worked to persuade his fellow San Franciscans that it should be theirs.

Phelan saw San Francisco's basic shortcoming as the lack of a selfless and public-spirited citizenry. Corporations had been able to corrupt officeholders, overcharge the public, and provide inadequate services because the people, especially the best elements, were negligent in their civic duties. They did not have the passionate, jealous attachment to San Francisco that tied Europeans to their cities. The newness of San Francisco, its short and rapid growth, its lack of tradition meant that people had not lived there long enough to develop those bonds of pride and love that would allow them to put the good of the city above their own personal interests. Most of them were newcomers; they had arrived from all parts of the globe. The ethnic and cultural allegiances they brought prevented them from melding into the devoted citizenry San Francisco deserved and needed. Struggles between employers and laborers added a further and often deeper cleavage.

The city suffered from the lack of local patriotism. Public policy was narrow, short-sighted, and perverted to serve individual interests and private ends. Instead of taking advantage of its remarkable natural beauty, San Francisco was a homely city, dirty, cramped, with few broad avenues, public places, or handsome buildings. It did not give its citizens the public services they needed or their children the education they deserved. With life so mean, San Francisco was losing its magnetism for new residents and tourists. San Francisco possessed incomparable natural advantages, notably the harbor that made the city the nation's great Pacific port. But unless the people could be aroused and convinced to take an active interest in public affairs, to see their lives bound up with the destiny of the city, these advantages would be squandered and San Francisco condemned to an inferior status.

In order to mould citizens out of residents, to stimulate a lethargic public and unite it in a devotion to the city, the city itself had to be made an object worthy of affection. Public money and private donations must go toward creating a beautiful and inspiring physical environment. Monuments and statues of past leaders, men of genius, and fallen heroes would teach history and instill patriotism.

Grand buildings, large parks, and broad avenues would bring the people together and expose them to the spaciousness and magnificence of their city. On a more prosaic level, the city would acquire the public utilities, supplying the citizens with better water, faster and safer transportation, and cheaper gas. The school system would be taken out of politics and education improved to implant in the children a concern for civic virtue and to train them in occupations essential to the prosperity of the city.

If San Francisco were refashioned along these lines, if it became physically beautiful and culturally harmonious, if it provided its residents with both the requisites and pleasures of urban life, delightful parks and efficient streetcars, it could again attract migrants by the thousands. New businesses would emerge, and the growth and future prosperity of the city would be ensured. The city's greatest asset was the prospect for the good life in the city itself, to be realized by the transformation of an apathetic population into a citizenry passionately attached to San Francisco. This is the vision that emerges from the statements and actions of James Duval Phelan.

The 22nd mayor of San Francisco, bank president, real estate owner, patron of the arts, and ultimately United States Senator from California, Phelan began his public career with the advantage of a wealthy father. James Phelan, the father, was a forty-niner. Wiser than most of his contemporaries, and more affluent, he had come to San Francisco not to dig for gold but to sell merchandise. When he decided to go to California, he prepared himself for the voyage by stocking up on two commodities sure to be in demand, liquor and iron safes. Shipping what he could from New Orleans to San Francisco, he next went to New York and bought more goods which he dispatched on three ships, one of which was lost. He himself followed by way of the Isthmus of Panama, where he contracted fever. When he finally secured passage to San Francisco by drawing a ticket in a lottery, he made money aboard ship by selling baking soda to the steamer's steward. Both Phelan and his goods reached the city safely; he sold them easily and went into business with his brother Michael, who had come to San Francisco in the party organized by David Broderick.

The Phelans continued to import goods from the East. James had invested $40,000 in merchandise bought in New York, and despite losses in transit, he made a good profit. Safes which had been bought for $100 each in New York sold in San Francisco for $1,500; almost all items brought at least twice their cost in the East. Another brother in New York, John Phelan, shipped goods to James. Phelan made his fortune very quickly. The profit margin was so high that even though he was burned out in June 1851, losing $75,000, he was able to recoup his losses almost immediately. Brother Michael was a more serious threat; James had to return hurriedly from a pleasure trip to England in 1851 to save the business from the foolish investments his brother had made. James continued to prosper. He was among the first California merchants to ship wheat to England, starting in 1865.

For the career of his son, James Duval, the father's most significant investments were in San Francisco real estate. He put his money into choice city lots, and because the income was large he did not often sell. His first and prime purchase was the corner gore bounded by Market, O'Farrell, and Stockton streets. The property had been sold in 1848 for $16. Phelan was the fourth owner, and he and his partner James Ross paid $14,000 for it in February 1854. Six years later Ross sold his half interest to Phelan for $6,125, and Phelan kept the lot, erecting a large building on it in 1882.[1] He also became an important banker, organizing the First National Gold Bank of San Francisco in 1870 and serving as its president. He owned real estate in the city of San Jose, and was a bank director there as well. He was an organizer of the Western Fire and Marine Insurance Company and the vice-president of the American Contracting and Dredging Company, which worked on the French attempt to dig the Panama Canal.[2]

James Duval, his only son, was born in April 1861. For business reasons, the family lived for a short time in New York, but Phelan spent most of his youth and received most of his education in San Francisco. He was graduated from St. Ignatius College in 1882. Though he enrolled in the Hastings Law College of the University of California, also in San Francisco, he did not earn a degree. Instead, his graduate education was informal and included a trip to Europe in 1882–1883, where he studied the workings of European cities and recorded his observations in letters and articles for San Francisco magazines and newspapers. Upon his return, Phelan was persuaded by his father to enter the family business. When James G. Fair died, young Phelan succeeded him as president of the Mutual Savings Bank. In 1892, the senior Phelan died, and his son, James Duval, became principal manager of the large real estate and banking interests his father had accumulated.³

In assuming control and direction of a family estate, Phelan's career was typical of the second generation of the San Francisco commercial elite. Many sons and heirs took on the management of the fortunes their fathers had made; the more energetic and clever of them succeeded in increasing the holdings or in diversifying them to keep the dividends coming in. Phelan differed from his contemporaries, however, in his active involvement in public affairs and in his political ability. His two chief concerns were the cultural life of San Francisco and the reformation of municipal politics. In the 1890s he fought political corruption as a member of the Citizens' Defense Association, worked for the introduction of the Australian ballot, and helped lead the reform wing of the Democratic party that finally drove blind boss Chris Buckley from power. In the same decade he served as president of the Bohemian Club, then a coterie of artists and businessmen interested in the arts, and of the San Francisco Art Association. He was vice-president of the California World's Fair Commission in 1893 and actually managed the California exhibit in Chicago. He helped to inaugurate the Mid-Winter Fair, San Francisco's continuation of the Chicago event. During this period he began to commission statues and monuments celebrating historic events and public figures, with which he planned to adorn San Francisco.⁴

In July 1896, shortly before he ran for mayor, Phelan published an article supporting a new charter, then before the voters of San Francisco, which called for civil service reform, increased power for the mayor, less state interference, and a different manner of electing the supervisors.⁵ Phelan approved of these changes primarily because they would encourage "better men" to take part in city affairs and weaken the control of bosses and machines. Though he admitted that the present condition of government in San Francisco was deplorable, Phelan did not want Americans to dismiss cities as unredeemable. He agreed that Jefferson had been accurate in predicting all the difficulties of the modern city, but insisted that Jefferson's "fears could not turn back the tide of civilization, for it is after all the modern city that stands for civilization." Cities, especially great ones, were both inevitable and indispensible; they "are the repositories of everything that science and art and invention have done for mankind and they are a dear possession of every country. We must make our cities habitable. We must make them fit for a free and enlightened people. . . . Whatever is defective must be made whole."⁶ A committed urbanite, Phelan loved the great city, despite all its shortcomings, as the locus and source of civilization.

San Francisco itself represented the glaring disparity between grim actuality and magnificent possibility. Campaigning for mayor in September 1896, Phelan sought to inspire the public with his vision of the city's ideal future, the new San Francisco, while reminding them that only through their efforts could that ideal be achieved. The city had an excellent location, "for it is and must be the chief outlet into the Pacific of the trade of the American continent." Nature, Phelan felt, "has dowered San Francisco." The gold rush had attracted a "superior population," but one that lacked a firm commitment to developing the city itself. Without a community of interest, without "civic pride in the founding of a commonwealth," the early residents had been hunters after fortune, "on whose wings they hoped to fly when she smiled upon their suit."⁷

Yet the city had survived:

Destroyed by fire, she rose in fairer form. Pillaged by her custodians in the name of law and order, despoiled of her lands by fraud or by conspiracy . . . compelled to suicidally surrender her water front to the State in order to avoid a threatened private monopoly, betrayed by her legislators in the granting of valuable franchises for long terms without reversions, safeguards nor consideration, she has been the outraged and neglected foundling of Fate, surviving simply because there is a necessity that she should live.⁸

Commerce helped determine her destiny. Phelan shared the commonly held belief that San Francisco would have an imperial future as the heart of America's Pacific empire.⁹ But his vision was broader than that of the Chamber of Commerce. San Francisco lives, he said, "to be the capital of an empire, and to foster the arts of peace; to yield for her citizens the fruits of a civilization, riper and better than those which gladdened the Athenian heart and fulfilled the Roman's boast—'to be a Roman was greater than to be a King.' " Trade and wealth were the means through which San Francisco would supply her citizens with a rich and cultured life.

Though he referred to Rome here, the two cities Phelan most often mentioned as models for San Francisco were the Athens of Pericles and the Paris of Haussmann. He told his audience that:

When Pericles was considering the best use to which he could put the treasures of Delos, which flowed into the Athenian treasury, he consulted the wise men of his city, who, with one accord, said: "Make Athens beautiful, for beauty is now the victorious power in the world, and that city will take precedence over others by the charms of the beautiful, and, like a lovely woman, will win fame, admiration, love, and influence. Appreciation of the beautiful will render the citizens cheerful, content, yielding, self-sacrificing, capable of enthusiasm. What could be more enviable than a nation to whose festivals people flocked from far and near?" So they put aside the gloomy and austere models of the Spartans and made Athens, garlanded like a bride, the mistress of all hearts.[10]

Athens for him became the temple of a religion of civic virtue; its citizens became worshippers, obedient, faithful, and free of petty egoism.

The renovators of Paris in the mid-nineteenth century had accomplished a similar, if more secular, transformation. Under the direction of Baron Georges Haussmann and Adolphe Alphand,

Paris rose to a position from which she teaches the world how to provide for the necessities, comfort, and artistic cravings of civilized people living within a city's walls, and develop the fine and useful arts and sciences to an unparalleled degree, combining work and play, profit and pleasure, in such a marvelous combination as to delight and stir the emulation of mankind.

By "necessities" Phelan meant that the city must guarantee a healthy environment; therefore he urged the scientific study of sanitation to eliminate infection and disease. But necessities for him also included culture and beauty. The very existence of a great city demanded that "it be clean and bright and healthful; that its children be properly instructed; that the convenience, culture, and happiness of its people be an object of solicitude, and that its burdens be equitably adjusted." If the city could ensure for its residents a life worth living, it would grow and prosper by attracting newcomers and visitors. The lessons that Paris taught Phelan included the understanding that beauty pays. He assured his listeners that "San Francisco could be thus made a great resort—a great summer and winter city," if only the people worked to make it so.[11]

European cities, especially Paris, showed Phelan another means to make and keep San Francisco rich. Industrial schools, especially in France and Germany, trained fine craftsmen whose excellent work gained access to any market. Phelan wanted San Francisco schools to do no less. To improve the system, he argued for school directors appointed on grounds of competence, not political patronage. In stressing the importance of craft excellence, Phelan may have been trying to use the city's educational system to give its manufactures a competitive edge. Higher wages in San Francisco meant higher priced goods, but superior craftsmanship would keep them in demand.

The one American city that appealed to Phelan was Washington, D.C. He admired its broad boulevards and the magnificent monuments erected in honor of the country's heroes. San Francisco should emulate the capital and construct columns to commemorate the explorers Vasco Nuñez de Balboa and Juan Rodriguez Cabrillo, the conquerors John D. Sloat and John B. Montgomery, heroes in the history of the Pacific and the city. The pillars, he said, "should stand in our streets as an inspiration to the rising generation." Inspiration was crucial to the creation of a new San Francisco. The only way to transform the city, to make it beautiful and life in it humane and worthwhile, was:

by stirring the public spirit of the people; by teaching them that these objects are desirable, not only for their health, comfort, and lucrative employment of themselves and their families, but for the delight and pleasure of strangers who shall be attracted to their city, and thus add to their municipal and individual prosperity. Civic capacity will follow close upon the footsteps of civic pride![12]

Phelan's speech attracted widespread attention; some said it won him the nomination and the election.[13] He was elected in November 1896, again two years later, and for a third time in 1899. A skillful politician and forceful administrator, he removed an uncooperative Board of Supervisors and gave the city a government less corrupt and more attentive to its welfare than had his predecessors.

In his campaign, Phelan had pointed to the city's need for a new charter to replace the antiquated, oft-amended Consolidation Act of 1856. In 1897 he chose a Committee of One Hundred to draft a new document. The majority of the committee and Phelan desired a more modern, centralized, businesslike government in which the mayor would appoint administrative officials and be responsible for their actions. The new charter was adopted the following year, despite some opposition from spokesmen for organized labor, who argued that it was antidemocratic and antiworking class. In addition to strengthening the office of the mayor, the charter increased the number of supervisors from twelve to eighteen and made their election city-wide rather than local, a move intended to weaken boss control, and perhaps popular influence as well. The charter instituted a civil service system to fill the city offices and provided for a greater degree of home rule. It also expressed, as a statement of policy, the aim of the city to acquire and run public utilities, including a water supply, gas works, street railroads, and other monopoly services.[14] Given the primitive condition of the municipal undertakings the city then operated—the sewers, the hospital, the school buildings, even city hall—this nonbinding and extralegal inclusion may have seemed utopian. But it coincided well with the overriding intentions of the charter, which were to provide a more modern and capable government for the city as a means of directing the growth that most desired and prophesied.

While he worked for governmental reform, Phelan also sought to keep alive the idea of a new San Francisco, a beautiful and cosmopolitan city beloved by its populace. He personally commissioned the sculptor Douglas Tilden in 1897 to create a fountain commemorating California statehood. A year later he gave a library to the almshouse, and the following year donated libraries to two high schools. A fourth library, this one for the city, was presented in 1901.[15] He encouraged others to adorn the city with statues. When German-American citizens erected a memorial to the poets Goethe and Schiller, Phelan was on hand for the dedication in Golden Gate Park. A cosmopolitan San Francisco, he said, made up of all the races, appropriates to itself the German cultural heritage and makes it part of the city's legacy.[16] Phelan himself was chairman of the committee in charge of raising the monument to Admiral George Dewey in Union Square and served on another group presenting a memorial to California's volunteers in the Spanish-American War. He also gave or promoted the Native Sons of the Golden West monument, the University Football statue in Berkeley, the statues of William McKinley and the Irish nationalist Robert Emmet, and a group of statues in Golden Gate Park dedicated to Father Junipero Serra. Here again Paris was his model, for in that city the monuments to great men exalted the souls and awoke the emulation of the citizens. While honoring the brave, he wrote, we beautify the city.[17]

The project Phelan pushed most vigorously was a plan to carry that tongue-like projection of Golden Gate Park, called the Panhandle, to the intersection of Van Ness Avenue and Market Street. His second inaugural message to the Board of Supervisors, in January 1899, referred to the Panhandle extension as one of the most essential public improvements. Golden Gate Park was San Francisco's greatest public undertaking, the one symbol available to Phelan of the creative and life-enhancing powers of the city itself. Completing the Panhandle to Van Ness and Market, "the two main arteries of the city, reaching, with their tributaries, every section," would bring the park to the people, "would be as a welcoming hand reaching out to the residents and visitors alike, extending them the hospitality of woodland, sea, and shore. It would lure them from their busy haunts in the congested districts of a great city to the charms and restful atmosphere of nature." The park, if more accessible, would help San Francisco become the country's leading resort city. Phelan succeeded in convincing San Franciscans of the desirability of the Panhandle extension. A bond issue to finance purchase of thirteen blocks carried with the necessary two-thirds majority. The state supreme court declared the issue invalid, because it had originated under the old charter and was completed under the new.[18] Phelan promised to resubmit the question, but the opportunity to do so did not arise while he was in office. The need to secure money for improvement of utilities overshadowed the Panhandle matter.

Important as it was, acqusition of the Panhandle formed only a part of the more general desire to reshape parts of the city for aesthetic, recreational, and sanitary improvement and to ensure that future development would follow approved lines. The San Francisco Art Association, of which Phelan, the private citizen, was president in 1894–1895, requested that Phelan, the mayor, appoint a committee to draft a comprehensive plan for the "adornment" of San Francisco. Naturally he complied, selecting architects, artists, lawyers, and businessmen as the nine members. He told the Board of Supervisors of Mrs. Phoebe Apperson Hearst's plan to establish a prize competition, inviting architects of the world to submit plans for artistic improvement. He assured them that the new charter contained the necessary mechanisms to accomplish such proposals.[19]

Although nothing material seems to have resulted from the Hearst offer or the appointment of the adornment committee, the Democratic Municipal Platform for the 1899 elections reiterated, in Phelan's rhetoric, the demand for a plan:

When a city realizes that its future is secure, it should act with confidence. The great and varied resources of the Pacific Coast behind us and the vast ocean before us point unerringly to the greatness of San Francisco; and hence, we, who are laboring in its behalf in this generation, should plan for it while we still have time, on broad and liberal lines, that will ultimately conduce to the health, comfort and prosperity of its inhabitants.[20]

The platform called for a bond issue to finance a new sewer system, a city hospital, and the purchase of public utilities; it also advocated the extension of the Panhandle, the creation of a parkway to connect Golden Gate Park with the United States military reservation called the Presidio, and the establishment of public squares throughout the city. San Francisco, it implied, was economically an imperial city, but needed a physical presence commensurate with its material importance. If it were made beautiful, it would prosper as a pleasure resort and "attract winter and summer the people of other States and lands."

In Phelan's mind there seems to have been an integral connection between adorning the city and filling it with monuments, on the one hand, and municipal regulation or ownership on the other. The beautiful city would be a delight to its residents only if beauty extended beneath appearances, only if it included health, convenience, and efficient service. Good hospitals, clean water, an improved sewer system, and safe and rapid transportation were as necessary for well-being as magnificent parks and patriotic monuments. Though hardly a socialist, Phelan was more than willing to replace private undertakings with public ones wherever private interests were too concerned with profits to provide adequate services.

In his first message as mayor, he pointed to the city of Glasgow as an example of successful municipal enterprise. Glasgow would levy no municipal taxes in 1897; it earned enough revenue to meet its expenses from operating the streetcars, the water department, the gas works, and other public utilities. While not proposing that San Francisco immediately follow this course, he did remind the supervisors that quasi-public corporations were subject to regulation to restrain "their natural desire to augment their profit. The representatives of the city should stand between the demands of the corporations and the rights of the consumers," he added, and if regulation proved inadequate, municipal ownership under a reformed civil service might be the answer to the demands for efficiency, better service, and less corruption. Two years later he advocated that the city construct its own light, gas, and water plants, so that the city itself would furnish its people "these prime needs of civilized life."[21] The fact that the city would satisfy these needs seems as significant as the efficient provisions of goods and services; the utilities would be another bond between San Francisco and its people, another reason why the city should be the object of their affection.

A huge gulf separated Phelan's beguiling vision of the new San

Francisco from the actual city in the 1890s, especially the condition of public undertakings. The sewer system, for example, was a mess. Private real estate developers had built additions cheaply, using poor materials, and without reference to the system as a whole. More than 125 outlets discharged sewage into the bay and ocean; the mains ended so near to the shoreline that tides often beached the garbage.[22] The city hospital had been constructed in 1868, for a population of about 120,000. It was put up quickly and inexpensively, built of wood because it was intended only as a temporary structure. Yet it still stood in 1900, and its 400 beds had been supplemented by a mere 72 additional free beds elsewhere for the city's indigent. One observer referred to it as "a time-dishonored municipal monstrosity, . . . which in private hands would be open to criminal indictment." If the choice were between sleeping in the hospital or in the street, he said, he would choose the latter. Another critic said in 1905 that it was the worst city hospital in the nation.[23] Whereas the hospital suffered from inadequate funds, the city hall had cost over $6 million and was still a disaster. Built over a period of twenty years, with numerous changes of architects and designs, the completed building covered almost seven acres. But all the money and size did not make it any less garish; it was "a cyclops of a city hall."[24] Worse, the construction had been so shoddy and corrupt that the walls were to collapse under stress from the 1906 earthquake, leaving a grizzly skeleton.

The San Francisco waterfront presented another depressing instance of the inability of the city to build and operate necessary structures and services. In this case the fault lay as much with the state of California, since the waterfront had been under state control since 1863.[25] Instead of using public money to create an efficient and attractive commercial facility, the constant policy of state officials had been to make the harbor duties pay for both upkeep and improvement of structures. Successive governors had used positions on the Harbor Commission and in the administrative machinery as "an asylum for the liquidation of political debts," and the port suffered from the ineptitude and lack of concern of its supposed managers. "In the days before the fire," wrote a magazine editor,

> it was to the observer a matter of constant wonder how the miles of shacky sheds, of inflammable piers, rotting, toredo-pierced piling, extending along San Francisco's waterfront . . . could endure for a single year. These flimsy structures seemed to extend a perennial invitation to fire.[26]

Unlike the sewers, the hospital, or the city hall, the port had a direct bearing on the prosperity of San Francisco and California. It seems ludicrous that the city should have allowed the state to assume management and that the state should have done such a poor job with so important a resource.

Civic improvements festered in part because San Francisco voters were reluctant to authorize and pay the money necessary for construction and upkeep, either through taxes or bond issues. Citizens distrusted their city officials and feared, with good reason, that any large sums would be squandered by corrupt administrations. Candidates for city office had to pledge themselves to strict economy and to maintain a low tax rate, the so-called "dollar limit," which fixed the maximum property rate at $1 per $100 of assessed property. Voters also refused to approve bond issues. New projects were financed on a pay-as-you-go basis, so that while the city had practically no bonded debt, it had a miserable municipal plant. By 1900 this attitude was beginning to change. The new charter gave the impression, at least, of more responsible government, and civil service replaced some political appointees with disinterested administrators. The improvement clubs and commercial organizations campaigned for necessary public works. Phelan's energetic endorsement of the new projects certainly helped, as did the return of prosperity after 1896. Probably as significant was the emergence of Los Angeles as an active rival; a look to the south convinced some San Franciscans of the need to act in order "to redeem the City from the imputation of dry rot." Voters did approve $18 million of bonds in 1899 for a new hospital, for schools, and for park additions.[27] But the change was gradual and did not affect a large part of the population. Fewer than 30,000 people voted in the 1899 bond election, compared with over 66,000 in the general election the following year. Even Phelan's platform of 1899 pledged his party to observe the "dollar limit,"[28] though the pledge was probably more a ritualistic gesture than an indication of what Phelan thought desirable.

In many respects, then, the new San Francisco that Phelan urged his fellow citizens to work toward flew directly in the face of the long tradition of municipal penury. A city that would not adequately support its public hospital was not likely to spend fortunes on beautification or adornment. Phelan was certainly aware of the difficulties involved, and some of the concrete steps he took were attempts to overcome public resistance to municipal expenditures. The new charter more carefully fixed responsibility for the allocation of funds to make dishonesty at least more discoverable. Civil service was an important precondition for municipal ownership.[29]

As mayor, Phelan promised an economical and efficient administration and pledged to be guided by strict business principles. Even at his most visionary, Phelan tried to root his ideal city in economic reality. All the projects, from the sewers to the parks to the transportation network, were intended to increase the city's wealth through population growth and tourism. "If cities are made attractive," he wrote, "they will draw homeseekers and visitors, which make prosperity." If, conversely, the city were ugly and unhealthy, people would stay away. "So municipal art," he continued, "is not a dream of the dilettante, but should be the concern of the practical men of every community."[30]

As one of the largest landowners in San Francisco, Phelan himself stood to gain from a more populous city that also catered to wealthy tourists. Certainly he understood the relationship between the value of urban real estate and the size of a city's population. An unfriendly critic claimed that Phelan's own profit was his main incentive, that certain improvements like the Panhandle were pushed because of property Phelan owned in the vicinity, the value of which would be increased if the project were completed.[31] A more damaging accusation came from an anti-Phelan weekly. It charged that instead of developing his own holdings, he planned to sell them after others, encouraged by his fine words, had beautified the city:

> Mr. Phelan is a poet for revenue. He strikes the lyre with the plectrum of profit. He pictures in glowing diction a City Beautiful built for Phelan, but his own lily hands are not grasping the trowel. When his Timotheusian song has roused the civic ambition to the park and boulevard phase of energy, then will Mr. Phelan sell his holdings at enormous prices to the men that do things, thus at last permitting the improvement of that Market Street gore and all the property owned by himself and his brother-in-law. And when all is done he will point with pride to the colossal structures that he did not build, saying, "Talk about the Builders of the Commonwealth! What are they to me? Where would your City Beautiful have been if it hadn't been for Me? Therefore the least that you can bestow upon the author of all this grandeur is to name my city after ME—ever glorious PHELANOPOLIS!"[32]

Yet these accusations miss the mark. Certainly Phelan, a banker, real estate man, and aspiring politician, did not neglect his own interests, financial or political. Presumably he liked wealth and power; many people do. The creation of a new San Francisco with himself as principal agent would probably help to bring him both. But what must be emphasized is the long-run nature of his involvement and its deeply emotional quality. Phelan opposed those who would make quick and speculative profits from the city's growth by treating San Francisco and its people as a commodity to be exploited. If his fortune were to increase, it would do so with the well-being of San Francisco, not at its expense. There is no reason to discount his sincerity when he told an audience of city merchants:

Richelieu, the great servant of his country, said, with affection, "The State is my bride." And there are American citizens everywhere in every community who have the same instinct of loyalty and who, at the sound of alarm will give their support to the government, and who would regard the theory of converting the government to private uses for personal advantage as repugnant to them as would be the robbing of their neighbor.[33]

Phelan's attachment to San Francisco and his desire to have that emotion shared by his fellow residents might be described as a civic religion, but as that expression has other connotations, let us use the neologism "civicism" to depict Phelan's position.

Sincerity aside, there seems to have been a glaring weakness in Phelan's grand design for the social and aesthetic transformation of San Francisco. If he wanted to use the beauty of the city and the healthy social conditions that it fostered as a means of instilling pride and a sense of public responsibility in the populace so that the citizens might overcome their pettiness and selfishness and support measures to improve the city, then the means and the ends were virtually identical. San Francisco could be made beautiful only through the cooperative efforts of the citizens; it could provide in abundance and quality the necessities of modern urban life only if the citizens would agree to be taxed, would agree to submerge, at least partially, their private aims and interests. The force to produce this civic spirit was in large measure emotional—a devoted attachment to a beautiful and bountiful city. But of course San Francisco could become a fit object for affection only *after* it had been transformed, that is, only after bonds had been approved, taxes raised, building codes and other controls instituted, properties purchased, parks expanded, politics purified, public utilities acquired. Only the new San Francisco could motivate the citizens to create the new San Francisco. If pushed to its logical extreme, Phelan's plan had little chance of success.

San Francisco was not a closed system, running solely on internal energies. The prosperous years after 1896 brought both money and confidence to the city, and Phelan sought to tap this confidence and make it flow in progressive channels.[34] The challenge of Los

Angeles, conversely, produced a fear of being overtaken that helped stir San Franciscans. Phelan, on his part, always included an economic inducement in his proposals, arguing that a new San Francisco would be a rich San Francisco. In addition, his addresses and articles were probably intended as agents of inspiration. The prospect of a beautiful San Francisco, persuasively articulated, might instill a milder version of the same spirit as a realized new San Francisco. Finally, although only the total resources of the city could accomplish a complete transformation, private donations would certainly help. The monuments Phelan gave to the city would serve as small-scale examples of what the city itself might achieve and would begin the process of creating a patriotic, beauty-conscious population. Athens, Paris, Washington, three models for Phelan, all had required some resource outside the normal political and economic structures of the local communities to initiate a transformation. For Athens, it was the fortune of all the Greek cities, for Paris and Washington it was the power and wealth of the national governments. A question for Phelan, then, was where to get those resources necessary to begin the transformation. His answer was twofold: a volunteer group, the Association for the Improvement and Adornment of San Francisco; and the Chicago architect and city designer, Daniel Hudson Burnham.

The formation of the Improvement Association and the arrival of Burnham in San Francisco, which will be discussed in the next chapter, linked Phelan and his ideas to a national movement. Since the early 1890s, Americans who wanted to make their cities more attractive places in which to live had, by and large, subscribed to an aesthetic doctrine that is known as the "City Beautiful." The Columbian Exposition in Chicago in 1893, the shimmering White City, had presented a temporary yet potent example of what the "beautified" American city might become. During his work at the fair as vice-president of the California delegation, Phelan, like most visitors, was deeply affected by what he saw.

Aesthetically, the fair was dominated by two principles. First, the buildings themselves, monumental in size, were mainly classical, modeled after the great designs of antiquity. Second, they were arranged formally, harmoniously, and completely, so that a viewer would be struck as much by the relationships among the buildings as by the buildings themselves.[35] Thomas W. Palmer, president of the Fair Commission, felt that "the buildings, their grouping, and laying out of the grounds will in themselves do more good in a general way than the exhibits themselves, by the exhaltation that it [*sic*] will inspire in every man, woman and child." The man most responsible for the overall organization of the fair's architecture, Daniel Hudson Burnham, said that "the beauty of its arrangement and its buildings made a profound impression not merely upon the highly educated part of the community, but still more perhaps upon the masses, and this impression has been a lasting one."[36]

The City Beautiful movement found its inspiration in the architecture and the arrangement of the structures and their settings. After the Chicago event, many cities formulated plans to unite attempts at aesthetic improvement. The proposals for Washington, D.C., of the Senate Park Commission of 1901, also headed by Burnham, reinforced the idea that to do anything correctly, the city must do it according to a general plan.[37] When Cleveland in 1902 wanted to build some new government buildings and restore its village green, it called on Burnham and the architects John Carrère and Arnold Brunner to put the buildings into a unified whole. Although the entire project only covered slightly more than ten city blocks, a plan was thought necessary. The architects showed the influence of the Chicago Fair in the four principles they adopted for the new buildings: uniformity of architecture; classical Roman design; one material for construction; uniform scale. Plans for cities soon came to deal with more than architectural and site considerations; they included problems of circulation, adaptability, recreation, economy of transportation, and other matters. But as Charles Mulford Robinson, a leading advocate for the City Beautiful, said, "The spirit is the same throughout. It is the wish, in sudden apprehension of the physical possibilities of our cities, to realize them more fully, to make the community worthy of its present, to fit it better for its nobler future."[38]

While proponents of the City Beautiful stressed the need to plan for the whole city, they also paid attention to smaller details that affected the urban scene. Some proposed that outdoor advertising on billboards be limited or at least regulated, that street signs be artistic, that great numbers of trees be planted, and even that shopkeepers and artisans identify themselves by the colorful symbols of medieval heraldry. Most of them advocated building more and greater city parks and parkways. Robinson wrote that, as children of nature, we should bring as much of the country to the city as possible; "such pseudonyms as 'the Garden City,' or 'the Flower

City,' should suggest marriages not less lovely, and more practical and appropriate, than was the poetic wedding of Venice to the Adriatic."[39] The planners paid special attention to the design and placement of municipal buildings, of schools, libraries, city halls, museums; when brought together these formed civic centers. They favored classical architecture for public buildings and for the immense railroad stations that were integral to some of the major plans. Monuments themselves were important components of the City Beautiful, which as a movement could trace its origins back beyond the Chicago Fair to the Washington Monument, the Statue of Liberty, and the Washington Arch. In the words of a stern critic of the whole effort, "the aim of the City Beautiful was the City Monumental."[40]

As an ideal toward which to strive, most spokesmen for the movement pointed to Paris, which, "of all modern cities, . . . more than any other deserves the title of 'City Beautiful.' " It had streets both paved and clean; it had large public *places* encircled by harmoniously related buildings, decorated with the best of modern statuary. Attractive bridges spanned the Seine, and the whole city was put into focus by a cathedral "of immense proportions." Though the French spent huge sums on Paris, the monies had not been squandered needlessly or hedonistically, for Paris was the best example of the maxim "that beauty of municipal adornment pays." One observer estimated the worth of that beauty to the Parisians at about $200 million per year. The money came from tourists and new residents, drawn to the city because of its loveliness, and from the increase in land values that greater trade and convenience produced.[41]

Phelan's proposals for San Francisco were obviously part of a broad movement. The desire for a comprehensive plan, the emphasis on monuments and classicism, the veneration of Paris, and the hope that beautification would support itself through tourism and urban growth, these attitudes were common to a generation of city improvers. In most cases they faced similar problems, as the rapid and uncontrolled growth of cities in the late nineteenth century created chaos and ugliness on a grand scale. The Chicago Fair, expressing the best thoughts of the most respected architects of the age, provided a solution with wide appeal. In addition, both urban political reformers and architectural planners grouped together in the late 1890s into organizations such as the National Municipal League and the American Civic Association. They exchanged ideas and programs, and their political proposals and aesthetic tastes became systematized.[42] So it was no accident that the spokesmen for the City Beautiful talked the same language.

In Phelan's vision of the new San Francisco, one sees a program for social change intimately bound to the search for beautification. To a large extent, the same is true for the national movement. In the first place, the kind of planning that the beautifiers advocated demanded some restrictions on individual tastes and desires, such as limitations on building heights and the imposition of uniform design for a group of buildings.[43] More radical spokesmen thought it necessary to go further. Herbert Croly, an editor of *Architectural Record*, pointed to real estate speculators and large landowners as the chief obstacles to all kinds of municipal improvements, but especially to planning. It was "a gigantic real estate speculation," rather than the large corporations, which dominated municipal governments in the United States, and "which has ignored economy, good looks, convenient planning and all other considerations of general public interest in the efforts to encourage rapid and unregulated growth." Croly could foresee no significant improvements until the public authorities were willing "to assert the public interest . . . against the special interest which most insistently opposes almost all such improvements . . . the owners of real estate in our large cities."[44]

Croly's attitude, however, which implied that severe restrictions be placed on the rights of property owners, appears atypical. Other proponents of the City Beautiful did not see a clash of interests to be overcome by assertion of political authority, but a potential harmony uniting all citizens for the good of the whole. One optimist noted that businessmen were beginning to understand that art was a good commercial asset, that handsome buildings brought profitable rewards. Some of the major accomplishments of the movement were the work of philanthropic individuals who donated libraries, museums, and monuments, and who put up fine houses that adorned the cities.[45] While it was true that the city governments had lagged behind wealthy private citizens, few writers followed Croly in blaming hostile business interests that dominated or resisted the public authorities. Instead, the focus of attention was not on men of wealth and power at all, but on the middle and especially the lower orders of society. It was these people toward whom the social purpose of the City Beautiful movement was directed.

In the most general sense, the movement hoped that by bettering the quality of life of the average city dweller, it might improve the dweller himself. The improvement, or "uplift," would come in part from a democratization of the good things in life, as "beauty, cleanliness, and art are no longer reserved for the few, are no longer the perquisites of the aristocrats, but are made the common heritage of the common people, for the benefit and uplift of all."[46] The rich had always had their art treasures, their superb buildings, even their private enclaves of nature. The City Beautiful movement wanted to make these things available to everyone in order to civilize the populace. Schools, for example, were of particular importance because of their influence on the young. The school buildings should be well built and attractively decorated as a means of teaching civic virtue; art would serve as a corrective for crime. In the same vein, the great emphasis put on splendid public buildings was a recognition that the city halls, court houses, and libraries were the houses of the people and had to be built with the same care as had been lavished on temples and palaces. Beautiful buildings would nurture a civic religion, "which means the redemption of our American communities from the sordid and the selfish and the base."[47] This civic religion would act as a purifier of urban politics; it would also elevate and educate the masses. In the modern city, "the highly cultured, the less cultured, and the barbarian (as to refinement) must dwell together." The purpose of beautiful buildings and other aesthetic undertakings was to ensure that whatever leveling took place would be leveling upward. Civic pride would make the barbarians into citizens; architecture would stimulate such pride. Preference for classic design rested in part on the notion that the buildings of Athens and Rome had played this role: "What an uplift the Greek must have felt as he approached the Acropolis! and how the pride of citizenship must have stirred within the Roman as he passed through the public places of the Eternal City and entered the Great Forum with all its wonders of architecture."[48]

City Beautiful planners and architects considered efficiency and convenience in their designs, especially as they became more experienced, but they seem to have been primarily concerned with visual effects. Robinson, for example, could tolerate skyscrapers because the "steel skeleton construction gives free hand to the architect in the facade, and art must find in it a worthy theme."[49] The design of buildings, the size, the harmonious arrangement, the site, all were intended to impress, to inspire, to elevate, and to uplift. Burnham had spoken of the profound and lasting "impression" of the Chicago Fair, particularly on the "masses," and other beautifiers used similar expressions in describing the impact of civic adornment.

The plans themselves were supposed to work in the same way. Burnham's famous though disputed dictum began, "Make no little plans; they have no magic to stir men's blood and probably themselves will not be realized."[50] In an argument about the success of city improvement plans in general and a New York City proposal in particular, both Croly and Robinson admitted that the New York scheme had been too modest; had it been more magnificent, more inspiring, it might have received a better reception.[51] The inspiration of the plan would educate and enlighten the public to build the City Beautiful; the City Beautiful would elevate the populace, refining taste and, more important, instilling civic pride and patriotism. The masses, in short, would be civilized. Some beautifiers endowed art with almost magical powers. For example, one writer commented that French and German military prowess were responses to the Arch of Triumph and the Walhalla in Bavaria. "Why should not the American people be taught patriotism in a similar fashion?" he asked. The monuments would help to make good citizens out of the foreign-born population which "cannot read English books, but . . . can read monuments which appeal to the eye."[52]

Militarism was probably not a major goal of the proponents of the City Beautiful. Still, there was a particular social and political cast to their work. Though it is extremely risky to equate architectural and urban design with specific political and social systems, the effort has been made. Louis Sullivan attacked Burnham and the Chicago Fair as embodying a feudal, as opposed to a democratic, conception of power.[53] But feudalism is a fuzzy term that does not accurately characterize either the centralization of authority evident in the designs and arrangement of the fair or Burnham's own career as an architect of commercial buildings.

Other critics have found "imperial" a more suggestive word to describe the architecture and planning of the period. Patrick Geddes, the Scottish biologist turned urbanologist, was struck by the imperial tone of the plans for great cities displayed at the London Town Planning Exhibition of 1910. Despite the "dark austereness" of some plans and the "meretricious beauty of others," at the core was "the imperial, the Caesarist, type of city; . . . whether it be imitated from the Paris of Louis XIV or of Napoleon I, or from the correspondingly magnificent designs of Washington." In the "proposed transformation of Chicago," a reference to the Burnham and Bennett plan of 1909, he saw a restatement of "the strategic boulevards of Haussmann and Napoleon III."[54] Lewis Mumford, an admirer of Geddes, called the architecture of the American 1890s "The Imperial Facade." His dazzling chapter on the subject, in *Sticks and Stones*, suggests a number of connections between the urban aesthetic of the era and the social, economic, and political organization that was emerging.[55] Architectural historians John Burchard and Albert Bush-Brown noted the "imperial" quality in the Chicago Exposition and later fairs, a quality that set the tone for building design and city planning. In their view, "the Imperial aspect of this age dominated the reform aspect." The contemporary drive for garden suburbs and model industrial towns was a contrary and weaker influence.[56]

Imperialism is as troublesome a term as feudalism, but it may nevertheless be more accurate and more helpful, for it does convey some generalized sense of the emotional content of the City Beautiful. The beautifiers, Phelan included, almost always chose as their models three cities that were the capitals of empires. Pericles had adorned Athens by using treasures appropriated from the common treasury of all the Greeks.[57] Rome was the heart of the *Imperiam Romanum*. The Paris that the City Beautiful people adored was created by Haussmann under the second empire of Napoleon III. Washington, D.C. was laid out by L'Enfant as a "Seat of Empire,"[58] and perfected by Burnham to be just that. In the designs for governmental and public buildings, they preferred classical architecture of a grand scale, to glorify the image of the governments that built and occupied them. Monuments and statues would plant seeds of patriotism and increase loyalty to the country and its past. Planning itself necessitated an enlarged governmental authority with more control over choices that had previously been decided upon privately.

None of these facts alone is sufficient to identify the City Beautiful as the aesthetic of a new American empire. Even taking them together, they do not say a great deal about foreign policy or economic penetration. But they do, in a vague and indirect way, indicate that City Beautiful planners, in reacting against the ugliness and disorder of an environment created by laissez-faire capitalism and architectural eclecticism, projected a vision of a potent and active state in the process of taking its place among the world powers. The mantle of Athens, Rome, and Paris had fallen on the shoulders of American cities, and not merely on Washington, but on every wealthy, progressive, and optimistic metropolis that saw itself as one center of a continental and international power. For San Francisco, with its vast and rich hinterland, facing the Pacific and the hundreds of millions of people in Asia waiting for the influx of American goods and American ways, an identification with the cities of empire was not so far-fetched.

At the center of this imperial school stood Daniel Hudson Burnham. In 1904 he came to San Francisco to create a plan for the metropolis of the Pacific Coast.

4
An Image of Order

The Burnham Plan for San Francisco

By 1904, Daniel Hudson Burnham had established himself as the most prestigious city planner in America. He had already served as chief of construction for the World's Columbian Exposition in Chicago in 1893, as head of the commission for the Washington plan of 1901 to 1902, and as chairman of the Cleveland planning commission of 1902 to 1903.[1] It was an accomplishment for James Phelan that he could induce Burnham to undertake a plan for San Francisco. When it was presented in the fall of 1905, his work constituted the most comprehensive treatment of urban design to date. While offering innumerable suggestions for improving the city, Burnham concentrated his attention on two areas: a radical redesign of the street layout, and an enormous extension of the park system. A general theory of the city worked out from observations of European capitals guided his handling of both subjects. The theory, and the treatment of San Francisco, rested on a set of assumptions about the relationship between planning and society. Burnham believed that a properly designed city, filled with monumental public buildings, magnificent vistas, and vast open spaces, would serve as a lesson on the virtues of order. He intended his plan for San Francisco to reshape the social as well as the physical structure of the city.

On January 4, 1904, the *San Francisco Bulletin* carried a front-page article under the heading, "City Awakes from Long Sleep;

Magnificent Scheme is Outlined for Making San Francisco the Most Beautiful and Attractive Metropolis in America." The headline was misleading, for the story that followed was simply an interview with Allan Pollok, manager of the new St. Francis Hotel. Pollok complained that San Francisco was losing out to Southern California as a mecca for tourists and wealthy home-seekers from the East. He wanted more vigorous promotion of the city's virtues and a modest spending program to make it more attractive. There was no "magnificent scheme" here.[2] Yet something was up, for a few days later the *Bulletin* devoted several pages to the theme, "Make San Francisco a Great Pleasure City." Amidst a number of short pieces by prominent business and professional men, each calling for some specific improvement, one statement stood out. It came from James D. Phelan, who warned that San Francisco "will either be a great and beautiful and attractive city, where men and women of civilized tastes and wants will desire to live, or a great and ugly and forbidding city, which people will shun instead of seeking." After pointing to the new charter, the recent bond issue, and other projects as signs of life, Phelan turned to the big question. The city needed a general plan, "prepared by a competent person or commission, as has been done recently for the city of Washington, D.C., and Cleveland, Ohio." It should cover street widening, location of buildings, laying out of new roads, and extension of the Panhandle. Let us "have a plan made and back it up with that civic pride, spirit, and capacity which we all know exists in good measure, but which is not always awakened or wisely directed."[3]

The following day an editorial in the *Bulletin* supported all the proposals, referring to them as a symposium.[4] Other papers did not mention the story. Rather than a symposium or a spontaneous outburst of popular feeling regarding the future of San Francisco, these statements, including Pollok's "magnificent scheme"—which was neither a scheme nor magnificent—appear to have been a planned attempt to put this subject before the people of San Francisco, an opening salvo in the battle for civic beautification.

The *Bulletin* continued the campaign on January 9 with another page of articles on suggestions for civic improvements.[5] On January 13, Phelan, J. W. Byrne, and Willis Davis, presidents respectively of the Bohemian Club, the Pacific Union Club, and the Art Association, jointly issued an invitation to a select group of "representative men," requesting them to attend a meeting on January 15 to be held in the office of the secretary of the Merchants' Exchange. The first item on the agenda was the construction of a convention hall to seat at least 6,000 persons. But the most important issue was the need to direct the future of the city. "The civic spirit must be aroused," wrote the *Bulletin*, "the people must be taught to take pride in the beautifying of the city as they take pride in the beautifying of their homes. This city belongs to the people. It should be a credit to the people."[6]

The Association for the Improvement and Adornment of San Francisco (AIASF) was born at that meeting. The 26 founding members elected Phelan president and offered a host of proposals about what should be done: a great outdoor coliseum for open air sports; boulevards leading to Golden Gate Park and the army reservation at the Presidio; a boulevard around the bay shore; the adornment of Telegraph Hill; an ornamental hotel to crown Ashbury Heights. Phelan announced that he had already sounded out Daniel Burnham about designing a plan for San Francisco, and that Burnham had provisionally agreed.[7]

Actually, Phelan must have contacted Burnham at least eight months prior to the formation of the association, for on May 11, 1903, Burnham sent him the following telegram:

Would consider making design of general improvement of your city if given single charge of it. Could not accept any pay for myself but should desire to be free to employ others, such as landscape and building architects. All traveling and other expenses to be paid in addition to their salaries. Also a tour of Europe would be imperative in order to gather existing data found in cities similarly situated. Should want at least one year before reporting when should expect to make a full presentation. I ought not to be expected to accept any associate or associates except those I may select myself.[8]

Phelan tried unsuccessfully to see Burnham in Chicago in October 1903. Still, the architect wanted to do the plan, provided that he have a free hand. He wrote to Willis Polk that he would only do it as a labor of love, and he insisted as a precondition on the need to study the old hill towns that border the Mediterranean.[9]

This exchange shows that Phelan had wanted Burnham to do a plan for San Francisco for some time before the founding of the AIASF. Phelan's views about the relationship between civic adornment and the social and political situation in San Francisco dictated Burnham as precisely the man to choose. On his side, Burnham must have seen in San Francisco the perfect setting for a true City Beautiful. He offered his service as a labor of love, but insisted on complete control. Some sort of meeting of the minds had obviously taken place.

Phelan's task was to transform Burnham's enthusiasm first into a plan and then into a reality. No longer mayor, he had to find some extrapolitical mechanism to foster the endeavor. So he helped create a committee of public-spirited and prestigious citizens, formed in response to the well-publicized demand that the city do something positive about its appearance or lose its metropolitan status to the more energetic and unified Los Angeles. The committee could enlist the support and cooperation of powerful citizens as members of the sponsoring organization, and thereby educate a part of the social and economic elite to the need for a plan. It could raise the funds necessary to underwrite the plan. It could give widespread publicity to the plan, once it had been completed. Also, the larger the number of sponsors of the plan, the fewer its potential opponents. Finally, Phelan's political career had made enemies for him as well as friends. Any major proposal that had to stand largely on his endorsement would face difficulties from the start. The project of a respected civic association, on the other hand, even one that had Phelan as president and most active member, would fare much better when the struggle over enactment began. These conjectures help to explain the origins of AIASF, though they may overemphasize Phelan's role. Focusing on Phelan, however, connects the Burnham plan to local conditions in San Francisco as well as to the City Beautiful movement in general.

The men who assembled on January 15, 1904, to form the AIASF were not a random selection of the city's population. Of the twenty-six founding members, no fewer than twenty were listed in city directories as early as 1885: fifteen were merchants, generally presidents of large wholesale or retail firms; five were identified merely as "capitalists"; three held executive positions with the railroads; one was a hotel manager, one a lawyer, and one dean of a local school. Most of the founders lived in the fashionable Pacific Heights section; a few commuted from the Peninsula or the East Bay. Many were members of the exclusive Pacific Union or Bohemian clubs; one was secretary and another president of the Merchants' Association; a third the secretary of the San Francisco Produce Exchange and the Merchants' Exchange. Phelan had been mayor; Edward R. Taylor, a doctor, a lawyer, and the dean of Hastings Law College, became mayor in 1907. Henry J. Crocker had been an unsuccessful candidate in 1903. The founders of the association, by and large, were longtime San Franciscans and members of the city's social and economic upper crust. There were no architects among them, but

Edward W. Hopkins, a capitalist and former executive of the Central Pacific Railroad, was related to an architect and city planner—he was Daniel Burnham's cousin.[10]

The twenty-six founding members set out to recruit others, hoping to attract into the organization every man materially or sentimentally interested in the city, especially businessmen and professionals. A notice sent out by the board of directors informed prospective members that the association would work "in every practical way" to beautify the streets and places of San Francisco, "to make San Francisco a more agreeable city in which to live." Its proposals ranged from advocating ordinances to curb outdoor advertising and encouraging the adornment of private homes with flowers and shrubs to recommendations for new buildings and parks. The association promised to push for an auditorium and an opera house, a college of music, an observatory, an art museum, and an open air amphitheater. The amphitheater was especially important because it could bring some of the benefits of country life to the crowded and busy city; "in an open space . . . protected by the walls of an amphitheater, we have the nearest approach to the cathedral of the forest; and there our highest nature finds expression in music, oratory, poetry, and the drama." The AIASF would pressure the city government to enforce building codes and to put up municipal structures of the highest architectural standards. The keystone was a comprehensive plan to unify all the smaller projects. The plan would indicate where to locate boulevards and new public buildings, what direction park extension should take, and what should be done with the harbor. It would guide private benefactors wanting to donate something of value to the city. It would uplift the citizenry and elevate the public taste. To make the benefits more concrete, the plan would "be given the widest publicity, both in this country and abroad, thereby serving as a great advertisement for our city, its future and its opportunities."[11] The plan, in short, would save San Francisco.

Burnham himself arrived in May 1904, and the AIASF gave him a banquet at the St. Francis Hotel. Phelan opened the festivities with a speech that stressed his favorite themes: the riches that nature had bestowed on San Francisco; the new imperial destiny in store for the city; and the need for a new spirit of cooperation and achievement to take advantage of both opportunities, to make San Francisco "worthy of its position and destiny." Burnham spoke and modestly defined his role as producing a skeleton design for the city that local architects would flesh out. At the end of the dinner, a sense-of-the-meeting resolution unamimously invited Burnham to draft a plan for the beautification of the city. Two days later, Burnham spoke to another gathering at the Palace Hotel. He repeated his belief that he could not do the work unaided, that he would need the ideas and cooperation of residents more familiar with the wants and capacities of the city.[12] He appreciated the suggestions that were immediately forthcoming. He struck a more somber note when he said that it would be necessary to know both the willingness and the ability of the city to pay for any suggested scheme.

Burnham left San Francisco in early summer and did not return until September. While he was away, local groups offered their ideas about what San Francisco, as a City Beautiful, must have. Burnham himself solicited advice from Phelan. In July he wrote Phelan, then in London, asking him to stop in Chicago on his way back to San Francisco. "Can you give me a day or two here so that we may talk things over?" he asked, "I very much desire you to do this."[13] There is no record of whether Phelan did pay a call, but Burnham's insistence suggests that if he did not see Phelan in Chicago, he almost certainly spent time with him in San Francisco in September and October.[14]

Burnham only stayed in the city from September 22 until October 13, 1904, when he left hurriedly for the Philippines. A firm supporter of American colonialism, he eagerly accepted the offer to draw plans for a redesigned Manila and a new summer capital at Baguio. He saw this work as an extension of his efforts at home, to bring the benefits of modern planning to the masses, and he was not troubled by the fact that in the Philippines his employers were American military authorities serving as imperial rulers of a conquered territory. He returned to San Francisco in February 1905, picking up the work he had dropped to go to the East. He admitted that "it is too early yet for me to say just what I have in mind. The general scheme will be broad and the suggestions of the citizens considered and carried out as far as possible." To aid his vision, he had a small studio constructed on the slope of Twin Peaks, near the geographical center of the city. There he and some of his assistants lived and worked. Using a high vantage point from which to get an overview was Burnham's custom. The AIASF paid $2,500 for the cottage, which Willis Polk designed. Burnham himself was in and out of San Francisco, never staying for more than two or three weeks; much of the plan, especially the details, was probably the work of his assistant Edward H. Bennett and others. The master returned to San Francisco in May 1905, and this time he had with him another eminence in American architecture, Charles Follen McKim. Phelan could soon report to the association that McKim had collaborated with Burnham—almost certainly an exaggeration—and that McKim had approved wholeheartedly of the work, saying that it was now both possible and practicable for San Francisco, within a reasonable period, to become "a beautiful city worthy of its unique and superb location."[15]

Phelan diligently spread word of the work Burnham was doing. He sent a long letter to the *New York Tribune* in January 1905, informing it of the plan and what it would do for the future of San Francisco. The AIASF, he wrote, was confident of success and felt that money spent on beautifying the city "will attract a large population, both permanent and transient, and add not only pleasure and comfort of living, but greatly increase the city's prosperity."[16] The promotional aspects of the endeavor were pursued as ardently as the plan itself.

In September 1905, work on the plans was completed. Phelan was away on one of his frequent trips to Europe, studying the beauty of Paris. William Greer Harrison, president of the Olympic Club and a founder and director of the AIASF, represented Phelan in presenting the plans to the Board of Supervisors. He said, in language that might have been Phelan's, that "the highest form of civilization is the beautiful—beauty of character and beauty of environment, and one is a complement to the other." It would be criminal to allow the city to be ugly when it could so easily be beautiful. The task for San Franciscans was to make the city so attractive that all Pacific Coast residents would consider it their home, to make it nothing less than one of the most glorious cities in the world. For the most part Harrison confined himself to generalities, but his speech included one specific statement of some importance because of its prophetic accuracy. Making San Francisco a pleasure city, he said, meant regulating and limiting manufacturing establishments. "When manufacturing comes here some day," he stressed, "it will be established outside the city."[17]

Burnham could not attend the presentation either, but he sent a letter in which he gave his assistant Bennett a share of the credit. He advised that the first two projects should be the extension of the Panhandle and the construction of a boulevard circling the city. "As soon as these two improvements shall have been made," he wrote, "I am confident that thereby a demand will arise, on the part of the citizens themselves, for a continuance of the development of the city on broad lines." Mayor Eugene E. Schmitz was at his cordial best. He said it was a pleasure to receive the plans, he pledged himself to support them, and he echoed Burnham's choices as to what part should be undertaken first. At a banquet given that night by the AIASF, Schmitz toasted the new San Francisco. Harrison epitomized the feeling of harmony by raising his glass to all assembled, whom he called "neophytes in the temple of beauty, a temple within whose doors no discord should enter."[18]

If the daily press is any indication of the mood of a city, these calls for harmony were merely wind. News of the presentation of the plan and the banquet received minimal coverage. What filled the pages of the local newspapers was the heated election of 1905, in which the Democrats and Republicans, representing most of the "respectable" citizens and probably almost all of the members of the AIASF, had united in order to rid San Francisco of Schmitz and Abraham Ruef. If Schmitz and the association could sit down together and talk of harmony, beauty, and progress in the midst of a virulent campaign stressing corruption and class strife, either they were hypocrites of the first magnitude or else the abusive political rhetoric is misleading. One suspects a little of both: that the love feast was not totally sincere, but also that intense vilification in a political campaign is not a totally accurate index of the depth of division. Most likely the members of the AIASF, including the absent Phelan, a confirmed political opponent of Ruef and Schmitz, did not expect Schmitz's reelection. On the other hand, any beautification scheme calling for an ultimate expenditure of $50 million, as the Burnham plan did, would require participation from the city administration, no matter how personally obnoxious or corrupt the mayor and his advisor. So, if only to hedge their bets, the association had to deal with Schmitz.

Burnham's plan had as its core a "General Theory of the City," extracted by the architect from a study of the finest European examples, Paris, Berlin, Vienna, Moscow, and London. The layout of these cities approximated a series of concentric circles, with each circle identified by its most important function. Boundaries between circles were marked by successive boulevards that spread like ever-widening ripples from the center of the city. From the heart ran radial arteries, intersecting the boulevards and providing through avenues from one side of the city to the other. The innermost ring surrounded the Civic Center, those buildings devoted to administration and education. The Civic Center was "the real being of the city proper; all else should contribute to its honor and maintenance. In its national character it guarantees the city's relation to the country and in its civic character to the citizens." Municipal, state, and federal buildings, city hall, court houses, and the post office were situated here. The center also contained "those structures, public or private, of monumental character and of great civic interest, relating to matters literary, musical, esthetic, expositional, professional or religious." Burnham included the library, opera house, municipal theater, academy of art, museum, technical school, assembly hall, and the like. Since San Francisco had too many buildings to be grouped satisfactorily around one grand *place*, Burnham proposed several subgroupings, located on the radial arteries and the innermost ring, which he called the "perimeter of distribution." Removed from heavy traffic and "press of business," the structures and their "extensive settings" would contribute to public rest and recreation, and be well adapted to ceremonial events.[19]

The general theory identified two other "elements" of the city, the economic and the residential. Economic referred to the production and movement of goods and the flow of money and credit. San Francisco financial institutions were already so well grouped that the plan could identify an existing center of finance around the intersection of California and Sansome streets. Burnham offered no major changes, but he did mention as an ideal "a financial forum" that "should exclude vehicles from its center." It might take the form of a court or a series of courts with the stock exchange as the focal point. Commercial and manufacturing activities were less neatly arranged, and Burnham confined himself to a few general recommendations. Replanning certain streets would ease problems of transportation between warehouses on the waterfront and manufacturing and wholesale establishments. All the facilities, including freight depots, docks, and wharves, should be designed for indefinite expansion. He recommended that a sea wall be built to contain a system of docks that would enlarge and concentrate the city's wharfage capacity. But he felt that explicit suggestions were beyond his province; "it is not the aim here to solve the problem of property interests or to lay down in detail the scheme suggested, but merely to indicate the direction in which it should be studied."[20]

Burnham's treatment of the residential district was also brief.

He viewed the spread of housing as an ineluctable process; single family homes retreated to the outskirts before the advance of multiple dwelling places. The planner's task was to establish beforehand, in the most desirable districts, a proper size for the blocks and streets, and to see that the landscape was arranged to preserve viewpoints and park spaces. He did suggest that in some of the poorer and flatter areas, some streets be replaced by "a chain of park-like squares, formed in a measure by the unused or misused back-yard areas."[21] Without vehicular traffic, these chain parks "would become public avenues of beautiful planting, in which one could walk with great comfort, and where children could play, free from the danger of traffic." It is interesting to consider Burnham's suggestions as a forerunner of the superblock arrangement favored by some later planners,[22] but it may be more to the point to recognize that even when dealing with housing, Burnham thought primarily in terms of streets and parks.

"A city plan," he wrote, "must ever deal mainly with the direction and width of its streets."[23] In San Francisco, many of the most important streets were too narrow to handle the traffic, and they were laid out in the familiar gridiron pattern, so common to American cities and so frustrating to City Beautiful planners. As early as 1839, a Swiss surveyor named Jean Vioget had plotted a rectangular street plan in the downtown area now bounded by Sacramento, Montgomery, Pacific and Dupont streets.[24] Eight years later, surveyor Jasper O'Farrell extended Vioget's plans. Supposedly he tried to change the layout to make it conform better to the hilly terrain but was frustrated by the opposition of landowners. O'Farrell also laid out Market Street as a broad avenue running diagonally from northeast to southwest, parallel to the old road from the waterfront to Mission Dolores.

South of Market, O'Farrell planned streets to run parallel and perpendicular to it rather than continuing the north-south arrangement of the original survey. Each block north of Market consisted of six square lots, 137.5 feet on a side. A block had three lots running east and west, two lots north and south. O'Farrell thought that larger blocks were more desirable, so in the south of Market area he designed the blocks to contain six lots, each 275 feet on a side. Blocks to the south of Market were four times the size of those to the north. Successive later surveys extended these original arrangements.[25]

The cumulative results produced a street plan that severely

hampered the efficient flow of people and goods, kept local districts isolated from one another, and took little advantage of the aesthetic possibilities afforded by the city's hills. Market Street was 110 feet wide and it carried much of the downtown traffic. But it lay like a barrier between north and south, with the blocks in these sections of different size, and with few streets crossing Market directly. Streets ran straight over the hills in the area north of Market, with no thought given to impassable grades. Cable cars could move people over the hills, but many of the streets were too severe for horses and heavy wagons. Finally, the gridiron plan ignored the visual delights made possible by the elevations within the heart of the city. Burnham's plan attempted to alleviate the faults of the gridiron pattern.

The changes that Burnham proposed for the streets are literally countless. Sometimes he treated new diagonals and curving streets as units, sometimes as multiple entities. Including the cutting of new streets, the extension of old streets, and the widening of streets already in existence, the *Report* contained at least seventy alterations. The proposals embraced every district in the city, from the built-up downtown area to the practically unoccupied sand hills of the Sunset district south of Golden Gate Park. Yet in drawing up the plans Burnham was guided by his theory of the city and by the needs of San Francisco. Most of the recommended new streets can be understood by reference to these two considerations.

Burnham's general theory pictured the ideal street plan of a city as a spiderweb of concentric circles intersected by diagonals. The geography of San Francisco, especially the tallest hills near the center of the city and the concentration of population in the northeast quadrant, made a single-centered web impossible. Burnham did not abandon his ideal; rather he adapted it to local conditions and proposed a plan with multiple centers, from each of which radiated new diagonal arteries. These centers he called *places* or Round Points—good Parisian designations—and he spread them throughout the city, from the Richmond district in the northwest to the South San Francisco area on the southwest.

The most important center stood at the junction of Market Street, Van Ness Avenue, and the proposed extension of the Panhandle. The complex of buildings around this *place* formed the crucial Civic Center, which was encircled by the Perimeter of Distribution. More a seven-sided polygon than a true circle, the Perimeter of Distribution was to be created by widening four existing streets and cutting three diagonals to connect them. At each of the seven angles of the polygon, Burnham located a *place*, smaller than the one at the center but still quite spacious. A union railroad station was proposed for one of these *places*, to be balanced on the opposite side of the polygon by an opera house. A diagonal street would be cut to connect them, crossing Market through the central *place*.[26]

The only other full-fledged circular thoroughfare Burnham proposed was the Outer Boulevard, to which he gave special emphasis because of its feasibility and its importance to the theory. Unlike the Perimeter of Distribution, which would have to be hacked out of the heart of the city, the Outer Boulevard largely avoided the built-up portions of San Francisco. In those places where it ran along the commercial sections of the waterfront, Burnham wanted to elevate it and make it the roof of warehouses.[27] Because it would not involve great dislocation or expense, it could be built quickly to induce completion of the major portion of the program. For most of its 30-mile course, the Outer Boulevard was to follow as closely as possible the bay and ocean shore. Only when it entered San Mateo County, south of San Francisco, and crossed from the ocean to the bay, did it leave its coastal route, although the plan called for it to run inland past Hunter's Point until a sea wall on the bay side was built. Then the route would follow the sea wall and girdle the city.[28]

Functionally, the boulevard served two distinct and ultimately antagonistic purposes. First, it would be a means to alleviate traffic congestion within the city. Travelers going from one part of town to another could circumvent the interior by using the Outer Boulevard. Second, the Boulevard would be a pleasure route, a source of refreshment to those who followed its scenic path. Its coast-hugging location would offer vista after vista, from the Golden Gate on the north to the ocean shore on the west to the Laguna country and mountains on the south. The eastern portion provided glimpses of Mount Diablo, the hills of the East Bay, and the charms of the harbor itself. Describing the part of the boulevard that he projected across the roofs of yet unconstructed warehouses, Burnham felt it would be,

an ideal place for a ride or a walk, the passer-by looking down on the shipping below, and when he tires of watching the activities and listening to the voices of the men engaged in the work of the port, he may note the changing aspects of the sea and study the effect of sunshine and shadow on islands and mountains seen through the masts of the ships. This treatment will lend delightful variety to a drive on the boulevard and will add a special charm to the life of the city.[29]

City Beautiful planners took pride in merging utility with beauty; Burnham obviously delighted in marrying these aims into the Outer Boulevard. But what the builder had joined, the automobile put asunder. High speeds and traffic on a scale Burnham could not have predicted make those highways that do more or less follow his suggested routes merely utilitarian. They create tension, for the driver at least, more than they encourage contemplation.

The Outer Boulevard was not intended as the ultimate means to improve the traffic flow. It was more of a transitional measure, to carry the burden until the other changes could be made. These alterations fall into four categories. First, Burnham proposed widening important existing thoroughfares so that they might carry more traffic. Market Street, for example, although already more than 100 feet wide, would be made even broader to accommodate its many users. To connect San Francisco with the Peninsula to the south, Burnham suggested that Mission Street be widened to 210 feet and the roadway divided into five sections, two of which would be planted lanes for bridle paths and promenades.[30]

A second set of improvements was intended to aid traffic in the central area, especially to cross Market Street. New streets were cut directly across the avenue, and existing ones were extended to carry them across. In the business section northeast of Market, from Sansome on the east to Van Ness on the west, every third, or in one case, fourth street would be extended due south to cross Market. The Civic Center area would contain three additional direct crossings, two of them bisecting the great *place*. All the new diagonals throughout the city would shorten distances between given points; the most important of them would also connect terminals like the Ferry Building, the proposed Union Station, and the Pacific Mail docks.[31]

The original surveyors had treated the hills largely by ignoring them and continuing the checkerboard pattern as if they did not exist. As its third aim, the Burnham plan envisioned some modifications to eliminate the steep grades and to take advantage of the charm of the hills. Most of the proposed changes were located in the less inhabited regions in the southern and western parts of the city, particularly the area around Islais Creek. But Burnham wanted radical alterations of some of the well-populated hills in the northern section, Russian Hill and California Street (or Nob) Hill. He drew in long, curving roads that avoided a frontal assault on the crests and swept up gradually. He planned bridges to carry streets over some existing roads; elsewhere he wanted to lessen the grades. The results would ease communication, making the hills less an obstacle to traffic and more an invitation to pleasure seekers.[32]

A fourth and crucial intent of the proposed street system was to increase recreational opportunity by making existing parks more accessible, by providing pleasant approaches to parks not yet built, and by creating parkway streets that would themselves serve as natural breathing spaces the crowded city needed. Completing the Panhandle by extending it beyond Market Street all the way to the bay shore was the first and most important of a large number of new streets designed to bring residents easily from their homes to the city's gardens. Other streets, many of them diagonals, would connect the Panhandle with the Presidio, the Twin Peaks area, and the populated Mission district. A parkway one block wide would run from the Presidio to Golden Gate Park, and another of equal breadth through much of the Sunset. He planned an even larger scale boulevard as an entrance to the proposed park on Potrero Heights in the eastern part of the city. Burnham placed his parkway there because "its axis corresponds with the axis of Twin Peaks, and it would therefore yield the most beautiful view of them." Also "it would afford direct communication between the park on Potrero Heights and the superb park spaces at the west end, and at the same time it would furnish wide breathing spaces and playgrounds for the numerous residents along its entire length." A last justification superseded the others; "probably no other expenditure of money will bring surer returns in health, happiness and consequent good citizenship than the sum required to construct this parkway."[33]

Burnham considered street layout as the vital center of any city plan. He valued streets almost as works of art. They should be "faultless in equipment and immaculately clean," he wrote, and until they become so, "monuments and statues are out of place; men and events can be much more effectually commemorated by street improvements." The tone of the *Report* also reveals that Burnham's imagination was less excited by the details of a plan for traffic than by consideration of the majestic views, gentle undulations, and intercourse with nature that the parkways and boulevards would afford. Language becomes almost poetic when one follows the Outer Boulevard as it "rounds Fort Mason and emerges on a straightaway run" enters the Presidio "sweeping around the parade ground," "climbs the slope," and shortly "sweeps down across Lobos creek, reaching the headlands."[34] The extension of the Panhandle, "rising gently from Van Ness avenue, ... reaches its summit at Steiner street and thence sweeps gently down and up to join the existing Panhandle at Baker street. A certain sympathy is thus obtained between the drive and the natural contour of the land." Proceeding westward, the way is increasingly adorned with richer plantings until, at its highest grade, it is banked by terraces "with hanging gardens of flowers." From there it "dips down almost imperceptibly and with increased picturesqueness of planting reaches the point of transition, a public Place with central motif," before emerging into "the sylvan beauty of the original Panhandle."[35] These descriptions mark Burnham's concern with the aesthetic and recreational possibilities the new streets would offer. When he treated projects whose functions were more exclusively to supply refreshment and enjoyment to the residents of the city, he gave his imagination even freer reign.

The city had less park acreage than contemporary standards considered adequate, and much of its open space was not readily accessible. The national average for metropolises was one acre of park per 206.6 persons; Boston, with one acre per 42.2 persons, was the most generously parked city. San Francisco's total park area amounted to not more than 1,400 acres for a population of more than 400,000, or 285.7 people per acre.[36] Of the 1,400 acres, Golden Gate Park accounted for more than 1,000; the congested residential sections in the eastern half of the city were virtually parkless.

Burnham attacked the problem on three fronts. First, he advocated that small parks and playgrounds be established regularly throughout the city. He left the details of site selection to others.[37] The small parks should be developed "in accordance with one general idea," although some variety would of necessity be allowed. They must be attractive to passers-by, offering shade and pleasant surroundings to those who use them. The playgrounds might vary in design, but each "should provide uniformly for the wants of all the people, men, women and children." Their location would depend upon the population density in the different parts of the city. Though he recognized the need for them, Burnham's discussion of small parks and playgrounds is both cursory and vague, a mere half dozen short paragraphs, and contrasts with the extensive, detailed, and convincing treatment given to other aspects of the plan.[38] He obviously preferred to concentrate on recreational areas of vast proportions or with commanding sites.

San Francisco's hills distinguish it from most other American metropolises. Before the construction of the Golden Gate and Bay bridges, with their immense towers, before the erection of 20- and 40- and 50-storied office buildings destroyed the natural contours of the site, the hills were unchallenged in providing the city with a vigorous, appealing skyline, and with strategic vantage points from which to see the area as a whole.[39] Burnham and his assistants had used Twin Peaks to get an overview of San Francisco while working on the plan, and the architect was somewhat surprised to find that so few residents ever came to the summit to be inspired by the magnificent scene.[40] Perhaps as a way of enticing blasé San Franciscans to scale the city's heights, Burnham proposed that the tops of all high hills not yet densely populated "be preserved in a state of nature, while their slopes below should be clothed with trees." On those hills already covered with houses, all vacant land too steep for building should be reserved for parks and lookouts. Proposals for Telegraph Hill, although somewhat unclear, suggest that Burnham even wanted to replace some existing residential areas with hilltop parks. Taken together, the plans for the treatment of the hills would crown almost all the peaks in San Francisco with a garland of parks, playgrounds, gardens, and belvederes. At lower levels, the slopes and bases would be encircled by contour roads, accented with terraces, and connected to the rest of the city by the new avenues that Burnham had outlined in the street plan.[41]

The third and final portion of Burnham's answer to San Francisco's need for additional recreational space called for the creation of a series of new, major parks ranging in size from 31.20 acres for Telegraph Hill to 4,764.00 acres in the combined Twin Peaks–Laguna de la Merced parks. Plans for the hills and for the large parks often overlap. Of the eleven hills or hill groups described individually, six reappear under the suggestions for parks; almost all the proposed parks either contain or are situated on hills and high ground. Burnham chose the hills for several reasons. They were naturally beautiful yet unsuited for residential purposes because of steepness, inaccessibility, or difficulties of drainage. The system of hill parks would "shelter the city from the west by inclosing it with a girdle of planting. . . . In case of a great conflagration this system of parks and parkways would form an effective barrier to its spread."[42] Burnham was preoccupied with vistas and viewpoints. Placing parks atop the hills would provide glimpses of the city from above and views of the parks from below. He ignored the fact that the city's most popular and attractive existing park, Golden Gate, was mostly flat and offered playing fields, conservatories, museums, and music stands rather than majestic outlooks.

Burnham justified only one of the proposed large parks, that in the Potrero Heights section south of Market Street, on the grounds that it would serve a heavily populated and poor district. In fact, the list of thirteen new parks includes only three located in areas of dense residential concentration, Potrero Heights, Telegraph Hill, and Fort Mason.[43] But since Burnham considered parkways as recreational spaces, and since he planned many of the new streets to lead directly from the residential sections to the new parks, it is inaccurate to conclude that he was only concerned with impressive sites for the parks themselves and disregarded the convenience of prospective park users. His aim instead seems to have been to put the parks in ideal locations and bring the people to them, rather than to select less desirable spots while bringing the parks to the people. Of course he was restricted in his choice by the availability of vacant or lightly used land. He could not situate a large park in the midst of expensive real estate. Still, he seems to have preferred hilly and somewhat wild sites to any tamer, flatter ones, no matter how obtainable.

The area of the large parks described in the Burnham *Report* amounts to 7,700 acres, with another 500 acres given over to parkways. Burnham wanted to increase the total park area from 1,400 to 9,855 acres, which meant one acre per every 200 residents—for a city of 2 million people![44] Burnham made no small plans.

The two largest of the proposed parks were the Presidio with 700 acres and the Twin Peaks–Merced parks with 4,764 acres. The Presidio, an artifact of Spanish settlement practices, had fallen after American conquest to the United States Army. More than 1,500 acres in size, on a magnificent site in the northwest section of the city overlooking the Golden Gate and the Marin County headlands, its importance as a military base revived with the Spanish-American War and American involvement in the Orient. San Franciscans already used its lovely walks and tree-shaded slopes as a pleasure resort. Burnham wanted to make it more accessible and develop it as "a monument to the United States Army." Drives and concourses would be arranged to provide "the best possible views of the landscape, and to allow the public to participate in the military maneuvres." The parade ground would be enlarged and a great drill ground created, with a forecourt connecting the two. Both fields would be enclosed by terraces, "from which the public in large numbers may watch the maneuvres, the bay making a fine background for the spectacle."[45]

For the Twin Peaks–Merced parks, Burnham envisioned more varied but no less impressive spectacles. This huge area, over seven square miles in size, extending from the 900-foot-high summit near the center of the city southwestward to the ocean, embracing several small mountains, two lakes, and countless superb vistas, gave ample scope to the architect's grandest dreams. This park was to be the brightest gem in San Francisco's sylvan crown, and here Burnham let his imagination loose. "Twin Peaks," he wrote, "ought to be not only a public park, but a center for great public fêtes in which the natural beauties of the city and country would be the chief attraction. Every improvement directed towards this end would contribute to the growth and beauty of the city."[46] Careful plantings of trees, fruits, and flowers, some of them irrigated by a cascade of water falling from a reservoir near the summit all the way to Lake Merced, would make the area ideal for floral festivals. The landscaping must also allow for lines of sight from the heights to all parts of San Francisco, accentuating the peaks as a focal point.

The classical motif, so strong a current in the City Beautiful movement, reached new heights in Burnham's plans for Twin Peaks. Slightly to the north of the summits, in a natural hollow, he located "an amphitheater, or stadium, of vast proportions." Here lacrosse, football, polo, and other games might be played, and horse shows held. Spectators sitting on the southern slope would take in both the event itself and the Golden Gate beyond. Burnham was delighted with the spot: it reminded him of a similar amphitheater "in the hills of Delphi, which overlooks the Gulf of Corinth, and the theater of Dionysos, at the foot of the Acropolis, from which Piraeus and the Sea of Aegina come finely into view." South of the stadium, on the eastern side of Twin Peaks, he put an academy, "arranged for the accommodation of men in various branches of intellectual and artistic pursuits." This early version of the modern research institute would bring together men of genius "for independent study or collaboration and [they] will enjoy the constant inspiration of ideal surroundings, an association the city will do well to cultivate." In addition to buildings for living, study, and administration, the academy would include "a little open-air theater, after the ancient Greek model."[47]

The third institution based on ancient models was an athenaeum. Though Burnham wrote that "the Athenaeum, so called, should receive some few of the greatest works of art," he was not particularly explicit as to its exact functions. Instead he concentrated on the location and design. The architecture he modeled after parts of the Villa Hadrian; it consisted of courts, terraces, and colonnades to protect visitors from the winds while offering them the major vistas of San Francisco. He placed the athenaeum at "the termination of the great vista from the hills north of Twin Peaks to the Merced country and the ocean." This location would shelter the structure from prevailing winds in summer and winter. More important, it would provide an ideal spot for a monument, in "the form of a colossal figure symbolical of San Francisco," at the geographic and moral center of the city. So situated, the figure "would hold the eye from every part of the great glade that sweeps down to the Laguna de la Merced."[48]

The final and most revealing expression of classicism on Twin Peaks is the suggestion for private homes. Burnham did not want the whole area acquired for park purposes; "the idea is to weave park and residence districts into interesting and economic relations." Along the level contour roadways on the less steep slopes of the area, land should be reserved for "villa sites." To ensure unobstructed views from each villa, the city should prevent building on the lower side of each roadway for up to 100 feet.[49] Burnham says little more about these villas; he does not specify who will live in them. But the context in which they are placed makes the answer obvious—the patricians of San Francisco.

The Burnham *Report* made a number of suggestions that fall outside the three principal categories of Civic Center, streets, and parks. Some of these recommendations seem remarkably modern and problem oriented; others are more trivial in their concern with "adornment." The *Report* endorsed subways for rapid mass transit. The major diagonal arteries should be equipped with underground lines, the first to run under Market Street. Tunneling through Ashbury Heights would aid cars traveling from the Mission District to the northwestern part of the city. A general system of traffic regulation should be developed, including one-way streets and restrictions on heavy trucking on some boulevards. Burnham regarded it as inevitable that San Francisco would some day get its water from the Sierra Nevada. He wanted to locate the reservoirs that would hold this supply high enough that "the water may be used for fire purposes, fountains and water works of all descriptions." His most sumptuous proposal called for a number of reservoirs at descending levels, the water moving down from the top in cascades, "producing a veritable 'Chateau d'Eau.' "⁵⁰

The *Report* concludes with a list of "General Recommendations": that an art commission to control matters pertaining to civic art be established by charter amendment; that a study of street adornment be made; that trees be planted in streets; that a uniform cornice height for buildings in public places and on important avenues be adopted; that pavement width and material be adapted to the localities; that statues in parks be confined to formal areas; that cutting into hills for mere commercial gain be prohibited; that factories producing smoke be pushed as far east and south as possible; that the city hospital and almshouse be relocated; that cemeteries be removed from the city and be arranged so as to encourage "thoughts of consolation and peace" rather than "gloomy meditation."⁵¹

The variety of the general recommendations, the number of street changes and new avenues, the size and lavishness of the proposed parks, all attest to the scope of Burnham's imagination and his desire to be definitive. The plan was certainly not intended for immediate execution; it was too vast and too drastic, despite the effort to work within the given street system, and it required the expenditure of too much money. Instead, it was to "be executed by degrees, as the growth of the community demands and as its financial ability allows." Only an overall plan, to be completed in parts, could avoid a piecemeal approach and still have some reasonable expectation of being implemented. The plan, Burnham wrote, "should be designed not only for the present, but for all time to come." He advised San Franciscans to look at what their city had become in a mere 50 years and project the future accordingly. "A meagre plan will fall short of achievement," he added, "while a great one will yield large results, even it if is never fully realized."⁵²

By what standards does one assess a city plan such as Burnham's for San Francisco? Measured against prior and contemporary achievements, the San Francisco plan was a decided advance. It moved beyond the design for Washington, which had been almost exclusively concerned with park improvements and public buildings. Herbert Croly thought that if even only a portion of the suggestions were carried out, San Francisco would become the most conveniently planned city in the nation.⁵³ Not until Burnham completed a plan for his own city of Chicago in 1909 did city planning produce a document with a deeper and more thorough comprehension of a great city.⁵⁴ The San Francisco plan moved beyond existing achievements, but that may attest more to the limitations of the field rather than to the excellence of the plan itself. A modern reader of the *Report* thinks of all the important facets of city life *not* treated: no study of the economic base; scant attention to commercial facilities; little mention of housing; no method for carrying out the plan; no discussion of financing it.⁵⁵ Burnham's primary concern was aesthetic, although he certainly worked on the practical question of traffic. But to castigate him for this emphasis, as both contemporary and later critics have done, calling it "mere adornment," or "mere beautification," is to ignore a central theme that makes the plan both an embodiment of James Phelan's vision of the new San Francisco and a fitting representative of the City Beautiful movement.

"Although the romantic treatment of parks is admirable," Burnham wrote,

it should at least be accompanied, in a certain proportion, by a more formal disposition of tree-planting, which will lend the added charm of contrast and color. In the smaller parks this amounts to a lesson of order and system, and its influence on the masses cannot be overestimated.

He cited Parisian examples to buttress his point: "The striking beauty of the vista in celebrated European gardens, and in particular in the masterpieces of Le Notre, in France, is a sufficient argument for its application where conditions are favorable to its use." An underlying assumption permeates the plan; it is that the aesthetic quality of an environment, its shape, organization, and appeal, become stamped on the character of the inhabitants. Orderly and systematic tree planting makes for orderly and systematic people, or at least people who respect order and system. Grand vistas of the beauties of nature, especially views from great heights, elevate and inspire character. Noble, dignified, and harmoniously arranged public buildings "strengthen the public sense of the dignity and responsibility of citizenship." Small parks with individual characters, named for a distinguishing tree or flower will "have the effect of stimulating the interest of the residents in the park located in their neighborhood." A "Maternity," sitting amid the Greco-Roman splendors of Twin Peaks, "in surroundings of the most ideal character, yet not far removed from the city," will have an influence "of great moral value."⁵⁶

The two principles that dominated Burnham's aesthetic for San Francisco are segregation of functions in the city and great visibility.

Governmental and other public buildings are brought together into a Civic Center, and they are made manifest by uniform and "vigorous architecture" that "impose[s] a sense of order." Banks, stock brokerage firms, insurance companies, and real estate offices are grouped into a financial center, whose ideal form should be a forum of courts with the Stock Exchange "as the focal point on the main axis."[57] Shipping, wholesale and retail trade, residences, all have their allotted and segregated locations, their axes and focal points. Even the private homes, too diffuse to be harmoniously grouped, have discernible *exempla*—the villas of Twin Peaks. Most of the functional organization Burnham set forth in the plans already existed in San Francisco, shaped by factors such as level land, accessibility to docks and rail yards, the money and real estate markets, and the propensity of many types of businesses and services to form subcenters of their own.[58] Also, the notion that functions, especially work place and residence, should be separated was in Burnham's time and probably still is the prevailing belief for both planners and laymen.[59]

Burnham's aim was not simply order; he wanted the order to be apparent, the shape of the city to be seen and understood by the citizens. From the hill-top parks, one glimpsed San Francisco's magnificent natural surroundings. Just as important was the view of the city. Each elevated park was to have a playground, "arranged, if necessary, in terraces from which a good view of the city may be had. By thus affording the young appropriate places for recreation and giving them at the same time a broader outlook a twofold educational purpose will be served." San Francisco iself, efficiently organized, comprehensive, and visible, becomes a grand version of the small park with formal tree planting; it embodies "a lesson of order and system, and its influence on the masses cannot be overestimated."[60] The city plan brings order to the social as well as the physical structure of San Francisco.

What kind of order? On that question, the plan is vague and incomplete. Daniel Burnham was primarily an architect and designer of cities; his views of society were a reflection of that professional outlook. He wrote about the shape of the city, and whatever he thought about the organization of life within that city has to be coaxed from his statements about physical arrangements. Therefore it is hopeless to expect a great degree of precision or sophistication from him about social matters. Only later would planners begin to claim expertise in areas other than design.

The point to understand is that order, unmodified by any

descriptive adjectives or qualifications, had a substantive meaning for Burnham. It meant, first of all, the opposite of disorder and chaos so apparent in most American cities of the era. It meant healthy surroundings, clean streets, and nature, even if formally planted. It also meant civilian participation in military maneuvers, mass spectator sports, and yacht harbors on the bay. It meant progress for San Francisco in the form of rapid and prosperous growth. It meant some political arrangement capable of mobilizing enough authority to enact the proposals in the *Report*, and it meant a disciplined public enlightened enough to vote the necessary funds. It meant, all in all, that San Francisco was to be a version of an imperial city, a new Athens, Rome, or Paris, dominating rich hinterlands and the Pacific Ocean, physically beautiful and socially sound.

Designing a plan for a new San Francisco took talent, but transforming so grand a conception into a reality, especially in light of San Francisco's past and present social and political situation, would be considerably more difficult. In the rebuilding of Paris in the mid-nineteenth century, Baron Haussmann operated under the aegis of Napoleon III's imperial authority. Until the late 1860s he was "unhampered by an elected municipal council, . . . spent the taxpayers' money without their consent, withheld information on the use of public funds, and defied efforts to control his activities."[61] When boosters called San Francisco an "imperial" city, their language was largely metaphorical. They referred to economics, not politics. Haussmann, with his blind disregard of public opinion and organized interests, would have been a failure in San Francisco; the question was, could anyone, even James D. Phelan, succeed?

5

The Ideal and the Real

"Civicism" and Shady Politics

Now that they had the Burnham *Report* in hand, Phelan and his allies had to face the really arduous labor of making the city conform to the plan. They began to publicize it before local organizations and in the press. They must have hoped that favorable coverage would be an important first step in gathering support. But even with these cautious moves, they quickly ran into trouble. Phelan and several of his friends became embroiled in two conflicts. One concerned the site of a new library; in the course of the dispute, Phelan was charged with altering Burnham's plans for his own enrichment. The other centered on competing proposals for electrifying the street railway system. Here again, there were accusations of dark forces at work, bending civic improvement to serve personal gain. The conflicts point out how easy it was to divide San Franciscans over the issue of urban development, how little they trusted one another, and how difficult it would be to convince them that the Burnham plan would serve the best interests of the city as a whole.

For James D. Phelan, the Burnham plan was both a design for the new San Francisco and the means for reforming the old. He wrote a "Historical Sketch of San Francisco . . . with Special Reference to Townsite, Early Plans and Public Reservation," as a conclusion to the *Report*.[1] He narrated a bleak story, a series of opportunities missed because of individual greed, official laxity, and the mistaken belief that trees and lawns could not flourish on San Francisco's shifting sand dunes. A few bright spots, such as the reclaiming of Golden Gate Park, the widening of Kearny and Dupont streets, and the extension of the shore line, lightened the gloom and stood out as proof that natural obstacles might be overcome and established street patterns changed. The future looked even better:

> The commercial and industrial greatness which had been predicted for San Francisco from the earliest times has been fulfilled, and, as in older communities, a love of the true and the beautiful, a craving for artistic betterment and a sense of public duty have succeeded the hard struggle to tame the wild earth, explore its secrets, raze the forests, build the city and command the sea.[2]

The city was rich enough to finance major improvements, and it was developing the will to undertake them. In the Burnham plan, its people had the one essential ingredient: "an ideal with which to nourish their imagination and to give them a goal towards which to labor with confidence."[3] Phelan hoped that the plan would inspire San Franciscans to overcome their petty jealousies and animosities, to constrain their desires for personal gain when these desires ran counter to the good of the city. "Civicism," uniting San Franciscans on their journey to the City Beautiful, would eclipse the contest of private interests that had characterized the history of the city since its birth.

This vision foresaw no less than a transformation of the social, economic, and political culture of San Francisco. It was quickly confronted by the reality of those animosities and suspicions Phelan sought to transcend. Soon after the presentation of the Burnham *Report* in September 1905, bitter conflicts emerged to reveal how far San Franciscans were from converting to Phelan's version of "civicism." In the climate of suspicion that prevailed in San Francisco politics, even the motives of the supporters of planning, including Phelan himself, became suspect.

A whiff of scandal reached the provenance of the Burnham *Report*. Burnham had encouraged suggestions from people in San Francisco, and he acknowledged the assistance of some local architects in the formation of the plans. But a more sinister side to the question of influence arose around a seemingly trivial issue, the site for a new library. The bonds that San Francisco voters had authorized in 1903 for public improvements included $1,647,000 for a library, $1 million for the building and the remainder for acquisition of the site. The bonds failed to sell on their own, but Phelan found purchasers for $2,009,000 of the $17,174,000 total. These funds would be used to buy land; they would be spent by the Democratically controlled Board of Supervisors rather than the Schmitz appointees on the Board of Public Works. Among the parcels to be acquired was a site for the public library, then housed in the city hall.[4] The Board of Supervisors, in directing the trustees of the public library to select a location, instructed them to choose Western Addition block number 67, two streets west of the city hall, or another lot of similar size and value in the immediate vicinity.[5] The library trustees chose Western Addition block number 73, two blocks south and one block west of block 67.

It took three meetings for the Board of Supervisors to accept the decision of the library trustees. They heard arguments from owners of property in the two blocks, each group trying to convince them to purchase their land. More confusing was the question of which site fit better into the still uncompleted Burnham plans. Phelan, appearing as a representative of the AIASF, pointed out that block 73 would front on an extended Panhandle. If the library were situated there, it would be part of the approach to Golden Gate Park. B. J. S. Cahill, a local architect, countered with the claim that block 67 would form part of the great quadrangle being planned to face city hall. He said he was speaking for the absent Burnham. What finally decided the question for the supervisors was the impassioned oratory of the Reverend Father Allen of St. Ignatius Church and College. Representing his 500 parishioners—and voters—he convinced the supervisors to locate the library on block 73, across from the church. The selection was affirmed by a vote of thirteen to four, but the issue did not disappear.[6]

In San Francisco in 1905, all decisions by the city government, whether mayor, supervisors, or Board of Public Works, on how to spend large sums of money were open to charges of graft or favoritism, and the library site was no exception. A short time after the action of the supervisors, *Town Talk*, a San Francisco weekly that darted frequent barbs at Phelan, accused him of manipulating the selection of the library site. The magazine charged that Phelan actually made Burnham change the plans for the entire Civic Center complex to accommodate Phelan's preference. His motive, *Town Talk* speculated, was his desire for a straight Panhandle, unlike the zigzagged one that Burnham had provisionally adopted. But perhaps other considerations were involved. The magazine argued that Burnham had actually revised his plans for the civic center area after Phelan's friend Mrs. Eleanor Martin had bought part of block 73 "through the agency of Mr. Phelan's friends and business associates, the Magee brothers, real estate agents." The revised version of the plan designated this block as the most appropriate for the site of the library. Now, according to *Town Talk*, "the Library Trustees favor it, Mr. Phelan urges the purchase of it, and his friends, the Supervisors, who are properly regarded as part and parcel of his political machine, have voted in favor of putting through the deal."[7] Having made the charge, the magazine then denied that Phelan was acting for selfish motives, but observed that if Phelan had Schmitz's reputation, there would be a grand jury investigation.

Town Talk's habitual hostility toward Phelan[8] might lead one to discount the accusations. The arguments were based, however, on some hard facts. Property records show that Mrs. Eleanor Martin did indeed purchase a large part of block 73 on December 14, 1904, from the Hibernia Savings and Loan Company.[9] The date was only two days before the original conference between the library trustees and the supervisor's committee, so it seems unlikely that any shifting of plans was done at that time, although Mrs. Martin may have been informed of the forthcoming changes of the library site and moved to take advantage. On the other hand, there was the less mercenary charge that Phelan's attachment to a certain route for the Panhandle led him to have a preliminary version of the Burnham plan altered. The question is whether there was such a preliminary plan, and, if so, how *Town Talk* learned about it.

The internal evidence points to Cahill as the informant. In an article written in 1909 during a dispute over locating a new city hall, Cahill recalled the library site issue. At that time, he remembered, Phelan supported an extension of the Panhandle in a direct line between Fell and Oak streets to Van Ness Avenue. According to Cahill, Burnham and Bennett had decided against this route and in favor of one Cahill sponsored, the diagonal zigzag to Fulton Street. The Fulton Street route would make block 67 preferable as a library site; the Fell-Oak streets route favored block 73. Phelan worked on the library trustees and the supervisors, Cahill contended, and was about to succeed in having them select block 73 until Cahill appeared and "with much effort succeeded in causing them to suspend judgment for a few months until Mr. Burnham should arrive from Manila." When he returned, Burnham assured Cahill as late as three days before the supervisors were to meet that he, Burnham, favored block 67. But at the meeting, Burnham enthusiastically recommended the selection of block 73. Phelan had triumphed, and his favorite route for the Panhandle appears in the Burnham plans, rather than the Fulton Street route of the "Plan of 1904."[10]

Such were Cahill's recollections. How accurate they were is open to question. Newspaper accounts of the meeting at which Cahill claims to have delayed action until Burnham's return—the meeting of December 23, 1904—discuss Cahill's speech but do not say that he spoke for delay. Nor is there any mention that Burnham appeared at the supervisors' meeting at which final determination of the library site was made—the meeting of March 6, 1905. Finally, the "Plan of 1904," presumably an early draft of the final *Report*, was not discussed in the newspapers or periodicals, nor is it mentioned in the Burnham *Report*, though Cahill did reproduce some illustrations from it.[11] Was this "Plan of 1904" anything more than Cahill's own design which failed to get approval from Burnham? Did Cahill then blame Phelan for the rejection and relate his side of the story to the sympathetic *Town Talk*? Cahill had done an earlier plan for beautification that included a civic center, and perhaps felt that his pioneering efforts were now being overlooked.[12] There is certainly reason to believe that his account of the episode is not wholly accurate. But there is in his favor one pertinent fact. Though the printed version of the Burnham *Report* did not stipulate a definite location for the library, the grand semicircular *place* at the crossing of Van Ness, Market and the Panhandle extension practically eliminates block 73, the site chosen by the supervisors.[13] Thus, there is some credibility to Cahill's charge that a switch, for whatever reason, was made in earlier plans, but overlooked when the final illustrations were drawn.

Neither the selection of block 73 by the supervisors nor the faint odor of corruption *Town Talk* thought it detected received much notice in the press. An editorial in the *Bulletin* approved of the site chosen as central and accessible,[14] but other than that, the whole issue evaporated. Yet the charges brought by Cahill and *Town Talk* raise two questions: First, To what extent did individuals influence the details of plans in the Burnham *Report*, whether for monetary or other reasons? Second, Was there a widespread feeling among San Franciscans that such influence had been exercised?

There is no satisfactory answer to the first question; the case of the library site and the Panhandle route is the most fully documented instance of such influence, and certainly the evidence is cloudy. The second question is equally thorny; one cannot poll the citizenry of San Francisco in 1905 to ascertain prevailing opinion. The story in *Town Talk* may have been an isolated instance of suspicion that went unnoticed or unremarked upon. But if the Burnham plan managed to survive more or less unscathed from charges that private and particular motives had shaped the proposals, the potential for such accusations remained high. San Franciscans had seen too many examples of jobbery, during the Schmitz administration and before, not to be sensitive to hints of corruption. One of the tasks of the AIASF, in publicizing and promoting the Burnham plan, would be to convince the citizens that the plan as a whole and in each of its parts was a disinterested, professional accomplishment, and not merely a series of deals.

The plan was presented to the Board of Supervisors on September 27, 1905. They accepted it and referred it to the committee on streets, sewers, and parks for consideration and report. The supervisors appropriated $3,000 to have 2,358 copies of the *Report* printed.[15] No other official action was taken. The strategy of the AIASF seems to have been to concentrate on making the plan known to the citizens of San Francisco through the press and by speeches to organizations in order to build a base of support within the population at large and among powerful interest groups. Such backing would be necessary to allow, or perhaps coerce, the city government to initiate action. As Burnham had pointed out, the plan was not intended to be realized instantly, or even in one decade. In the course of time the details would have to be refined and altered. But implementation would have to begin sometime, with some particular features. It was hoped that completion of the first stages would generate enthusiasm for the rest of the undertaking.

Measured by newspapers, magazines, and resolutions of organized groups, the reaction of the city's commercial and civic bodies to the Burnham plan was uniformly favorable. An article in the *Merchants' Association Review* appearing shortly after the presentation of the plan endorsed the suggestions. Several months later, San Francisco's realtors applauded Phelan when he told them, at the first banquet of the newly formed Real Estate Board, that they must get to work to execute the Burnham plan in their own lifetime. To begin, he called for an immediate extension of the Panhandle, at a cost of $6 million. Board President J. R. Howell advised the audience that the people should be educated to understand the value of beautification. He also warned them not to ask of each project whether the author of it would benefit, but whether it was good for San Francisco. The audience at a Commonwealth Club banquet two weeks later heard Phelan deliver yet another plea for the plan, and also listened to an endorsement from Club President Harris Weinstock. An editorial in the *Bulletin* commended Burnham's work. In fifty years San Francisco would be the city of two million people for which the plan was intended, and if it were to avoid the ugliness so common to most American cities, it must begin now to direct development with a proper regard for utility, convenience, and beauty. "If there were in San Francisco," the editorial concluded, "a Carnegie having millions to give away for public weal he could not employ them better than in conforming the city, so far as he might, to Burnham's ideal."[16] This wish for a Carnegie suggests that the *Bulletin* had doubts about the capacity of the democratic process, as embodied in San Francisco's government, to accomplish something of the magnitude of the Burnham plan. Some great power, independent of petty and selfish interests, armed with vast resources, might be necessary. The *Chronicle* also endorsed the plan, noting that the beauty and enjoyment of beauty that the plan would create were even more important than the economic gain to the city which would probably occur.[17]

While the local press and organized groups were pledging support to the City Beautiful according to Burnham, others spread the word nationally of San Francisco's glorious future. Before the plan was made public, Charles A. Keeler, an authority on architecture, published an article setting forth the strides already made toward municipal adornment and promising that much more would follow. Several months later, Herbert Law of the AIASF revealed "The San Francisco of the Future as Planned by Daniel H. Burnham, Builder of Cities." Reproductions of the Burnham plan, in whole or in part, appeared in magazines.[18] By and large these articles were summaries of Burnham's work, introduced by enthusiastic comments. It took the perceptive Herbert Croly to put the plans into the context of San Francisco's development and the growth of the Pacific Coast, and to pinpoint some of the problems that so large an undertaking would encounter.

According to Croly, the Burnham plan was of national importance because San Francisco would shortly become one of the three or four leading metropolises in the country, a New York of the Pacific Coast. It would be the center of finance and industry, and the home of the intellectual leaders of the West. It had grown so rapidly since 1897 that, if the rate were maintained, in twenty years only New York, Chicago, and Philadelphia would be larger. San Francisco would profit from the inevitable expansion of the West's economy. It already attracted many tourists, drawn by its climate, location, and cosmopolitan tone. Adoption of the Burnham plan would combine with the natural advantages to enhance the resort qualities of the city. Croly endorsed Burnham's recommendations almost without exception; if the plan were realized only in part, he said, San Francisco would become the most conveniently arranged city in the nation. Yet his understanding of political and economic realities led him to identify several obstacles that might stand in the way of execution.

In the first place, implementation would necessitate collective action. Individuals, "acting in obedience to innocent and unconscious personal motives," would undoubtedly do the bulk of the work, "but the essential task must be achieved by the community acting with the fullest and most definite determination to make San Francisco a great city." Only the community, wrote Croly, "can make the plan of the city—its physical constitution and appearance—adequate at once to its extraordinary situation, the manifest industrial needs of its future, and to its (possibly) higher destiny." Uniting a city as divided as San Francisco into a community would be a Herculean task, but it was made even more difficult by the rapacity of private interests. The gridiron street layout, which Burnham sought to alter, was the creature of "that generally ignorant and obnoxious individual, the real estate speculator, whose selfish interests demanded lots and blocks of uniform size and with rectangular corners." This villain of San Francisco's past had not disappeared with the end of the gold rush or the coming of the railroad; he was still at work, busily laying out new subdivisions in the same disastrous way. Only when the whole community organized against the speculator would the city realize its magnificent physical heritage. And organization had to take place quickly, for in ten or fifteen years the land for the Civic Center—linchpin of the whole plan—would become prohibitively expensive. Finally, the economic feasibility of the plan depended upon a continuation of the current rate of growth of the city. If population increase slowed to a still considerable 30 percent each decade, Croly thought it unlikely that enough wealth would be accumulated to allow for even a gradual implementation. The role of the Burnham plan, as seen by Croly, was both to stimulate growth by making the city attractive and to regulate development in the interest of beauty.

Despite its crucial significance for the future of San Francisco, the Burnham plan was not to be enacted in haste. Croly did not regard it as another, larger Chicago Fair, to appear suddenly and artificially, imposed on the landscape, complete in all details. Rather it must grow organically:

> There must be about it much that is accidental and mysterious as well as much that has been foreseen and proposed, and it must within certain limits be judiciously left to itself. Above all, it must be allowed to ripen slowly, so that it may not wear the aspect of a modern improvement, but will really be the outcome of the better sense and taste of the people of San Francisco, helped out by the informative imagination of a few.[19]

Paris, Croly reminded his readers, was the product of French temperament and tradition, not the child of Haussmann.

Although Croly accurately perceived that Burnham's proposals would find opposition from powerful economic interests, he erred slightly in predicting that real estate speculators would be the chief enemy. Instead, the role was played by the street railway companies. The AIASF had taken as part of its self-imposed mandate the job of constantly agitating for aesthetic improvement. It called for the "removal of artificial creations that destroy what there is of natural beauty, such as telegraph poles and the hideous advertisements and signs."[20] By pledging itself to act as watchdog of the beauties of the streets, the association joined a dispute of some fifteen years standing: Should overhead trolley wires be permitted in the downtown area? The trolley controversy was the first indication that beautification would not go uncontested.

During the 1870s and 1880s, cable-car lines were built on many San Francisco streets, and owners of older, horse-drawn lines were hurt by the competition. Electric trolleys became practical by the late 1880s, and the horse-car men wanted to convert their equipment to trolleys and regain their profits. They succeeded in 1891 in having the state legislature legalize electricity as a motive power for city transportation. The owners of the cable systems, which had by this time been consolidated, wanted to maintain their monopoly. They sponsored a propaganda campaign directed against the dangers of live overhead wires. "If a person was killed in any part of the world by a trolley wire mishap," political boss Martin Kelly recalled,

> the incident was multiplied into a million. In saloons, corner groceries and other places where men used to congregate you could hear vivid descrip-

tions of how a trolley wire broke somewhere in Siberia or Patagonia and went hissing and twisting on its way licking up a large assembly, composed mainly of women and children.[21]

More to the point, the cable interests bribed the Board of Supervisors to pass an ordinance prohibiting the use of overhead wires. Cars could still be driven by electricity, but the current would have have to be carried by conductors set in conduits beneath the pavement. This arrangement cost much more to install than trolley wires.[22] The horse-car owners, however, were able to reach the supervisors in the same manner as had the cable company. After public hostility to the trolleys had subsided a bit, the supervisors repealed the ordinance, and the horse-car lines were converted to electricity. They were quickly purchased by the cable-car company, and by 1893 almost all the transit in the city had been organized into the Market Street Railway Company.[23]

Financial reorganization did not mean operational consolidation or a uniform system. Cable cars continued to be used on steep hills and on busy Market Street. Also, the prejudice against the trolleys did not disappear. The city engineer issued a report in 1901 to the Board of Public Works contending that the conduit would certainly replace the overhead system in the densely populated sections of major cities. The city, he felt, should definitely adopt a conduit system when it took over the Geary Street, Park, and Ocean Railway road at the expiration of that company's franchise in 1903. The existing cable slot would make conversion to a conduit less costly.[24]

The Market Street Railway and three smaller lines were purchased in 1901–1902 by a syndicate of Eastern investors headed by Patrick Calhoun. Stock of the new company, called the United Railroads of San Francisco, was owned by a holding company incorporated in New Jersey, the United Railways Investment Company of San Francisco. After paying an inflated price for the companies it bought, United Railroads issued $40 million of stock to its owners with no basis other than increased earnings anticipated from rapid population growth in San Francisco.[25] The earnings did in fact increase and net income rose even faster.

United Railroads paid its parent company $600,000 in dividends in 1904 and $760,000 in 1905, a return of 3.8 percent on the $20 million of preferred stock.[26] These dividends were in addition to $1,524,000 paid as interest due on the bonded debt. The company was proving its organizers correct; it was paying dividends on watered stock.

Table 2
Earnings and Income of the United Railroads of San Francisco

	1903	1904	1905
Gross earnings	$6,243,219	$6,652,630	$7,066,892
Operating expenses and taxes	3,760,062	3,676,438	3,617,821
Net income	847,473	1,216,395	1,687,480

SOURCE: *Moody's Manual of Railroads and Corporate Securities, Seventh Annual Number, 1906*, (New York: Moody Manual Company, 1906), p. 1244.

Net earnings depended on both gross receipts and operating expenses. Receipts would rise and expenses decline if the remaining cable and horse cars could be converted to trolleys. The need for transfer points wherever electric cars from the outlying districts arrived at Market Street probably cut down the number of riders and certainly cost the company money. Cable cars were smaller and slower than trolleys. They created havoc during rush hour because their speed could not be increased. The most inefficient line was the Sutter Street. Its passengers rode cable cars to Market and Sansome streets, where they had to discharge and board horse-drawn cars to ride down Market to the Ferry Building. The original franchises for these lines, issued in the almost forgotten past, stipulated the kind of motive power for each route; any change necessitated approval by the Board of Supervisors. Since popular feeling against the overhead trolleys had not entirely dissolved, the board was cautious about allowing new wires to be strung. To induce public acceptance, the United Railroads undertook a propaganda campaign in 1904, focusing primarily on the benefits that would ensue if the Sutter Street line were electrified.[27]

This campaign quickly met resistance from some property owners along the Sutter Street route, who organized the Sutter Street Improvement Club in the spring of 1905. Frank J. Sullivan, Phelan's brother-in-law and also a founding member of the AIASF, was president of the group. Its active membership included millionaire Rudolph Spreckels, who lived on Pacific Avenue, which was served by the Sutter line. He also owned property on Sutter Street, both in his own name and as a partner with Phelan and others in the Real Property Investment Company. Phelan had a lot on Sutter Street, and his sister Alice owned a large parcel that she leased to the White House Department Store.[28]

The trolley question was Spreckels's initial foray into politics. As spokesman for the Sutter Street Improvement Club, he complained that poles and wires were ugly, dangerous, and would lessen the value of real estate. The conduit, though expensive, was more modern and attractive. New York City and Washington, D.C., both used the conduit system; San Francisco should not settle for anything less. Patrick Calhoun, as president of the United Railroads, argued that rain would flood the conduits in the wet season. Spreckels countered by offering to pay for drainage pipes on an experimental line, but Calhoun refused.[29]

The uproar raised by the Improvement Club presumably influenced the Board of Supervisors against giving in to the United Railroads. At any rate, the board took no action during the spring and summer of 1905. But merely preventing the railroad from stringing trolley wires was not a satisfactory victory for the Sutter Street Club nor for the commercial interests of the city. All agreed that the existing system was inadequate and that some immediate improvement was necessary in order to hold San Francisco's population. The inconvenience of travel in the city, especially from outlying districts, was forcing people across the bay, where car service was much better. In Southern California, an extensive network of trolley lines helped to spur the growth of Los Angeles. Meanwhile, San Franciscans wrangled over the question of conduits or overhead wires. In an effort to end the stalemate, the Merchants' Association invited William Barclay Parsons, an internationally famous engineer, to come to San Francisco and advise the city on planning a street railway system.[30] Perhaps an impartial expert could cut the Gordian knot of discord.

Parsons was in San Francisco by August 1905. Daniel Burnham sent his assistant Edward Bennett a letter of introduction for Parsons, who, wrote Burnham, was visiting San Francisco to give advice "regarding the proper system of sub-ways for that city." The letter instructed Bennett to acquaint Parsons with the features of the Burnham plan so that Parsons's work would harmonize with it.[31] Whether Parsons did consult with Bennett is unknown. The engineer must have busied himself examining the city's transportation needs, for his report was completed by November 20, 1905. It was formally presented on December 5 at the eighth annual dinner of the Merchants' Association and published, in the form of a letter to Association President Frank Symmes, in the December number of the *Merchants' Association Review*.

Parsons based his recommendations for San Francisco on a

study of the existing routes, equipment, quantity of traffic, and population density in all parts of the city. He took into account the limitations imposed by steep grades, and he evaluated the performance of electrically driven cars using storage batteries, conduits, and overhead wires. He frequently referred to the experience of other cities in America and Europe. Underlying his recommendations was one explicit assumption, namely that a system with all cars driven by a single type of power from a uniform source was most efficient and therefore most desirable.[32] Even the proponents of the conduit admitted that its greater cost confined it to the heavily trafficked areas of the city, and that extensions into outlying districts would call for the stringing of overhead lines. But they argued that it was possible to combine both methods into a workable system, using cars equipped to handle power from above and below.[33] Parsons implicitly rejected this approach. He advocated overhead trolleys for the entire city, in preference to conduits and subways, which were too expensive, and to battery operated cars, which did not work well enough.

A major objection to the trolleys was the unsightliness of poles needed to carry the wires. Parsons pointed to European cities in which artistically designed poles also held street lights, signs, and mail boxes. They were spaced at 200 or even 300 feet, rather than at 100 as in San Francisco. The terrain presented a more formidable obstacle to the trolley. Cable cars, after all, had been invented to scale the city's heights, and the first one had followed Clay Street over Nob Hill. Trolleys could not make the grade. As a remedy Parsons suggested that trolleys run through two tunnels cut beneath Nob Hill. The cars would stop at one station in each tunnel, where elevators would carry passengers to and from the crest of the hill. Elsewhere minor rearrangement of routes and regrading of streets would complete the changes needed to make the cable car obsolete.[34]

Parsons concluded his report with an assurance and a warning. The Panama Canal would enhance San Francisco's position on the major trade routes, he believed, but this advantage must be accompanied by a progressive policy on the streetcar question:

For the growth of a modern city many things are necessary, but none is more important than a proper system of internal transportation. Commerce and trade, as well as public convenience, are promoted and stimulated by good and rapid means of going from residence to business, or from one trading center to another. With proper development the future population will be attracted to the peninsula, and your municipal lines will be extended. If the development is checked, the residential area, which always follows the line of least resistance, will be deflected to the outlying suburbs across the bay, and in degree, according to the difference in facilities, availability of land, and general economy. People will cross the bay to do business in the city, but will build residences, make investments in improvements, and pay taxes in other communities.[35]

The message was unambiguous; to capitalize on its location on the bay, San Francisco had better increase its desirability as a residential city by modernizing its transportation system.

If the directors of the Merchants' Association had invited Parsons to San Francisco in the hope that he would settle the trolley issue once and for all, then the invitation had been totally in vain. At the very dinner at which Parsons's suggestions were made public, the controversy flared with renewed vigor. After the report was read, Frank J. Sullivan assailed the overhead trolley and the corporation that wanted to foist it on San Francisco. He even intimated that there had been some collusion between Parsons, the Merchants' Association, and the United Railroads. Was it not curious, he asked,

that, when we poor citizens who are interested in Sutter street are trying to have an underground conduit on Sutter, a report of this character, to all intents and purposes a plea in favor of an overhead electric system, should be given to the public[?][36]

The terrain of the city would not allow for a uniform system, Sullivan argued, and the people had repeatedly expressed themselves against poles and in favor of conduits. The trolley wires were unsightly and unsafe, a constant threat to electrocute pedestrians and set fire to homes. The experience of other cities demonstrated that the overhead system had become antiquated for central areas.

Sullivan also attacked the street railway corporation. Progressive mayors like Hazen Pingree of Detroit and Samuel Jones of Toledo, and, he added, pointing to his brother-in-law, James Phelan, were against long-term franchises or any franchises at all. But in San Francisco, these valuable rights, belonging to the people, had been purchased for next to nothing from corrupt boards of supervisors and had become the most valuable assets of the corporation. Now the United Railroads, which had paid $35 million for property worth $10 million and then watered the stock by an additional $45 million, wanted to construct a "cheap and nasty overhead system." San Francisco had the opportunity, thanks to Burnham's work, to be a beautiful city. But beautiful cities did not ruin their streets with hideous poles and wires. The question boiled down to one of home rule versus profit for foreign owners. "Shall you own these railroads," asked Sullivan, "or shall they be controlled by the bondholders who live six thousand miles away? Shall we have this city that we love as we want it, and of which we shall always be proud?"[37] Or, by implication, would the future be directed by profit-hungry financiers in New York, London, and Amsterdam?

In the course of his speech Sullivan had dealt roughly with Patrick Calhoun, reminding him that his grandfather John C. Calhoun, in his devotion to states' rights, had been the great advocate of home rule. But Sullivan closed on a more conciliatory note. If Patrick Calhoun could see the question through the eyes of San Franciscans, said Sullivan, "and is not guided solely by his relation to it as the representative of a foreign interest," he would certainly give the city what it wanted, "home rule in the traction system for our people."

Calhoun followed Sullivan as speaker, and he quickly let Sullivan and the audience know where his fealty lay. While he yielded "unquestioned allegiance to the great principle that home rule should control Americans," he rejoiced "that local pride may be merged into a broader Americanism, and that the citizen of New York may indeed call himself the fellow citizen of the San Franciscan." Calhoun was telling San Francisco capitalists that they had no monopoly on the local scene, that franchises, rails, and rolling stock could be bought on the open market, and that investors from the East and Europe had as much right to profit from the transportation needs of San Franciscans as did any Native Son of the Golden West. Calhoun also claimed that Sullivan had undervalued the amount United Railroads had spent on the properties and overestimated the amount of water in the stock. The railroad, according to Calhoun, was returning only 4.96 percent on actual capital invested. But the owners were not disappointed. They had faith in the future of San Francisco, and to demonstrate it were about to spend $8 million to improve the system. They would not throw away money on conduits. Of all the street railway mileage in Europe and America, conduits accounted for only 2 percent, overhead trolleys for 93 percent. Certainly the rest of the world had not been entirely in error. Calhoun ended by assuring his listeners that, as the holder of a public franchise, the United Railroads took seriously its responsibility to provide the best possible service. An economic law dictated that the interests of the city and the interests of the company were the same.[38]

Despite these assurances and Parsons's endorsement of the trolley, not all San Franciscans were convinced that what was good for United Railroads was good for the city. The directors of the Merchants' Association polled the members on their preferences for the streetcar system, mailing out a series of questions about different aspects of the problem. Asked whether they favored Parsons's view of a uniform overhead trolley for the entire city, 121 voted yes, 204 no. The proposal for an underground conduit for Market and adjacent streets currently served by cable cars, with an overhead trolley for the rest of the system, received 198 yes votes, 84 no votes; 217 respondents indicated that the conduit was their first choice for Sutter Street, compared to 93 who wanted the trolley and 5 who preferred cable cars.[39]

The directors of the association chose to ignore these votes. Arguing that the 364 members who returned ballots represented less than a quarter of the total membership, they took it upon themselves to endorse the major portions of Parsons's report. Because of the unwillingness of the United Railroads to construct conduits, and because there was no legal way for the city to compel the company to do so, the choice was not between conduit and trolley but between trolley and cable. Given those alternatives, the interests of the city dictated a conversion to electric trolleys. Cities in the East Bay were growing at San Francisco's expense because of the terrible transportation system. Visions of the City Beautiful were all right in their place, the directors asserted, but "it should be remembered that San Francisco is a commercial city, and while every effort should be made to beautify the streets, the city's growth and prosperity should not be sacrificed simply to give business districts an aesthetic appearance." The action of the directors received criticism in the press on the grounds that they had taken a poll of members and "then proceed[ed] to act precisely contrary to the instructions thus given." Within the association itself, the directors' support for Parsons and the trolley raised hostilities to such a level that long-standing friendships were shattered.[40]

Meanwhile a constant stream of criticism of the United Railroads appeared in the editorial columns, news stories, and even illustrations in the *Bulletin*, and, to a much lesser extent, in the *Chronicle*. In addition to the conduit-trolley question, the main points of attack were that the railroad provided inadequate service, that its cars and overhead wires were hazardous, that the company was interested exclusively in paying interest on its watered securities, and, most emphatically, that absentee owners in Wall Street and Europe were robbing San Franciscans and retarding the growth of the city. "The owners of the company's stocks and bonds are Wall-Street magnates whose only interest in San Francisco is that of a tax-farmer in the province which he has been commissioned to squeeze," charged a typical *Bulletin* editorial.[41] Photographs showing cars at rush hour jammed with passengers appeared above captions asking whether the straphangers were getting their money's worth.[42] Although the *Bulletin* approved of the city attorney's plan to halve fares for riders unable to get a seat, in general the 5 cent fare was not an issue.[43] *Bulletin* editor Fremont Older was a political ally of Phelan and Spreckels; the newspaper's castigation of the United Railroads was almost certainly an effort to weaken the company's position regarding the trolley application.

If the Phelan-Spreckels axis had its friends, so did Calhoun and the United Railroads. At a meeting of the San Francisco Real Estate Board on March 14, 1906, realtors unanimously supported a set of resolutions calling upon city authorities to allow the company to substitute the overhead trolley for underground cable. While the conduit might be better, argued real estate owner and AIASF member Herbert Law and his brother Hartland, it was not feasible because of the company's opposition. Those who held out for the conduit were delaying progress.[44] The *Bulletin* refused to accept this logic. It accused the realtors of being speculators who, for the sake of quick profits, were willing to sell out the best interests of the city to Wall Street financiers. Instead of giving in, the city should hold out for a few years and force the railroad to come around. San Francisco deserved the very best; it "must become a first-rate city, and this it will not be while its best streets are marred with poles and wires."[45]

In late March 1906, it seemed for a brief time that the *Bulletin* had been correct, that the United Railroads would have to modify its plans for electrification. A newspaper story appearing on March 21 told of secret negotiations between Patrick Calhoun and representatives of the Sutter Street Improvement Club and the AIASF that had been going on for several days. The two sides had agreed that the cable lines on Market would be converted to conduit as far south as Valencia Street, and the Sutter line would be run as a conduit from Market westward to Polk Street. Everywhere else in the city, the cables would be replaced by overhead trolleys with the approval of, or at least without opposition from, the two organizations. Herbert Law, with a foot in both camps, and Rufus Jennings, secretary of the California Promotion Committee, had acted as mediators.[46]

Either the story was premature or else its appearance put a damper on the negotiations, for in the next three days the agreement fell through. Spreckels did not want the trolley wires in front of his house on Pacific Street, which would have been the case according to the arrangement. Calhoun announced on March 21 that the Sutter line would be a conduit only from Market to Powell Street, a mere six blocks; the seven blocks from Powell to Polk and all the route thereafter would get overhead wires. He also said that if the people of San Francisco did not want the conduit at all, if they in fact preferred a trolley, he would accede to their choice. He then would donate the difference in construction costs, which he put at $200,000, to the city for improvement and extension of the Panhandle. This pledge was a sop intended to appease Phelan, but whatever possibility for acceptance it may have had was vitiated by the last item in his statement. Asked how he proposed to ascertain the will of the people, Calhoun answered that the Board of Supervisors, as representatives of the ideas and wishes of San Franciscans, would make the decision.[47]

As early as February 1906, the *Chronicle* had commented on the general feeling of conduit supporters that the United Railroads was ready to get its way through corrupt means, if necessary.[48] Even before then, however, Older, Spreckels, and Phelan had taken definite steps to initiate an investigation and prosecution of Ruef, Schmitz, and the Union Labor Administration.[49] Calhoun's promise to elicit public sentiment through the Board of Supervisors was certainly no assurance that popular feeling would in fact be consulted. The Sutter Street Club and the AIASF met immediately after Calhoun's announcement and both demanded from him a clarification of intentions. He sent them a letter breaking off negotiations and declaring that he would proceed with plans for a uniform overhead system for the entire city.[50]

Perhaps as early as the fall of 1905, Spreckels, with Phelan and others, had decided upon another battle plan.[51] Instead of trying directly to compel the United Railroads to adopt the conduit, local capitalists would build and operate a competing transit system, using only the underground conduit as a source of power.[52] Fears that the United Railroad and its backers might outbid the Spreckels-Phelan group for any new franchise were dispelled with the news that multimillionaire Claus Spreckels would be a principal backer of the local group. According to Rudolph Spreckels, their motives were entirely civic and in accord with the goals of beautification. "The people must understand," he said,

> that we are all united on this question for the benefit of San Francisco, that this is every man's fight, and that every man in town is concerned in it—the beauty of the city. The mere advertisement of it abroad that the city is equipped with the most modern and sightly street-railway system in the world would be of incalculable benefit to San Francisco.[53]

Phelan also stressed the importance of the city's appearance if it wanted to be a tourist haven. Since eastern men of culture opposed overhead wires, he said, San Francisco must follow their lead if it wanted to attract Easterners. Ironically, he blamed "Eastern capitalists" for trying to impose the trolley system on San Francisco.

Plans for the new road developed rapidly, suggesting that it may have been in preparation for some time. The organization was to be called the Municipal Railways Company of San Francisco. Its backers claimed they would capitalize at actual cost of construction, estimated to be $14 million for 200 miles of single-track road. At that price, they said, the road would pay a reasonable profit and still provide the best car service in the country. The city might purchase the road at any time by paying the owners for their capital outlay plus a fair interest, thus bringing the new system into a city-owned one that had been in the offing for years.[54] To speed the undertaking on its way, property owners on Bush Street, probably at Spreckels's suggestion, petitioned the Board of Supervisors to grant the new company a franchise for a conduit road on Bush.[55] On April 17, 1906, the Municipal Street Railways Company filed for incorporation. Its directors were Claus and Rudolph Spreckels, James Phelan, George Whitell, and Charles S. Wheeler.[56]

Calhoun and his assistants were not idle in meeting this challenge to their virtual monopoly in streetcar transit. According to the *Bulletin*, "dummy clubs, called into being by the United Railroads, are industriously resolving and whereasing in favor of poles and overhead wires for the purpose of making it appear that public opinion is divided on the question." Canvassers, presumably employed by the company, were busily gathering signatures of Market Street merchants supporting conversion to the trolley.[57] But the railroad's major effort was a secret one. Abraham Ruef had been receiving $500 a month from the company since 1902 as a "retainer." The amount was raised in November 1905, after the Union

Labor Party's landslide victory, to $1,000. For this money, Ruef gave advice to the United Railroads. He told Calhoun, for example, that public hostility to the company would be abated if the company provided the city with some aesthetic ornamentation. Later he suggested that the company put up electric lamps on its trolley poles and illuminate the streets free of charge. The company, through its counsel Tirey L. Ford, accepted these proposals with modification. But Ruef's main service was not public relations. In April, after some negotiation, Ford agreed to pay Ruef $200,000. Although nothing explicit was said, it was clear to both men that the money was a bribe, to pay the supervisors for granting a trolley permit.[58]

In the struggle between the United Railroads and the conduit proponents, the city government was, for a while at least, a third force. The Charter of 1900 had called for municipal ownership of public utilities. When the franchise of the independent Geary Street road expired in 1903, the Board of Supervisors refused to renew it, but did permit the Geary Street, Park, and Ocean Railway Company to operate on sufferance, paying a proportion of its receipts to the city. The Geary route was intended to be the core of a municipally owned system. Though the process of acquisition was complicated and progress slow, the Geary line put the city more or less in the transit business.[59] Also, the Board of Supervisors could regulate the privately owned lines regarding fares, extension of routes, and types of power. In February 1906, City Attorney W. G. Burke urged the Board of Supervisors to pass an ordinance fixing the fare at 2½ cents for passengers unable to find seats.[60] A month later, just after the Spreckels group had announced its decision to build a system to compete with the United Railroads, Burke brought forth a plan of the administration to do precisely the same thing. This new road would be built with private capital, but would then revert to the city. From all appearances, Burke was trying to preempt the field from the Spreckels group, which, he said, "seems to have made itself a third house in the municipal government." But no private effort was necessary; "our administration, our incorruptible Board of Supervisors, and I may add, the City Attorney, are determined to wage vigorous and unrelenting warfare on the United Railroads." As if to show his sincerity, Burke added that a 3 cent fare for rush hours, when most passengers had to stand, would be enacted. But after several weeks of discussion, the incorruptible Board of Supervisors, in their customary secret caucus on Sunday nights, killed the measure at the insistence of Abraham Ruef.[61] Clearly Burke had promised a good deal more than he could deliver, if he had ever intended to make a delivery in the first place.

The Burnham *Report* and Calhoun's plan to convert cable cars to overhead trolleys were contemporary phenomena, and supporters of one conflicted sharply with those of the other. It is relatively easy to identify spokesmen of each side because they received coverage in the press. Burnham's most vocal and adamant champion was, of course, James D. Phelan, president of the AIASF. In the struggle over the trolley question, he was joined by his friend and business associate Rudolph Spreckels, by Spreckels's father Claus, by Phelan's brother-in-law Frank J. Sullivan, by local capitalists who owned property on Sutter Street or who invested in the Municipal Street Railways Company, and by Fremont Older of the *Bulletin*. Presumably many members of the AIASF and other beautification clubs like the Outdoor Art League, some owners of property elsewhere in the downtown area, and some members of organizations like the Merchants' Association and the Commonwealth Club, which endorsed the Burnham plan, took Phelan's side.

Supporting Calhoun and the railroad were the directors of the Merchants' Association, the San Francisco Real Estate Board, some downtown merchants, and, in secret, the Union Labor administration. Since both antagonists probably created or used local improvement clubs, it is difficult to decide how much credence to give the various petitions for or against the trolley. A San Francisco weekly, for example, contended that the United Railroads had possibly pressured some clubs in neighborhoods at the extremities of the cable lines to take a stand in favor of trolleys. But, said the magazine, the small property owners in these areas genuinely wanted service, did not care particularly how they got it, and so sided with the railroad against the downtown interests. Since the question of trolley versus conduit never came to a referendum, it is not possible to estimate how the electorate at large felt about the issue. Most likely the majority of San Franciscans were more or less indifferent, although the press, even the anti-Phelan *Town Talk*, noticed a general public hostility toward the United Railroads.[62]

The contest between the AIASF and the United Railroads cannot be understood merely as a battle between businessmen and aesthetes, between those who wanted a handsome return and those who wanted a beautiful environment. Certainly the members of the San Francisco Real Estate Board, which had greeted the Burnham *Report* with enthusiasm in February 1906, were moved by the desire for speedy profits when they favored the trolley in March. And of course it was a cash calculation that prompted Ruef and the Board of Supervisors to favor the trolley. But on the other side, Spreckels and Phelan spoke openly of the loss to property values from erection of wires and poles. Phelan had always promoted city beautification as a path to city prosperity, because it would stimulate tourist trade and population growth.

The situation is further complicated by the similarity of economic appeals. Both the Burnham plan and the electrification scheme were programs for development, both promised to bring wealth to the city and make at least some of the people richer. For owners of real estate in the settled districts and large merchants in the downtown area, the promises were made to the same people. A good example is Herbert Law, a founder of AIASF, who in 1906 had recently acquired the Fairmont Hotel and owned other valuable property. With other members of the Real Estate Board, he voted for the trolley. He and his brother were accused of accepting from Calhoun the offer of certain traffic concessions worth $20,000. They denied the rumor and argued that they were interested only in the good of the city. The Laws then worked to bring about a compromise between Calhoun and Phelan and Spreckels. When that compromise failed, the Laws endorsed Spreckels's plan for a competing railroad.[63] They may have been hypocritical, but it seems more likely that they were having genuine difficulty in choosing between two courses of action, each of which appealed to their economic interest. The problem for the Laws was one of perceiving where the true advantage lay.

The division over the trolley question, then, is only partially explained by reference to hard economic interests. For the United Railroads, certainly the cheapness of the overhead trolley was the principal consideration. But for San Franciscans, the case remained more complicated. Simple calculations of expected profit and loss do not tell us why Spreckels and Phelan saw their advantage to lie in one direction, while the Laws thought it lay in the opposite. Likewise, the Merchants' Association, made up of men with basically homogeneous interests, would probably not have divided so sharply had the economic elements of the issue been more clear cut. Something else is necessary to understand why certain people took the positions they did.

A helpful hint may lie in the rhetoric of the conflict. As noted above, *Bulletin* editorials pictured San Francisco as being despoiled for the benefit of outside financiers. In the *Bulletin*'s language, the "lords of Wall-Street," the "Eastern capitalists," the "absentee owners," were "tyrannizing," "crushing," "oppressing" San Francisco with their "silurian" and "rapacious" policy dictated by "greed."[64] Frank J. Sullivan had used similar expressions in attacking the Parsons report. Phelan spoke in the the same terms when he assailed Eastern capitalists for trying to impose a trolley system on the city. Claus Spreckels affirmed his commitment to build a competing transit system by saying:

> It is outrageous to have the overhead trolley in this city. Calhoun says we shall have it, and I say we shall not have it. Why should he come here and tell us what we should do? . . . We have a beautiful city and I do not want to see it disfigured with more trolley lines.[65]

From the opposite side, Calhoun felt that he was the target of hostility because he was an outsider. He was convinced that the Spreckels-Phelan group wanted to build a competing railway system and used the trolley issue as a blind. "San Francisco" Ruef reported him to have said,

> has always been regarded by the great financiers of the East as a local provincial field. My own little experience here has shown me it is not the fault of the people. They are warm-hearted and broadminded. The fault is with a group of petty, selfish financiers who have secured a powerful grasp on the city's affairs and who want a restricted field for their own operations. By their attacks and the difficulties they put in the way these men discourage the coming of Eastern capital.[66]

There is no question that those San Franciscans most powerfully opposed to the overhead trolley did make a distinction between local and outside interests. They may have demagogically stressed the alien ownership of the United Railroads to arouse hostility and help themselves profit from a competing railway. But it seems more likely that they were, as they described themselves, moved by civic consciousness, at least as they defined it. As the culmination of Phelan's hopes for a new San Francisco, the Burnham *Report* was the blueprint for a socially cohesive city, one in which the residents took pride in the beauty of their surroundings, loved the city for the life it provided, and saw their own welfare intimately connected with the good of the community. Phelan's aim was hardly collectivism, yet his "civicism" pictured a society in which attachment to place helped to modify, but not eliminate, individual interests in the direction of the common weal. Therefore, he could not accept the argument that the trolley was preferable because it was cheaper or more efficient, without reference to some wider social purpose. Phelan and his friends, remarked a *Bulletin* editorial,

gaze into the far future. They behold San Francisco rising, puissant, like a strong man after sleep—to use the language of the great publicity agent of another commonwealth movement—but in their dreaming they do not see the United Railroads press the chloroform to the mouth and nostrils of the awakening titan and send him back to drowsihood; while the realty brokers attend the operation and hold down the titan's legs.[67]

Calhoun did not understand this kind of commitment. He wanted to make a profit for his corporation, and he attributed a similar motive to his opponents. But for Spreckels, Phelan, and their associates, the vision made sense both socially and economically. Those who had been touched by Phelan's "civicism" or who had reached a similar position independently fought with Calhoun and those San Franciscans who had not.

A last aspect of the local-alien conflict is revealing. When the Union Labor supervisors took office in January 1906, the final vestiges of Phelan's hold on the city government were removed. Even after he had retired as mayor in January 1902, a majority of the Board of Supervisors remained Democrats from his wing of the party. The supervisors were mostly men of means: merchants, professionals, high-ranking employees of large firms.[68] As one of their last actions, the board rejected a petition from the United Railroads for a trolley permit.[69] The Union Labor supervisors were a different class of people: minor union leaders and union members, several small businessmen, a few incumbents.[70] They all owed their election to Ruef, and they were tainted by the connection.

Even before they took office, Fremont Older began to put together an organization and an agreement which would lead to graft prosecutions in 1906–1909. Older had long attacked Ruef and Schmitz, and in December 1905, he convinced attorney Francis J. Heney and government detective William J. Burns to undertake an investigation of the city government. Older also persuaded Rudolph Spreckels to supply the funds necessary to support the investigation. Spreckels tried to enlist about fifteen wealthy San Franciscans to contribute, but Phelan alone came to his aid.[71] For those men who did get involved, for Older, Heney, Spreckels, and Phelan, ridding San Francisco of corruption was a civic responsibility. As Heney said to Spreckels, in declining compensation, "I was born in San Francisco and raised here. I have always felt that it was my city. . . . I'll do it for nothing. I think I ought to do it, for San Francisco. It's my town."[72] As suspicion increased in 1906 that Calhoun would get his permit through some underhanded means, the men behind the incipient graft investigation must have been upset by what they believed was taking place. Though they made no statement, in part because of the secrecy of their preparations, it seems likely that the attacks on the United Railroads as a foreign intruder were coupled in their minds with tacit curses of the johnny-come-latelys on the Board of Supervisors who would sell out the city for a song. The Burnham plan and the civic ideal were threatened by an unholy alliance, they must have felt, between unscrupulous wealth from outside the city and cheap politicians from within.

6
Relief and Rehabilitation

The Power of Ideology

Early in the morning of April 18, 1906, a violent earthquake rumbled along the San Andreas fault, striking San Francisco with particular severity. The quake touched off scattered fires that merged into a giant conflagration. When the fire subsided on April 21, much of the city lay in ruins. Matters like the streetcar controversy were pushed aside, at least temporarily, while San Franciscans confronted enormous tasks: first, providing relief for the victims, meaning in some degree virtually everyone in the city; second, rebuilding San Francisco, perhaps along lines laid down in the Burnham *Report*. The operation of relief and rehabilitation, important in itself, would be a test of how effectively the city could employ its resources to serve the common interest.

The current city administration soon proved inadequate to deal with the unprecedented difficulties stemming from the earthquake and fire. Mayor Schmitz himself stood out conspicuously in the early administration of relief, but he largely ignored his political allies on the Board of Supervisors. Instead he appointed a committee of prominent citizens as a de facto government to supervise activities. He put James D. Phelan in what became the most important post, head of the finance committee in charge of spending more than $9 million donated for relief. The finance committee established the guidelines for all programs. In making key choices, it operated under the assumption that individual responsibility was essential for maintaining public order. When it decided not to build permanent public housing, for example, it revealed a crucial inconsistency between the ideal of public responsibility espoused by Phelan and his planning supporters, and the dread of doing anything that might undercut the free market and individual initiative. This contradiction was to reappear over the larger issue of how the city should be rebuilt.

The city of San Francisco sits several hundred yards east of the San Andreas fault line. In retrospect, the site seems a foolhardy testing of fate, but before 1906 there had been only one serious quake in the city's recorded history, back in 1868. The damage it inflicted was not nearly severe enough to counter the magnetism of a city in which some were making money in great quantities.[1] Other than preferring wood to masonry construction, San Franciscans took no special precautions. When steel frame buildings developed in the 1880s and 1890s, local capitalists put up structures of ten or more stories. By 1906, the Claus Spreckels building on Market Street, eighteen stories high, was merely the largest of over forty steel frame buildings in the city, with others under construction.

The earthquake of April 18 proved the builders correct: steel frame structures withstood the shock. But hundreds of other buildings did suffer. The walls of the garish and shoddily built city hall tower came crashing down, leaving the great dome suspended in the air as if by levitation. Elsewhere in the city, brick chimneys tumbled, plaster cracked, some walls gave out. Damage was greatest on land that had been reclaimed from the bay, as in the area east of Montgomery Street. Buildings on the rocky hills were least affected.

By breaking chimneys, gas pipes, and electrical lines, the earthquake precipitated scores of fires. It also destroyed water mains and service pipes, so that the already inadequate water system was rendered virtually useless.[2] As a grim irony, the quake killed the fire chief, Dennis Sullivan. Under such conditions, it is no wonder that for more than three days the fires ravaged San Francisco almost at will. When the conflagration finally exhausted itself, the front of the fire extended more than nine miles. Why it did not continue is something of a mystery, for facing the front were hundreds of wooden buildings separated from the fire by streets of only ordinary width.[3] If, as was thought in parts of the country, the calamity was

God's chastisement of a sinful city, surely the Lord had a sense of proportion.

By the morning of April 21, when it had been brought under control, the fire had virtually leveled 4.7 square miles of San Francisco. It razed more than 28,000 buildings, leaving only 303 standing within the 521 blocks of the burned area. By way of comparison, the area destroyed by the San Francisco fire was six times that of the London fire of 1666 and at least one and one half times that of Chicago's fire of 1871.[4]

Estimates vary as to the number of people who were killed by the quake or died in the fire. The British Consul General in San Francisco reported that whereas the local residents put the number of dead at around 300, he thought the total must have been at least 200 more. "The smell of decomposing flesh is strong from the ruins in certain parts of the city," he wrote, "but at the same time the local contention that the odour comes not from human flesh, but that of cattle, is not without a certain amount of truth." A semi-official committee investigating the extent of the disaster found that 315 persons were killed by either quake or fire, another 7 had been shot, and 352 were missing and unaccounted for. Some of these no doubt survived to leave the city in the mass exodus that followed the earthquake. Probably the number of fatalities fell between 400 and 500.[5] Property damage is even more difficult to estimate. A committee on statistics put the figure at $105 million for damage to assessed real property; it made no guess as to the value of merchandise and personal property destroyed. Other estimates appraised the total loss at anywhere from $350 to $500 million.[6]

Quantitative assessments of the calamity do not adequately convey the extent of the damage. What had burned was the heart of San Francisco: the financial district, the major retail business district, most of the wholesale, factory and entertainment sections, the great hotels and restaurants, almost all the important buildings. Gone was the city of the Forty-niners, the railroad barons and the silver kings, the great merchants and the financial giants. The gay, light-hearted, pleasure-loving city that history, abetted by legend, has told us was prefire San Francisco lay in ashes. Approximately one quarter of a million people, or about three-fifths of the population, lost their homes. These included Nob Hill grandees, denizens of Chinatown, and the workers south of Market.[7] Great as the damage was, it was initially overestimated by the outside world. The *New York Times* printed a map of the burned section that included about twice the

Relief and Rehabilitation   131

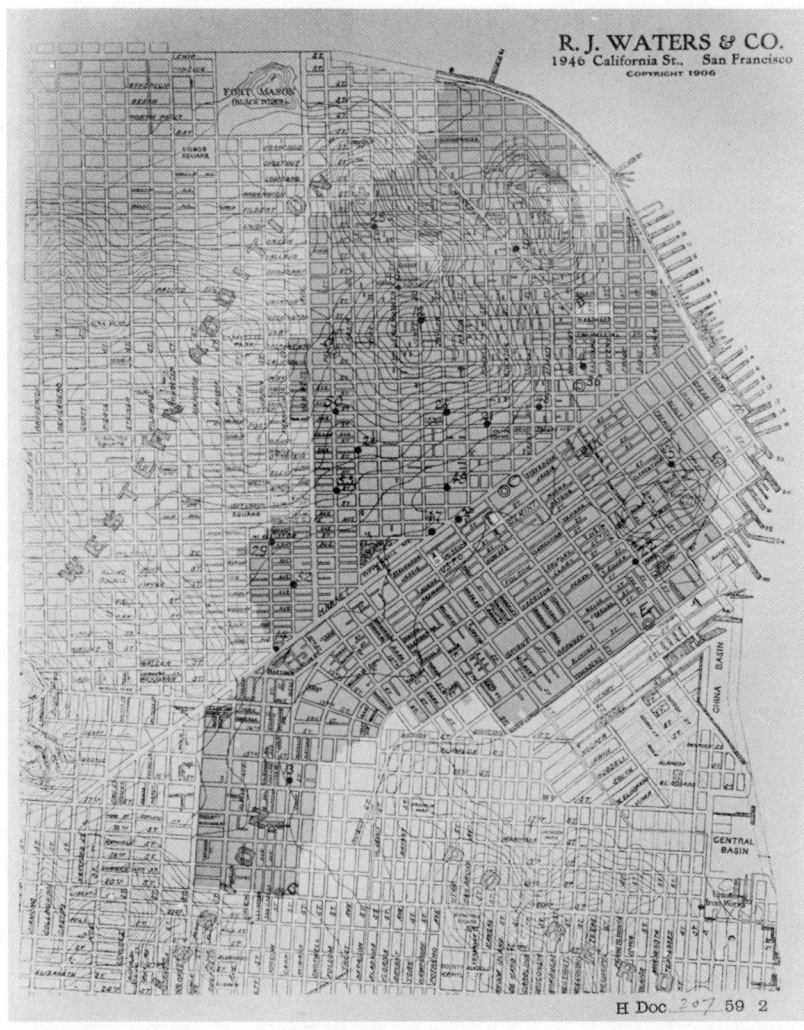

The extent of the fire (U.S. House of Representatives, 59th Congress, 2d. Session, Document No. 207)

actual area. The newspaper reported, as did other journals as close as Oakland, the erroneous information that the Cliff House had fallen into the sea.[8]

There were saving remnants. The waterfront had largely escaped, as had the Southern Pacific railroad terminal. Important federal buildings such as the Post Office and the Customs House survived, thanks to their stout construction, private water supplies, and the efforts of the employees. New steel frame buildings, including the Spreckels Tower, the St. Francis and the Fairmont hotels, the Mills Building, had been gutted by the flames, and some had suffered structural damage from the 2,000 degree heat, but the shells still stood, awaiting restoration. About 150,000 people were not burned out. And of course the city's priceless location was not affected. The idea so widespread before the fire, that the city's harbor and position on the Pacific had destined it to be the metropolis of a new American empire, did not evaporate when the buildings went up in smoke. Some men had become rich in San Francisco; with will and work, they would become rich again. As I. W. Hellman, president of the Wells Fargo Nevada National Bank, informed his correspondents, the vaults were safe, business was good, and "the business men of our community are in buoyant spirits, filled with energy and with determination, in rebuilding our city, to make it stronger and more beautiful than ever."[9]

During the first morning of the fire, Mayor Eugene Schmitz issued a proclamation intended to maintain public order. "The Federal Troops, the members of the Regular Police Force and all Special Police Officers," ran the broadside, "have been authorized by me to KILL any and all persons found engaged in looting or in the Commission of Any Other Crime."[10] In issuing the order, Schmitz expressed the widely shared fear that beneath the surface of civilized life in San Francisco lay a seething, lawless mob, waiting for the chaotic moment to rise up and commit all sorts of crime, especially crimes against property.

During the days of the fire, stories circulated that looters were rampant in the city, and that scores of them had been shot or hung by law enforcement officials. There was in fact both looting and shooting, but it was on a much smaller scale than anticipated or rumored. Almost certainly more property was lost because of soldiers who refused to let owners clear their residences, stores, or offices while the fire was still blocks away.[11] As John Young, the deeply conservative editor of the *Chronicle*, recorded, on the whole, considering the fact that before the fire the City was supposed to be harboring a large number of men who represented the extreme ideas of the syndicalists, there was a remarkable degree of that sort of orderliness which can only be secured by unquestioning acceptance of the assumption that the exercise of authority and the necessity of regulation are imperative if chaos is to be avoided.[12]

Shortly after issuing his "shoot to kill" proclamation, Schmitz took another step to guarantee the maintenance of civil order in San Francisco. Although the fire was then in its early stages, it was already clear that tens of thousands of people would be homeless, that the usual means of getting food and clothing would be interrupted, and that a massive relief effort would be necessary to care for the survivors of the earthquake and fire. To have expected the officials of San Francisco, from the recently elected and voracious Board of Supervisors on down to the civil servants who ran the almshouse and the hospital, to take the leadership in such a situation would have been foolish. Men of energy and talent in San Francisco in 1906 were not part of the city government; even Abraham Ruef was an unofficial advisor to the mayor. So Schmitz decided to create an ad hoc and extralegal committee of citizens to take control of the various aspects of relief for the stricken citizens. He appointed to this body, called by different names but officially known as the Citizens' Committee of Fifty, many of the leading lawyers, financiers, businessmen, architects, and clergymen of the city. His political opponents Rudolph Spreckels, James Phelan, and Francis Heney were on the original list; absent were Ruef, all the supervisors, and almost all labor leaders or other men from the class that had presumably put Schmitz in office. Ruef and many others were added to the committee during its seventeen-day life, so that ultimately the 50 grew to more than 130.[13]

Armed with uncertain authority, the Citizens' Committee quickly organized itself into subcommittees and set out to save what was left of the city. Though more than twenty subcommittees were established, the work of the Citizens' Committee involved four main tasks. First, the committee would help to supply food, shelter, and medical care for those who needed them, using its own resources and coordinating the efforts of others. For the majority of homeless, shelter meant tents or temporary barracks in a park, plaza, or other open space in the city. Food was pouring into San Francisco from nearby towns; the job of the Citizens' Committee was to facilitate preparation and distribution. Second, a subcommittee was appointed to oversee the migration of those who wanted to leave San Francisco. Third, two subcommittees assisted the police and fire departments in maintaining order and preventing a new conflagration. Finally, a number of subcommittees worked to speed the return of normal conditions by restoring the utilities and transportation networks, the government and the courts, the retail and wholesale trade.[14]

The single most important unit was the finance subcommittee. As news of the San Francisco disaster reached the rest of the country, city after city collected a relief fund to aid the stricken metropolis. Ultimately the cash contributions to San Francisco totaled almost $9 million.[15] The agency through which the great bulk of this money was to be administered was the Finance Committee of the Citizens' Committee of Fifty, whose chairman was James D. Phelan.

Accounts differ as to how Phelan became chairman. Either he was appointed by Schmitz on the mayor's own initiative or at the suggestion of some advisor, or he was elected chairman by the members of the committee, who were themselves appointed by the mayor.[16] In any case, Phelan's selection as chairman was an intelligent choice. He was a former mayor, a successful real estate owner and banker, and an officer of national civic organizations; he was widely known in the East, especially among those who would oversee the collection of contributions. The odors of corruption and radicalism that tainted Schmitz were effectively counteracted by placing Phelan in charge of the relief fund.

Phelan jealously guarded his position. When President Theodore Roosevelt announced to the nation that contributions should be directed to Dr. Edward Devine, who was sent to San Francisco as representative of the American National Red Cross, Phelan and others in the city strongly protested. They did not want direction of relief operations and resources to be removed from local control. Roosevelt agreed, and the Finance Committee was consolidated with the Red Cross under the title of the Finance Committee of the Relief and Red Cross Funds.[17] This reconstituted committee soon spawned its own subcommittees and assumed almost complete charge of relief and rehabilitation work. Phelan and other members of the original group, with some additional appointees, formed the executive committee.

Meanwhile, the other subcommittees of the Citizens' Committee of Fifty more or less ceased to function. After an initial spurt of energy and ingenuity, it became apparent that the scope and detail of organization necessary to relieve the homeless and other sufferers were beyond the competence of volunteer committees, whose members had their own affairs to care for. On April 24, the shelter subcommittee announced completion of temporary structures in Golden Gate Park to house 40,000 persons who had slept out of doors for the first week.[18] The following day, however, a meeting of the Citizens' Committee decided that the task of maintaining the temporary camps that had been set up would be better left to the army. Dr. Devine, the charity professional, approved of the move; "the work of restoring the city," he noted, "is a problem of such enormous proportions and private interests are of such vital moment to the vast majority of business men that the future of the city would be placed in precarious condition if some such move as was agreed upon today had not been taken." On May 5, Schmitz adjourned the Citizens' Committee *sine die*, leaving only the Finance Committee in operation.[19]

Several years after the disaster, the Russell Sage Foundation sponsored a study, the *San Francisco Relief Survey*, "to offer a book of ready reference for use on occasions of special emergency." The authors of the *Survey* were not impressed with the actions of the Citizens' Committee of Fifty. Writing from the perspective of charity administrators, they found that the committee, "with its list of subcommittees, hurriedly created, quickly to die, gives an excellent illustration of the futility of trying to effect an elaborate organization before the measure of a disaster has been taken or the extent of the means of recovery learned."[20] Although the judgment was probably too harsh, there was something frenzied and haphazard about some of the immediate relief endeavors. From the first day of the fire, for example, many refugees began to flee the city. The railroads offered free passage for those who could not pay, carrying some as far away as Chicago. The transportation subcommittee did not really organize this exodus; they merely publicized and encouraged it, seeking to lessen the relief burden within San Francisco. In the first nine days, the Southern Pacific railroad estimated that over 300,000 persons had been freely transported out of San Francisco.

By April 25, however, the transportation subcommittee was having sober second thoughts about the ultimate wisdom of this depopulation scheme. Recognizing that workers would be needed to rebuild the city, Thomas Magee, chairman of the Committee on Refugees, announced that free transportation to points in California would end the following day.[21] After April 25, the flow of refugees

Table 3
Persons Carried from San Francisco as Free Passengers
by the Southern Pacific Railroad, April 18–26, 1906

| Destination | Number of Persons |

Suburban points around the bay	226,000[a]
Elsewhere in California	67,000
Other states	7,684

SOURCE: *San Francisco Relief Survey* (New York: Survey Associates, 1913), p. 58.
[a]This figure includes thousands carried more than once.

did lessen.[22] The decline was due partially to a rapid return of livable, if not normal, conditions. Also, new procedures were adopted that made would-be refugees submit to personal interviews and investigation of their resources, and to inevitable long lines; these methods probably dampened the urge to leave.[23] Haphazard benevolence gave way to bureaucratic efficiency.

On May 5, as the Citizens' Committee passed from the scene, Schmitz appointed another body, known both as the Committee of Forty or the Committee on Reconstruction. Though some of the membership overlapped with the Citizens' Committee, the objectives of the Committee of Forty were different.[24] Its general purpose was to facilitate the physical and economic restoration of the city; its work will be fully discussed in the next chapter. It is necessary first to follow the work of the Finance Committee of the Relief and Red Cross Funds and its successors, after the expiration of the rest of the Citizens' Committee.

The Finance Committee had to make a number of crucial decisions: to define the purpose of assistance, how that purpose could best be accomplished, and to what extent the relief funds, as a quasi-public resource, should be allowed to compete with private suppliers of goods and services in rehabilitating the needy. There was also the overriding matter of who should control the funds and direct relief and rehabilitation.

During the first several months after the fire, a number of groups claimed the right to participate in decisions on how the funds should be spent. Donors such as the American Red Cross, the United States government, and private bodies demanded a say. The New York Chamber of Commerce restricted the use of the funds it had collected, and the Massachusetts Association for Relief of California sent investigators to San Francisco to check on what was being done with its donations. Both groups actually withheld money for a period in the summer and fall of 1906, pending investigation.[25] The Finance Committee based its claim on the fact that it was the legal recipient of the bulk of the funds. The city government, especially the mayor, at times sought to assert its authority. Established charitable organizations, particularly the Associated Charities of San Francisco, argued that their position among the poor was being undermined by the work of ad hoc committees, and that they should take over the relief. Otherwise, once the immediate crisis had passed, the city would be left with no effective agencies of charity.[26] Finally, there were the individual sufferers from the earthquake and fire, some of whom contended that they were the intended recipients of relief donations, and that the money and supplies should be distributed directly to them. The other claimants considered this position heretical.

With so many contestants competing for some measure of control, friction was inevitable. Most of it seems to have been minor and readily overcome, because of the urgency of the task at hand. Several disputes were more serious in that they raised questions about the distribution of power within San Francisco. The first concerned the actual administration of relief, especially the operation of the refugee camps. The army started to run the official camps a week after the fire. Around the middle of June, Phelan and Schmitz requested federal authorities to allow the army to continue on duty in San Francisco through September. General A. W. Greely, commanding officer of the Pacific Division, opposed retaining the army after the first of July, arguing that "the spirit of American institutions is obviously adverse to the quartering of troops in times of peace in large cities," and also that the relief funds could employ people who were out of work to do what the army had been doing, thereby aiding rehabilitation.[27] Greely convinced Schmitz that the army should go. He suggested creation of a three-man executive, one to represent the Red Cross, one selected by Mayor Schmitz, the third to be named by the Finance Committee.

Greely's recommendation worried Phelan and his friends. They feared that it gave Schmitz access to some of the patronage connected with relief, and that he would use these positions for his own political ends.[28] Three men were actually appointed to an executive commission in June. In July, the Finance Committee incorporated itself as the San Francisco Relief and Red Cross Funds, with Phelan as president. The major purpose of incorporation, which had been suggested as early as May, was to establish a permanent and legal body that could acquire land, loan money, and do other things the Finance Committee was unable to undertake.[29] The corporation also established its own committees, some of which rendered the Executive Commission totally superfluous. That body passed from the scene on August 1, having served only one month. Schmitz was kept away from the funds.

The expiration of the commission, and with it the only control the municipal government had over the relief funds, still left unanswered the vexing question of who, really, owned the money and goods that had been donated. Some of the disaster victims felt that it belonged to them and should be distributed equally among the sufferers. The city of Minneapolis sent a large supply of wheat flour to San Francisco, to be used to feed those in need, and the Finance Committee was beset by difficulties in deciding what to do with the flour. While arrangements to dispose of it were being made, Phelan received a pencilled note from a sufferer asserting that "We, refugees from the fire, are entitled to help which is sent from outside San Francisco, but at our Relief Station, No. 619, we haven't had any of the *surplus Flour* for two weeks."[30] Complaints about the quality of food in the refugee camps and about other adversities were fairly common, but more noteworthy were the challenges to the legitimacy and equity of the relief authorities. Part of the problem lay in the secrecy with which the Finance Committee conducted its business. Only after criticism in the press did the committee open meetings to reporters and allow accounts to be made public. As a result of the secrecy, rumors spread that favoritism was rampant, that no one with a claim could get his money unless he had influence, and that the list of employees on the relief payroll was filled by political friends of the committee members. According to "Autolycus," the charges were false. The suspicions developed because of the attitude of the Finance Committee; most of the members were businessmen who thought of the committee itself as a private business not accountable to the public.[31]

Matters between the Finance Committee, now incorporated as the Relief and Red Cross Funds, and aid recipients came to a head at the end of July 1906, when the corporation gave a banquet at the St. Francis Hotel to honor Devine on his departure. Devine had been instrumental in organizing relief operations, and it must have seemed only fitting to his local colleagues that he be feted when he left for the East. But to some of the refugees, particularly those in

Jefferson Square in the Western Addition, the dinner was just one more example of how the relief fund was being used to pamper the rich while the poor had to subsist on substandard fare. A group calling itself the Committee of Friends of Refugees circulated a broadside:

Dr. Devine, "The Generous" and his allies, The Finance Committee, "The Noble," will banquet on the fat of the land tonight with the relief funds which belong to us at the St. Francis Hotel, Tuesday night, July 31, 1906.

Meet, one and all, at Jefferson Square at 7 PM and march to the St. Francis Hotel, bearing the old clothes and soup as an emblem of their generosity to us. Let the whole world know that while we are starving they are feasting. Such infamy was never known.[32]

Both banquet and demonstration went on as scheduled. The local newspapers covered the event differently. The *Examiner* and the *Call* were sympathetic to the refugees, but the *Chronicle*, whose owner M. H. de Young, was inside at the banquet, treated them contemptuously. The gathering, according to the *Chronicle*, "degenerated into a meeting for the propaganda of socialism."[33]

There is not a great deal of evidence about other organized protests against the authority of the Finance Committee and the corporation.[34] Perhaps some form of newspaper self-censorship was in operation, keeping news of discontent from spreading. But observers noted that people resisted the authority of relief on an individual basis. For example General Greely complained that many girls at the Presidio camp, who had been servants before the fire, were making no effort to find work even though it was available. Others corroborated Greely's testimony and added that idle workmen in the camp were not answering the calls for workers. In an attempt to solve the problem, the committee passed a resolution offered by de Young requiring all able-bodied men and women to assist in keeping the camps clean.[35]

While the issue itself was probably minor, it seems plain that Greely and civilian members of the Finance Committee were eager to quash the notion that the relief funds were intended to support victims in idleness. In part they were motivated by that powerful current in Anglo-American culture that equates work with virtue and idleness with evil. Thus the weekly *Town Talk* could speak of people who had no real right to be housed in the relief camps, who were professional paupers to be turned out and made to hustle for a living. At a more sophisticated level, this idea expressed itself in the fear that unless the sufferers were given the opportunity to aid themselves, they would acquire the habits of dependency and become, to use the word of the day, "pauperized." Thus Devine, making recommendations for relief housing, could write that it was "no intention that the relief fund shall become a providence of the refugees, solving all their difficulties and relieving them of all individual responsibility." Instead, it was expected:

> that each family will to the greatest possible extent solve its own problems, find its own capital, decide on plans for its own home, discharge its obligations for any money advanced as soon as practicable . . . [so] as to preserve in full integrity the fundamental traits of American character, individual initiative and personal responsibility.[36]

The dread of pauperization and the desire to encourage "individual initiative and personal responsibility" were the joint foundations of relief ideology. Together they supported the principles that guided the relief officials. The first principle, which was arrived at after some dispute, was that expenditures for immediate relief should be held to a minimum and as much money as possible be reserved for the longer range objective of rehabilitation. Second, rehabilitation was directed at "giving those who have been left with the least a reasonable lift on the road to recovery of the standard of living maintained before the disaster."[37] Thus, when the *Relief Survey* said that the axiom of relief policy "was that help should be extended with reference to needs and not with reference to losses," what it meant in fact was that needs would be determined in part on the basis of prior circumstances. The businessmen would be set up in business, the home owner aided to rebuild, the renter accommodated with a small cottage, the worker helped in some other way. "It was not easy," the authors of the *Relief Survey* admitted, "to hold to the relief principle in the face of a sentiment by no means weak or voiceless that each sufferer was entitled to an equal share of the funds."[38] Third, rehabilitation, or the restoration of prefire conditions, would be hindered if the Finance Committee or the corporation competed in any substantial way with private business toward supplying food, housing, land, drugs, or other necessities. Wherever possible, the relief fund would give way to private enterprise.[39] The men who directed the relief organizations conceived of their function as restoring the social *status quo ante flamma*, and they understood this order to be based on individual initiative, capital, and ownership.

In their emphasis on the restoration of private enterprise as both the means and the end of rehabilitation, they found themselves in an anomalous position. As custodians of a large fund of quasi-public capital intended for the public benefit, they could hardly avoid competing with private interests. "Autolycus" commented that in assisting rehabilitation, they were engaged in a paternalistic experiment with socialistic overtones: "the government or private benevolence supplies the capital, the means of production for the use and advantage of the producer." In whatever enterprise they decide to engage, "they will be constantly accused of the crime of breaking markets." As businessmen themselves, "to whom a market is the most sacred thing on earth," they would be beset by "perplexity and mental anguish," no matter what they tried to do in the nature of relief or rehabilitation.[40]

In an apparent attempt to resolve the dilemma, Walter J. Bartnett, who had been a member of the Citizens' Committee and was a vice-president of the Western Pacific Railroad, proposed in late June that the Finance Committee cut the Gordian knot and simply give the money away. Sufferers would receive from $250 upwards depending on the size of the family, whether the wage earner had been killed, and other conditions. Thus the money would go into circulation immediately, creating work and forcing people to earn their livings rather than subsist on charity. The Finance Committee could pass out of existence and not have to worry if it were impinging on the territory of private enterprise.[41] The suggestion may have had some appeal, but it was not accepted. The Finance Committee remained in operation, but its actions continued to be circumscribed by a distaste for competing with private entrepreneurs.

The Finance Committee and the corporation directed relief efforts that touched on almost all aspects of urban life, but three areas adequately illustrate the principles and prejudices of the men directing relief. One was supplying food, especially in the days and weeks following the disaster. Later, after a permanent organization had been achieved, the corporation undertook two major rehabilitation projects, providing permanent shelter for those made homeless and assisting small businessmen to reestablish their undertakings. Taken together, the three programs embody a good part of the ideology of relief.

Food was an immediate necessity, even for those who were not burned out. Retail stores had had their surviving goods confiscated, so that even those who could pay for it were not able to purchase food. Yet food was available, train loads of it arriving from surrounding and even distant areas. The principal job of distribution fell upon the army, which officially took charge on April 29. Though some soup kitchens were set up soon after the fire, the great majority received rations and cooked them, either in the refugee camps or on the makeshift stoves that lined the streets of the unburned district. Fires in houses were prohibited until chimneys had been inspected. On April 19, an estimated 100,000 persons received rations. By April 27, the figure had climbed to 310,000 as private supplies were exhausted and no replacements commercially available. The number of recipients remained at over 300,000 until May 3, when it dropped to 280,000, and continued a more or less steady decline to 225,000 on May 8.[42] Clearly many of those who could afford to had begun to purchase their own food.

By May 11, only 187,000 persons were still receiving rations, but this decline was not fast enough for certain interests. According to the *Relief Survey*, persons outside the relief organizations applied pressure to change the policy of distribution, and the free allotment of supplies was curtailed at an even faster rate, "in order that the smaller traders might be encouraged to resume business and the funds be reserved in a great measure to give permanent relief."[43] Some of the relief stations were closed, and rations, now limited to meat, bread, and vegetables, were issued only three times a week. Registration of refugees, which had begun shortly after the fire, was accelerated. Rations were allocated according to family size. People who could work for wages were denied rations altogether.[44]

The Finance Committee had opened the first official hot meal kitchen around the middle of May. "The kitchens," reported the *Relief Survey*, "were intended to test the needs of those applying for free food, because the number of those willing to accept relief in food was expected to suffer diminution when a common eating room was offered." Food contractors provided the meals at 10 cents for a typical dinner of hot soup, roast beef or hash, one vegetable, bread, coffee and sugar. Those who could not pay cash were granted meal tickets by the Red Cross. The kitchens were also available to those with more money who could not, for whatever reason, supply themselves with food. These people, who paid 15 cents, had "the privilege of sitting at separate tables and ordering a better quality of food than that furnished at the free tables." The *Relief Survey* was uncertain about the success of the kitchens in reducing the distribution of free food, but found that "the new method did effectively help to weed out those who no longer needed free rations." By June

2, only 42,374 persons were still receiving free food, including both those who ate hot meals and those who received raw rations.[45] Since the other 270,000 were eating some place, one presumes that the retail food merchants and restaurant owners were on the road to recovery.

A second incident concerning the supply of food that illustrates the ideology of relief is the controversy surrounding the arrival of 70,000 barrels of wheat flour as a contribution from the millers and other citizens of Minneapolis. Some of the facts in this dispute are muddy, but the basic issues seem clear. The flour was clearly intended by the donors to be used to feed the hungry of San Francisco. On May 17, the Finance Committee decided to sell 4 million pounds of it. The *Relief Survey* contended that they were motivated by the fear that it would spoil. But other reasons were probably at work as well. Sometime in May—the letter bears no date—S. B. McNear, president of the Port Costa Milling Company, wrote that "the merchants, producers, and manufacturing interests of San Francisco are well equipped to supply San Francisco with all food supplies." Food was abundant, and there was no danger of famine. Instead McNear felt that:

the continued receipts of free food will work incalculable harm to the mercantile interests, wholesale and retail, of San Francisco. We admit the necessity of relief supplies, but we believe the supplies should be purchased from our own merchants, and request that further shipment of free donation be discouraged. Such relief as is found necessary should be furnished to the General Relief Committee in the form of money, which can then be put into circulation among our retail and wholesale merchants.[46]

Phelan and other members of the Finance Committee probably agreed with this reasoning, for the flour was soon sold by Allan Pollok, representing the committee, to the Port Costa Milling Company, the Sperry Flour Company, and the Stockton Milling Company. The firms agreed to keep the flour off the local market by shipping it all to London and China. Either the companies did not keep their word, or else there was a misunderstanding, for on May 26, a delegation representing other local flour dealers met with Pollok and Phelan to protest the transaction and express fears that the flour would remain in San Francisco. Pollok had not put the flour out to bid; he had merely contracted privately with three men he trusted, including McNear and Horace Davis of the Sperry Flour Company, who happened to be a member of the Finance Committee. The merchants who had been left out argued that the price of

$2.25 per barrel was only half of what the flour was worth. The Finance Committee was forced to break the original agreement and offer the flour to competitive bidding. It then was sold at prices ranging from $2.20 to $3.95 per barrel, for a total of $216,717.15.[47]

The controversy was not yet over. Disaster victims claimed that the flour had been given to them and should not have been sold at all. The millers of Minneapolis agreed. The chairman of the Minnesota Committee for California Relief sent a telegram to Devine demanding that he confirm or deny reports that "relief committee is selling flour given by Minneapolis for relief purposes to poor of S. F. at price ridiculously below its value that millers then are resacking it and dumping it on Oriental markets in competition with Minneapolis flour."[48] Most likely the reports referred to the already abrogated arrangement with the three companies. It is not clear what in fact happened to the flour in question, although it may have remained in the San Francisco area. Whatever the destination, the actions of the Finance Committee, as "Autolycus" chided, had been in error. The mistake, he contended, "was due to that confused habit of thought with which they are afflicted. They did not realize that

Table 4
Applications and Grants for Rehabilitation[a]

Nature of Grant	Applications Granted	Refused	Amount Granted	Average per grant	Percent of all money granted
Household furniture	9,064	1,274	$1,017,990	$112	33.9%
Business rehabilitation	4,740	547	872,437	189	29.0
General relief	3,635	581	486,509	134	16.2
Housing	1,709	337	567,301	332	28.9
Transportation	809	—	48,917	60	1.6
Tools	284	170	12,738	48	0.4

SOURCE: *San Francisco Relief Survey* (New York: Survey Associates, 1913), pp. 153, 158, Tables 33, 41.

[a]This table is based on records kept by the various rehabilitation agencies. Other assistance, such as tools provided by the Los Angeles Tool Fund, is not included, nor are the camp cottages, discussed below, which were given to the camp families. American National Red Cross, *Sixth Annual Report* (Washington: Government Printing Office, 1911), p. 52, gives $2,683,616 as the amount disbursed for "personal rehabilitation and relief." It used different categories and covered different time periods from the *San Francisco Relief Survey*. Also, some of the grants were treated as loans, which further complicated the bookkeeping. So the monetary totals are really estimates at best.

they were committing a grave breach of trust in selling the flour at all. They are business men, and in the eyes of such it is the most deadly sin to break a market."[49]

The task of getting people back on their feet began in May under the auspices of the Red Cross. In July the work was assumed by the Rehabilitation Committee of the Finance Committee, continued in August by several departments of the corporation, and finally taken over on a more modest scale by the Associated Charities on July 1, 1907. In all, more than 23,000 individuals or families applied for some form of assistance; a total of 20,241, or 86 percent of the applicants, received aid.[50] Applicants had to state the use to which they intended to put the money. The different uses and amounts granted in each category are shown in Table 4.[51]

Investigators examined all applicants and kept records. They sought to find whether the individuals were truly in need of relief. Absolute poverty was not a prerequisite; 79.6 percent of the property owners who applied received aid, including 62.2 percent of those who had more than $1,000. For some types of assistance, the applicant was expected to furnish part of the capital himself. The investigations weeded out those who had sufficient savings, were earning wages, had families who could help, or had no definite plans as to what to do with the money; 264 persons were turned down because of character defects.[52] The records enabled the rehabilitation workers to enforce the decision not to aid more than one person per family, and to provide only one kind of assistance, whether housing, business, or furniture, per applicant.

The plan for distributing the money combined the ideal of individual responsibility with solicitious paternalism. People would not be set up in business in which they had not been previously engaged. They would receive the lowest practical figure necessary to get a start. The intention of business rehabilitation:

was to supply the right sort of man with money enough to pay one month's rent, to buy the necessary fixtures, and to cover a deposit on stock or on machinery or instruments. The applicant went into debt for the rest of his equipment, with the idea of discharging the debt little by little from the profits of the business.[53]

The committee also required information about the scale of prefire business and current assets and liabilities. Applicants had to present detailed plans, including an option on what the committee judged to be a good location. "Every effort was made," the *Relief Survey* noted, "to prevent an applicant from starting business in a poor but costly location merely as an excuse for securing an allowance from the relief funds."⁵⁴

The people who received business grants constituted a homogeneous group. Most of them ran small establishments, and earned less than they might have by working for others. Either out of a preference for independence or because of age or other infirmities, they decided to resume their own businesses. Half of them were native born, the rest immigrants. In a sample of 889 recipients, there were 394 married couples, 286 women who had once been married but were either widowed, divorced, or separated, 93 single women, 55 formerly married men, and 61 single men. Clearly the selection committee had smiled on women, especially those with families to support. Boarding or rooming houses accounted for 256 out of 894 of the proposed businesses, tailor and dressmaking shops for 91. Very few hoped to set up manufacturing firms. A great many grants for $250 had been made, "a reflection of the committee's impression that there was little to distinguish many of the applicants, one from another, either as to plight or as to recuperative power."⁵⁵

Despite care in selection, the committee had moderate success in its results. The *Relief Survey* done in 1908 found that two years or less after receiving aid only 56.7 percent of a sample of 894 persons investigated were in business as planned. A full 28.7 percent were neither in business nor employed, including the 29 applicants who were known to have died. The failure of the 40 percent who were not in business was attributed to poor timing of the grant, not enough money made available, the wrong location selected, and poor health. The highest rates of survival were among professional people and those engaged in manufacturing, the lowest among those in trade and domestic and personal service, where capital was more crucial for success than skill. In some cases, especially for the old, the ill, the unrealistic, and those lacking initiative, the investigators felt that the committee should have provided more supervision. It had good results in those few cases in which it had supplied guidance; all 35 persons had started in business, and at least 23 had survived.⁵⁶ If anything, the committee had erred too much on the side of relying on individual initiative, especially in the uncertain economic conditions in San Francisco during the two years after the disaster. More paternalism would have helped.

The most ambitious project of rehabilitation dealt with housing. Almost $2.5 million was spent to provide shelter, both temporary and permanent, for the homeless.⁵⁷ As with business rehabilitation,

1.
Daniel Hudson Burnham, the master planner. (*Courtesy, The Bancroft Library*)

2.
The Burnham Plan in a bird's-eye view from the east. (From Daniel H. Burnham, *Report on a Plan for San Francisco* [San Francisco: City of San Francisco, 1905].)

3.
Downtown: the corner of Geary and Kearny streets, March 1906. (*Courtesy, The Bancroft Library*)

4.
Downtown: looking east down Geary Street. (*Courtesy, The Bancroft Library*)

5.
California Street looking up Nob Hill, with the shell of the Fairmont Hotel on the crest. (*Courtesy, The Bancroft Library*)

6.
Devastation seen from Nob Hill, with Ferry Building tower in rear. (*Courtesy, The Bancroft Library*)

7.
Lining up for rations in Golden Gate Park refugee tent camp. Note sign in Yiddish, suggesting that refugees may have clustered by ethnic group. (*Courtesy, The Bancroft Library*)

8.
Relief cottages in an unidentified town square, ca. 1907. (*Courtesy, The Bancroft Library*)

9.
James Duval Phelan, urbanist, enjoying the delights of nature at the Bohemian Grove, ca. 1906. (*Courtesy, The Bancroft Library*)

10.
Abraham Ruef, the Boss. (*Courtesy, The Bancroft Library*)

11.
Panorama three years after. The refurbished Fairmont Hotel is in the foreground;

12.
Downtown: Kearny Street in foreground. Note buildings on Montgomery Street in rear, still standing and awaiting rehabilitation. (*Courtesy, The Bancroft Library*)

the Ferry Building in the upper left; Yerba Buena Island in the bay beyond. (*Courtesy, The Bancroft Library*)

13.
Downtown: the same area during rebuilding, with Montgomery Street structures in use. (*Courtesy, The Bancroft Library*)

14.
Eugene E. Schmitz, the mayor. (*Courtesy, San Francisco Public Library*)

15.
Edward T. Devine, the charity professional. (*Courtesy, The Bancroft Library*)

the Finance Committee and the corporation combined paternalism with the desire to reestablish initiative and independence. Housing rehabilitation, however, aided three or four distinct classes of people rather than a single homogeneous group. First were those who had owned their homes in the burned district and needed assistance to rebuild. Second were some who had not owned property but were considered resourceful and might be stimulated to acquire their own homes. Third were "the non-property owners who had never lived in other than rental quarters and who were not likely to make wise use of a grant for the erection of a permanent house."[58] These would be sheltered for a year or two. Finally, there were the chronic dependents for whom the city would have to provide permanent care. In all cases except the last, which was customarily the province of municipal officials, the housing program of the corporation was an innovation and a potential intrusion into a field normally monopolized by the private real estate market.

Tents initially sheltered thousands made homeless by the fire. They were adequate for spring and summer, but Devine quickly realized that more permanent quarters would soon be required for perhaps 100,000 persons. On May 24, he presented to the Finance Committee a plan calling for the establishment of a nonprofit business corporation to buy land and build houses, using some of the relief funds as capital. The corporation would sell or rent houses to deserving refugees on a reasonable basis, and use the proceeds to build more houses. Devine received some encouragement when a special committee reported favorably on his plan to the Finance Committee.[59]

Before the proposal was acted upon, others recognized that the private home building industry would not be capable of putting up enough shelter quickly. General Greely wrote to Devine recommending that the Finance Committee spend $3 million or $4 million constructing emergency shelter for 10,000 in the form of small, individual homes on land belonging to the city. Additional funds could be borrowed at 3 percent from philanthropic people in the East.[60] M. H. de Young, as a member of the Finance Committee, proposed that the committee grant up to $500 to anyone who had owned a lot in the burned district and planned to rebuild there, the money to cover not more than one-third the cost of the new house. It was to be paid directly to the contractor upon completion of the work.

These three approaches to housing rehabilitation, Devine's,

Greely's, and de Young's, were consolidated in a series of recommendations submitted on July 10 by Devine with the concurrence of a volunteer board of architects and builders, the mayor, Phelan, and others. For those workingmen or others of moderate means who had owned homes and could not, on their own, secure enough capital to rebuild, the proposal followed de Young's plan, granting assistance up to $500 in the form of a loan or a bonus. No new relief mechanism or organization would be necessary to carry out the "bonus plan," as it came to be called. The Finance Committee would merely have to safeguard the distribution of the money. Devine and his associates doubted that this effort would go very far toward providing shelter for the families now in tents.

For the aged, infirm, chronically invalided, or others needing long-term maintenance, Devine recommended building permanent structures on city property. The method would be less expensive than paying for care in private hospitals, and would also secure for the city a modern home for its dependents. The plan would expand previously existing municipal services, but was not a new departure.[61]

The third part of the recommendations was aimed at wage earners who rented their dwellings. Extending the suggestions he had made in May, Devine advised relief and government officials to form a nonprofit corporation empowered to buy land and build houses. The Finance Committee would subscribe not less than $1 million as capital or a permanent loan, and the corporation would build and sell or rent homes to families who had been living in San Francisco on April 17, 1906. The profit from the sales and rentals would be reinvested in more homes or used for other philanthropic purposes. After a year, the corporation might sell its interests to savings banks and use the proceeds to aid any still suffering from the disaster.[62]

The novelty of this portion of Devine's plan lay in the means rather than the ends. The purposes, as he enunciated them, were to put money into circulation and stimulate the local economy, to provide sound shelter when the rains came, to help the city hold its working population, and to give workingmen the opportunity to own their homes. No person working for the relief of the disaster victims could have questioned any of these objectives. Rather, it was the mechanism by which they were to be achieved that must have raised doubts. "The intelligent and efficient carrying out of the plans proposed," Devine wrote, will enable the community to set a standard of attractive, sanitary, safe, and yet comparatively inexpensive dwellings which will have a beneficial effect not only in the immediate future but for the coming generation. The co-operation of the municipal administration in enforcing suitable conditions as to sanitation, light, ventilation, fire protection, etc., of the architects in making plans for convenient and attractive homes at moderate cost, of the building trades in getting these homes built, and of the Finance Committee in advancing capital and creating a corporation which will ensure the purchasers against fraud or injustice, will solve the housing problem and nothing less than this co-operation will solve it.[63]

In short, Devine's solution called for public housing, for taking at least part of San Francisco's housing supply out of the private market and making it the concern of official and quasi-official bodies, which would not merely house some 5,000 families but would also provide a yardstick to evaluate the shelter offered by the private sector.

Three days afterwards, on July 14, William Herrin introduced a resolution embracing Devine's recommendations. It was adopted unanimously by the Finance Committee. The sum of $500,000 was allocated for grants up to $500 to lot owners in the burned district to help them rebuild, the money not to exceed one-third of the cost of the house. Second, a like sum was to be used for loans to those who wanted to build anywhere in the city. Borrowers had to own the lot on which they planned to build, and the loan could not exceed $1,000 or be more than one-third the cost of the house. The money was to be lent at 3 percent, with a second mortgage on the building, and the lot was required as security. Third, up to $2.5 million was to be used to acquire land in the city and to build on it cottages, two-story houses, and flats of from three to six rooms each. The buildings were to cost from $750 to $2,000, and be sold at cost for cash or through an installment plan to bona fide residents of the city. A corporation would be established to transact all these proposals.[64]

The corporation carried out the three sections of Herrin's resolution, but with significant modifications. The bonus, or grant plan suffered the least alteration. In all, $423,228 was distributed among 885 applicants, with almost 90 percent receiving the full $500. The number of recipients fell below expectations, for it had been predicted that up to 5,000 workingmen were waiting to accept the offer. Also, the grantees included fewer wage earners than had been intended. The authors of the *Relief Survey* speculated that workingmen either did not apply or lacked enough money to make up their share of the cost of the house. So, many of the grants went to capitalists, some of whom had probably begun to build on their own when they learned of the offer. An investigation of 572 recipients selected at random revealed that 92 percent had carried insurance and had recovered at least a part of their loss; of 433 men for whom more information was available, 228 had been proprietors before the fire, and 205 employees. The committee in charge of distribution made no attempt to ascertain the actual needs of the applicants, so that more than half of the grants went to persons building houses costing over $2,500. Consequently, the homes built with the bonus money were substantial structures. The recipients were not wealthy; more than three-quarters of them rented a part of the houses they lived in. They were, however, a more prosperous group than that for which the program had been designed.[65]

For those persons who had not owned a home in the burned district but wanted to acquire or build a house in San Francisco, Herrin had proposed loans. In practice, they received both outright grants and loans. Some 1,572 people were assisted under what became known as the "grant and loan plan." The majority of them, 1,029 persons, built their own homes, many doing the actual work themselves. This group was given a total of $206,223 in grants, or about $200 apiece. The other 543 had homes built for them by the corporation. Each house was intended to cost not more than $500, but with plumbing, the average price came to $682. The corporation granted these persons $197,942 outright, and loaned $115,558 to 384 of them; 71 percent of the money loaned was ultimately repaid. The total spent under the grant and loan plan, exclusive of money repaid, was $567,301.[66]

As a group, the recipients of grants and loans were less well off than those aided under the bonus plan. Only 10 percent of those later surveyed had owned lots before the fire; 75 percent purchased land afterwards, in order to make use of the offer. Most of these lots were in outlying districts, where the cost of property was low. The houses were generally neat and clean, but smaller than the homes built by the bonus recipients. Occupationally, only 66 persons out of 896 who were surveyed had been proprietors of businesses before the fire; all the rest were employees. The grant and loan plan aided this group of people; it made them owners of their own homes and improved the quality of their housing, if only slightly.[67]

The most ambitious part of Devine's recommendations had called for the construction by the corporation of a large number of inexpensive but adequate homes to be sold or rented to those needing and deserving housing rehabilitation. It was this section that was altered almost beyond recognition. Sometime in August 1906, the directors of the corporation decided to abandon the attempt to build permanent housing on a large scale and instead determined to construct temporary shelters adequate for the winter season. They gave various reasons for the change in plans: not enough money, insufficient time, inability to acquire suitable and affordable land. Finally, it was alleged that if the corporation did embark on this enterprise, it would have to stay in business for a number of years and perpetuate the relief fund, rather than dispose of it as intended by the donors. On August 17, Phelan advised those who had been counting on securing the houses to be built by the corporation that they had better seek shelter elsewhere.[68]

Instead of permanent dwellings, the corporation decided to replace the tents with two- and three-room frame cottages in the same parks and squares. It was no easy task to put up enough of these structures for the people who needed them, and it was made more difficult by the unusual demand for lumber and construction workers in the city. Nevertheless, the work began on September 10, 1906, and was completed in March 1907. In all, 5,610 cottages, most with three rooms, were constructed, as were 19 two-story tenements, each with eight two-room apartments, at a cost of $884,559, or $55 per room. Five contractors did most of the work; the corporation had to build two planing mills to finish the timber. The camps sheltered around 17,000 persons until August 1907, when the population began to decline rapidly as attempts were made to close the camps.[69]

The people who found refuge in these cottages were generally of lower economic station than those who received either bonuses or grants and loans. The *Relief Survey* found that 380 of 415 men investigated had been wage earners before the fire; only 35 had been proprietors.[70] The median yearly income for families before the fire seems to have been in the $600 to $800 range.[71] If anything, income declined in the two years after the disaster. The prefire housing conditions of these people "were the least desirable in the city." The corporation decided that cottage dwellers should pay a rent of $2 per room per month on their houses. When Mayor Schmitz and the Board of Supervisors protested and passed an ordinance forbidding the collection of rents on city-owned property, the corporation responded by changing the rental fees into installment payments. Eventually, almost all the money collected was refunded, and those who had made the payments were given the cottages free and clear.⁷² The purpose of the rent and purchase charges had not been to meet costs, but to "establish the independence of the tenants," to separate "the worthy from the unworthy and to avoid pauperization."⁷³

In the summer of 1907, the city park authorities pressed the corporation to remove the cottage dwellers from the public parks and squares. The task was unpleasant, as not all the refugees moved willingly. In some cases, cottages were removed by force and deposited near the Ocean Beach.⁷⁴ Most of the dwellings were transported by the occupant or, in hardship cases, by the Associated Charities, to lots that the occupants had either purchased or rented. When the *Relief Survey* investigated a sampling of cottage residents a year after removal, they found the shacks generally crowded together on small plots; only 2 percent had bathtubs, only 15 percent had inside toilets, and only 40 percent were connected to the water mains.⁷⁵ Though the actual cost of removal was not very high, additional expenses were necessary to make the cottage, often shaken up by the trip, inhabitable.⁷⁶ In all likelihood it was only the substandard conditions of their prefire housing that allowed the residents to appreciate their present quarters.⁷⁷ The bright hopes Devine had expressed in June and the corporation had endorsed in July ended in 5,000 shacks.

When the authors of the *Relief Survey* came to assess the achievement of the cottage program, they found that the corporation directors had acted wisely "in providing shelter without consulting the wishes of those for whom it was intended." The cottagers were, after all, the "poorest class of homeless refugees . . . accustomed to comparatively low standards of living [who] consumed each day the daily wage, who were helpless when overtaken by the disaster." Some critics had "claimed that a more equitable distribution of the funds would have been to give to the poorest class as much as to the more fortunate refugees," but the authors disagreed. The corporation had been correct in recognizing that there were different classes of people to be aided:

Those who possessed vacant lots, or other property, or who could command means with which to build, gave tangible proof that the foundation of previous thrift and enterprise would serve as a guarantee of wise use of aid from the relief funds. The applicants who had owned no property, possessed no savings, and whose standard of living was low, could offer little, if any, guarantee of a wise use of funds. Had a body of expert social workers been engaged to study each family individually and to plan its future home, superintending the purchase of a lot and the construction of a house,—in fact, teaching each to be a good householder,—a more liberal housing allowance could have been safely granted. Such a constructive plan would have called for far more elaborate and efficient machinery than was at hand, and would have required a much longer time. However, it is realized that a situation which concerned practically the future home life of every camp refugee presented a wonderful and probably unparalleled opportunity for wise constructive philanthropy.[78]

For the charity professionals, the missed opportunity was not the provision of adequate housing by a quasi-public corporation; rather it was the chance to practice constructive social control on great numbers of individuals.

A set of ideas directed the various operations of relief and rehabilitation. Though never fully articulated and not entirely consistent, they formed an ideology. The most important aim was to restore people to the stations they had occupied before the fire, and in so doing, to avoid pauperization threatened by undue dependence upon the relief fund. In addition, the Finance Committee and its successors wanted to minimize if not avoid altogether any competition with private enterprise. There was also a streak of paternalism, or a desire for social control, that expressed itself in a distrust of what relief recipients, especially from the lower classes, might do if left to spend a share of the funds as they saw fit. Wherever the committee and the corporation did not rely on the market to rehabilitate the city, it was due to this paternalistic concern.[79]

If the relief and rehabilitation programs were an accurate indicator, successful replanning of the city by exercise of public authority was a poor prospect indeed.

7
Urban Phoenix

Broader Lines and Wider Streets

In the face of great loss and suffering resulting from the earthquake and fire, San Franciscans adopted a surprisingly buoyant attitude. The rest of the country declared its affection for the city, sent relief donations, and expressed confidence in the city's future. And the opportunity to remake San Francisco, to build from scratch a bigger and more beautiful city, appealed to a spirit of adventure that, San Franciscans were delighted to discover, had not entirely vanished with the passing of the pioneers.

There were two strains of thought about how the disaster had affected the people of San Francisco. One described a loving and egalitarian community that the fire had welded out of a stratified and contentious society. Perhaps this community might bury past divisions and seize the chance to remake San Francisco. The other also saw the fire as a great leveler, but it stressed opportunity, not community. Inherited wealth and status had supposedly been eliminated, leaving the way clear for a free and unfettered competition to sort out the capable from the losers in a pure Darwinian struggle. Individual ambition, not community good, would spark the rebuilders. Mistaken about the leveling, this view at least did not ignore the persistence of individualism in America.

The leaders of the planning movement thought less about social change and more about money and organization. James D. Phelan,

Senator Francis Newlands, and others who wanted to refashion San Francisco tried to draft the federal government as financial sponsor for reconstruction and replanning. They hoped that with federal funds could come centralized authority to direct rebuilding according to plan. But they were turned down in Congress, and they fared no better with private investors in New York. Planning would not be imposed on San Francisco at the behest of concentrated financial power emanating either from Washington or Wall Street.

Within the city, however, Mayor Schmitz did appoint a Committee on Reconstruction to provide some direction to rebuilding, and several subcommittees operating under its aegis managed to adapt Burnham's plans to meet the radically altered needs of the city. Leadership in this work was grasped by Abraham Ruef, of all people, but if his presence aroused suspicions of jobbery, they were somewhat allayed by the stamp of approval that Daniel Burnham himself bestowed on the performance.

In the confident mood that prevailed, few paid much attention to increasingly strident voices warning against replanning.

"San Francisco burned down last week," Henry Adams wrote to his English friend Charles Milnes Gaskell,

and I have been searching the reports to learn whether the whole city contained one object that cannot be replaced better in six months. As yet I've heard of nothing. Only the Stanford University at Palo Alto was a very charming group of buildings, and I'm sorry it was hurt. Yet San Francisco on the whole was the most interesting city west of the Mississippi. I was fond of it, and my generation made it. It produced many of my best friends and had more style than any town in the east.[1]

Harper's Weekly shared Adams's affection for San Francisco, "Columbia's most loveable and fairest child." She would rise again, not merely because she was beloved, but because "she is endorsed imperishably with an imperial future, with the queenship of the Pacific, by her vast and almost landlocked bay...."[2] The *New York Times* agreed. The great harbor in San Francisco Bay assured the future of the city. The "natural advantages" of location meant more than "artificial enhancements of investment."[3]

Though these opinions about the natural advantages of San Francisco and its future greatness merely reiterated what boosters had been saying for years, they must have been extremely comforting, coming in the wake of the physical destruction of so much of the city. The same message was broadcast almost daily in the local press, like an incantation that could produce results if everyone believed it. Now was hardly the time to quit San Francisco, proclaimed the newpapers. To leave now would be not only disloyal and cowardly but foolish as well, because rebuilding the city offered so many opportunities for the industrious to make new fortunes or reclaim old ones. The city was guaranteed a prosperous future; those who stuck by her would share in that prosperity.[4]

The earthquake and fire must have called forth a wide spectrum of emotions, including fear, rage, grief, despair, and other painful feelings. In reading accounts of the days following the disaster, one discerns another strain, more positive, even exhilarating. The pervasiveness of suffering produced a sense of fellowship, of community, of belonging. William James, who was teaching at Stanford in the spring of 1906, wrote to relatives that:

> everyone at San Francisco seemed in a good hearty frame of mind; there was work for every moment of the day and a kind of uplift in the sense of a "common lot" that took away the sense of loneliness that (I imagine) gives the sharpest edge to the more usual kind of misfortune that may befall a man.[5]

I. W. Hellman, the banker, informed a friend in Los Angeles that "San Francisco's citizens are now working in harmony; there is no distinction between rich and poor, all feeling kindly toward each other. Everything is being done by the strong to help the weak. . . . " Journalist Ray Stannard Baker corroborated Hellman's description of harmony. A miraculous brotherhood had replaced selfishness and animosity, and "for a splendid moment, this ruined city, San Francisco, was a Christian city."[6] The divided city, it would appear, had been united by a shared tragedy; community emerged from common suffering.

This feeling—"earthquake love," as some wags called it—expressed the sense that class distinctions had been obliterated, a new equality replacing the former stratifications that embittered society. Hellman attested to this leveling, and Baker went so far as to say that even racial discrimination had lapsed, if only for a while. The idea must have gained widespread acceptance. When French Ambassador Jean Jules Jusserand presented a medal to San Francisco in 1909 in honor of the rebuilding, he stated that "in one short hour before dawn all civil life had been abolished, all wealth had been annulled, all men and women were on a level, dispossessed of everything; it was really the equality of after death that was beginning among the living. All behaved as men and women of heart and honor."[7] If intended literally, these statements were obviously false. Not all wealth had been obliterated. Most of the wealthy had means of recovery, such as insurance, that set them apart from the destitute and the working class, and the operation of relief and rehabilitation worked to maintain distinctions of wealth existing before the fire. The idea reflects more a wish than a fact, more the desire for an end to invidious social differentiation than the realization of equality.

Others saw equality but in a different light—equality of opportunity in which all unfair advantages were cancelled and men were free to contest with one another on the basis of merit alone. An editorial in the *Bulletin* quoted an Easterner who, having been in the city on April 18, decided to make his home there. Because of the disaster, he felt:

all of us are starting from scratch and the race is to the best man. If I cannot rise to the top under these conditions then I will acknowledge that the fault lies in me, not in circumstances of conditions. In New York and in every going city society has crystallized and the possession of fortunes by some gives so long a start on poorer competitors that merit does not always win and it is hard to measure man against man by his position in the world.

San Francisco today is a homogenous mass of people, a perfect democracy. Within a few months there will be differences and inequalities as ability and industry gain the master over incompetence and sloth. I intend to be one of those that emerge from the masses.

The *Bulletin* agreed, calling the situation a "supreme test of manhood," which "has been morally and intellectually a benefit to the population of San Francisco."[8] Now the natives, those who had inherited fortunes from pioneer fathers and grandfathers, would have to regain their wealth in competition with vigorous young men, who would flock to the city to cash in on the opportunities. Gavin McNab, the politician, felt that before the fire, "the sons of the pioneers were living on memory, and, secure upon the high waves of world commerce, were talking day dreams." Now, however, primitive conditions prevailed, and more aggressive virtues were needed to survive.[9] Businesses would modernize as old-timers were shoved aside by enterprising newcomers.[10] New blood would pump through the veins of San Francisco, unhandicapped by sentiment, tradition, or the constraints of a social establishment. William F. Herrin saw "a new deal all around—a deal giving to capacity and energy opportunities which the old conditions denied as against established reputation."[11] Equality, for Herrin, meant that there would be no discrimination in favor of rich insiders against rich outsiders, such as E. H. Harriman and the Southern Pacific. It meant good riddance to the web of society that through sixty years had been spun in San Francisco. It meant, in short, the cash nexus, unhampered by sentiment, tradition, ties to place, or feelings of social responsibility, the ideal Social Darwinist world.

Like the fiction that class distinctions had vanished, the notion of absolute equality of opportunity was also too extreme. Though improvements on real property had perished, the ownership of real estate was unaffected. The fabric of commercial and credit relations had been torn but not demolished, and there was little reason to expect that bonds of affection, loyalty, and mutuality of interest had been sundered by the burning of buildings. Certainly Herrin, as chief counsel for the largest corporation in the state, did not anticipate that the Southern Pacific had lost all its advantages, its friends, retainers, and dependents. Nevertheless, so major an undertaking as the reconstruction of a city of almost half a million persons would offer numerous opportunities to men of enterprise and foresight. Also, the heirs of fortunes made during the early history of the city, whose wealth was now invested in real estate, office buildings, hotels, commercial and manufacturing establishments, would indeed have to stay on their toes to recapture the worth of their investments and return them to a paying basis. The city had not reverted to a state of nature, but it had been put in a state of flux. Nothing could be further from the stable, prosperous, cohesive society that Phelan had hoped would create and be created by the City Beautiful.

What would the new San Francisco look like? There was from the first no unanimity on this question. Still, of those expressing judgments, the majority seemed certain that the city would be rebuilt on "broader lines," and be larger and more solid. A *Bulletin* editorial claimed that the destruction was a disguised blessing. The fire had removed many impediments to improvement; "from the ashes of the old city will arise a great metropolis, solidly built, a monument to the courage, energy, and good sense of the people." The *Chronicle* agreed that the future city would be stronger and more solid.[12] From the East, the secretary of the National Municipal League assured Phelan that San Francisco would "re-establish itself on bigger and broader lines than ever." Hellman expressed his confidence that "before many years San Francisco will be built up more beautifully than ever." Not all the predictions of a larger city were unmixed endorsements. "There will be great buildings, many people, and much business," forecast an editorial, "but all that was unique and characteristic in old San Francisco has gone forever."[13] Nostalgia, however, had not yet become such a flourishing local commodity.

The terms *broader lines* and *greater strength* referred basically to two kinds of changes. First, the new buildings would be larger and more attractive than the ones they replaced.[14] Some changes in city ordinances might be necessary to guarantee that the new buildings were fireproof, but advances in building technology and the growth of the city would ensure that buildings constructed in 1906 and after surpassed those built in the 1870s or 1880s. Second, the street plan of the city would be altered; some existing thoroughfares would be widened, others regraded, and new streets would be cut. These improvements were essential to provide more efficient transportation in the congested districts, to control future conflagrations with wide avenues as firebreaks, and to make the city more impressive and thereby more beautiful.[15] Altering the street plan would be more difficult than putting up modern buildings. It demanded concerted action on a large scale, both to decide what changes were necessary and desirable, and to undertake them. Even if there were unanimous agreement, the costs would be high, especially considering the devastated condition of the city. If there were opposition to the changes, even to parts of them, then the financial difficulties would be compounded by political conflicts that might jeopardize the rebuilding program and would certainly shatter the feeling of harmony induced by the disaster.

By a miraculous stroke of fortune, San Francisco had a fully developed plan of a new street system, namely the report that the Association for the Improvement and Adornment of San Francisco had commissioned from Daniel Burnham. On April 18, the day of the quake, Burnham, traveling in France, received a telegram urging him to come immediately to San Francisco. Within a day he was sailing back to America.[16] To some in the city, the earthquake and fire took on the aspect of a providential and beneficial prologue, a necessary razing of impediments that had hindered the building of a city beautiful. "Now the way is clear for Mr. Burnham and the New San Francisco!" exulted a magazine writer. "He may glance down the city's highways and see no misplaced oddity to offend his architectural eye. Indeed, he will be fortunate if his vista includes more than a stray wall or so between his studio on Twin Peaks and the tall cone of the Spreckels Building."[17] Even the San Francisco Real Estate Board, not given to flights of fancy where land values were concerned, unanimously resolved:

San Francisco will arise phoenix-like from its ashes and will on lines of beauty and utility soon again take its place in the lead of Pacific Coast and Western cities. The disaster makes possible in a few years the fulfillment of the plans of D. H. Burnham for the adornment of our much beloved city, and the San Francisco Real Estate Board pledges the support of its members to the reconstruction of that portion destroyed by fire, and to the adornment of the entire city as proposed by the Burnham plan.[18]

A few sober voices cautioned against being swept up by the enthusiasm. The *Chronicle* noted that conditions had changed drastically since the Burnham plan had been drawn up, that the city would be financially pressed, and that hard-headed businessmen, not "artists or professional beautifiers," were the people to take the lead. Practical considerations came first; beautification would have to be put off until the city could afford it. Even the *Bulletin* warned that only those changes voluntarily agreed to by property owners could be accomplished. Condemnation proceedings to cut new streets would be too costly and too slow for the city. Haste and economy were the watchwords.[19]

The proponents of the Burnham plan, including Phelan, Walter Bartnett, and Francis Newlands, the United States senator from Nevada, ignored these early signs of doubt. They busied themselves preparing the groundwork necessary for adopting and enacting the plans. Three crucial areas demanded attention. First, financing would have to be found to enable San Francisco to rebuild rapidly and on the imperial scale contemplated by the Burnham plan. The reconstruction of the city would take money even if no streets were changed. The municipality would have to replace schools, street pavements, hospitals, sewers, and the like. Most of the building owners would need funds over and above whatever insurance they might collect. A project for new municipal expenditures would certainly increase the capital required beyond what local sources could supply, especially since investments in the city had suffered severely. Outside funds had to be attracted. Second, the original Burnham plan needed modification to fit the changed conditions. Some of the limitations imposed on Burnham by existing arrangements had been removed. Also, more attention could be paid to the needs of traffic in the downtown area, less to the plans for circular boulevards and broad avenues in the outlying districts. Third, a mechanism for enacting the proposed changes would have to be established; it must take into account the city government, property owners, the electorate, and even the state of California. A workable city plan must speak to the community's needs for beauty and utility; if it is to be achieved, it must speak with the voice of power.

The major potential sources of outside capital were the federal government and Eastern investors. Between the two, Phelan preferred turning first to Washington. On April 29, he announced a meeting for that day to examine ways in which Congress might be called upon to assist San Francisco. Local financiers and attorneys would confer with Representative Julius Kahn on legislation for the congressman to introduce. "It is of the very highest importance," Phelan warned,

that we should not fall into the old rut. Already we hear that for financial reasons we will be unable to realize the plans of Burnham, and there is danger that in our great desire to do things at once, and because we do not appreciate what we can do, this great opportunity, presented to us in the guise of a calamity, will not be taken advantage of.

Even without the Burnham plan, the business houses would require funds to rebuild, more money than San Francisco could supply. To lower the cost of borrowing, Phelan proposed that the federal government endorse up to $200 million of San Francisco municipal bonds. With a government guarantee, the bonds could be sold at 2.5 percent interest. They would be secured by the real estate in the city. The proceeds would be reloaned to private builders, who otherwise might have to pay up to 6 percent for the money they borrowed.[20]

Phelan's idea was supported by the *Bulletin*, which pointed to the government's guarantee of bonds of the Central Pacific and the Philippine railroads as precedents. Across the country, though, the *New York Times* deprecated it as a "cry of distress from one in sore straits, with a mind haunted by terrible present needs, and grasping desperately at the nearest and most obvious suggestion." San Francisco would be rebuilt, intoned the *Times*, "not as a work of philanthropy," but as a strictly business proposition. Large-scale interests including the transcontinental railroads, the banks in New York, Chicago, and San Francisco, and the major insurance companies might unite to direct the undertaking and supply credit; the government should not become involved. Within the city, the members of the San Francisco Clearing House also opposed Phelan's idea, calling it a plea for charity and warning against "untried methods of finance which may be found to be illegal or otherwise impractical."[21] The bankers were apparently apprehensive of government intervention into what they regarded as their exclusive domain.

Meanwhile, encouraging reports promised that eastern capitalists stood ready and willing to loan money to a renascent San Francisco. A vice-president of the National City Bank of New York came west shortly after the disaster. On April 25, he announced that his bank would do all it could to aid in the rebuilding. In his opinion, "Eastern capital in general, realizing that the disaster which has wrecked San Francisco may not be repeated before the end of time, will not hesitate to again invest largely in this city." On the same date, Walter Bartnett of the Western Pacific Railroad gave assurances that leading financiers throughout the country were willing to advance money to San Francisco, especially to aid the city as it rebuilt along lines laid down in the Burnham plans.[22] Several days later, Senator Newlands began discussions with bankers in New York about the formation of a giant investment company, to be capitalized at no less than $100 million, which would loan money for the construction of new buildings in San Francisco.[23]

In statements about the influx of eastern capital, the Burnham plan was not always mentioned as one of the uses for the money. Although Bartnett, Phelan, and Newlands seemed confident that some aspects or variants of the plan would be adopted, they realized that both the municipality and private real estate owners needed funds in any case. When they referred to the plan and to Burnham, they were aiming to quiet the fears of potential investors about the security of new buildings in San Francisco. Burnham's name was associated not merely with the Chicago Exposition and the City Beautiful, but with solid commercial structures and sound building practices. For many reasons, some of them material, San Franciscans minimized the role of the earthquake in the destruction of the city and emphasized that the fire had been responsible for almost all property loss.[24] For one thing, most insurance contracts specifically excluded liability for damage directly caused by earthquake. Also, it was feared that if outsiders thought San Francisco vulnerable to earthquakes, they would invest elsewhere, since earthquakes, unlike fires, represented a danger over which humans have little control, and for which insurance was not obtainable. To counter this apprehension, San Franciscans proclaimed with vehemence that fire and fire alone had leveled the city. In the rebuilding, precautions of all sorts would be taken to prevent a recurrence. Burnham's reputation was a partial guarantee of that promise. As the architect himself wrote to Mayor Schmitz, "outside capitalists will be disinclined to furnish money for San Francisco buildings unless strictly enforced municipal laws shall make conflagrations, and the shaking down of walls and partitions practically impossible in the future."[25]

In Washington, San Francisco's case was argued by Francis Newlands, senator from Nevada. Newlands was a son-in-law of the late William Sharon, who had made a fortune in the Comstock silver country of Nevada and had been a close associate of William Ralston, builder of the Palace Hotel and other flamboyant enterprises. When Ralston died in 1875, just before the completion of the Palace, Sharon became a principal owner of the hotel and of the Bank of California, another Ralston undertaking. Later he won election to the Senate from Nevada. Newlands married a daughter of Sharon, inherited a third of the large Sharon estate, and, like his father-in-law, went to Washington representing Nevada. A large part of his fortune, though, was invested in San Francisco real estate, including the Palace Hotel and other properties.[26]

On May 2, Newlands introduced a resolution calling upon the Ways and Means Committee of the House and the Finance Committee of the Senate to investigate ways in which Congress might assist San Francisco to rebuild. He suggested two methods. One was a restatement of Phelan's proposal, that the federal government guarantee the credit of the city of San Francisco, which would then sell bonds and loan the proceeds "at fair rates of interest by the city to property owners upon note and mortgage." The other was for the government to support, either by a loan or a subscription of stock, the creation of a great financial corporation. Half of the stock of this corporation would be taken by investors for cash; the other half would be sold to property owners in San Francisco for real estate. The cash would then be lent to individual owners of property, or be used to build upon real estate owned by the corporation, with the corporation gradually selling off the improved property. This enterprise was intended to produce a profit to the stockholders. The resolution concluded by calling on the president to appoint "a board of national commissioners experienced in exposition building, . . . with such powers and control over both plans and expenditures as may be deemed advisable."[27]

Newlands had not intended, he declared in motivating his resolution, to bring up the matter of the private corporation, for negotiations were still in their infancy. Since news of the affair had seeped out, he decided to make the matter public. It was most important for the federal government to act in one way or another. San Francisco was not just any city; it was a great port for both interstate and international commerce. The nation was vitally interested in its speedy restoration. The banks of San Francisco had their assets invested in real estate and commerce of the city, and so would not be able to provide the additional capital. More than money, the rebuilding of San Francisco required direction. Individual action would be insufficient because it was random. "The restoration of San Francisco," Newlands declared,

> must be upon broad and comprehensive lines, involving a greater strength and beauty in the development of the city in the future than has been displayed in the past. The development of that city requires a central control—a central control of the plans and a central control of the finances, such control as has been exhibited in the great expositions of the country, the World's Fair at Chicago, the great exposition at St. Louis, and the exposition at Buffalo, where, through the aid of the nation and through the aid of various States, great white cities have sprung up almost in a nighttime, with a perfection of plan and a beauty of detail unequaled in the history of the world. If we trust to individual effort, if each man in San Francisco who owns a lot seeks to put up some kind of structure upon it, we will, of course, have an accidental growth, a dangerous growth, so far as fire is concerned.[28]

For Newlands, the great expositions served as models in several ways. First, the federal government had donated money to the promoters of the fairs. Second, the expositions had been assembled and constructed very quickly. Third, and most important, the architecture of the buildings and their arrangement had been planned and coordinated by a few people, rather than left to individual whim and to chance. If the federal government supplied credit to San Francisco, it could also exercise some measure of control. The president could appoint a commission to approve all plans and expenditures, and he could fill the body with "exposition builders," men like Burnham, John Carrère, and Charles McKim. Newlands reminded the Senate that Burnham had recently completed plans for San Francisco, plans that doubtless would be followed. Burnham's design called for wide parkways dividing the city into four sections. These parkways would act as fire barriers, preventing a conflagration from spreading from one section to another.[29]

Newlands's eloquence was punctured by questions from Senator Alfred Hopkins of Illinois, who asked if the Nevada senator would approve of loans to farmers when the crops failed. Not wanting to antagonize Hopkins, Newlands hedged. All he was asking for, he stated, was an inquiry by congressional committees into the possibility and desirability of federal assistance. Perhaps the committees would decide against any aid; possibly Newlands would concur.

Neither senator from California, Frank Flint or George Perkins, supported Newlands. Flint urged speedy action on the resolution, if only in order not to mislead Californians with false hopes. He said that help was necessary for the poor people of San Francisco, who needed bread and meat, as well as "those who are desirous of steel-frame buildings." Perkins regretted that Newlands had acted before hearing from the government of California or the municipal authorities of San Francisco. Without moving into outright opposition, both Flint and Perkins displayed a visible lack of enthusiasm that must have undercut support for Newlands's resolution. As Republicans, they may have been moved by partisan considerations to oppose the Democrat Newlands; or perhaps they were hurt that Newlands had acted without consulting them. Also, the State of California was itself an applicant for aid, and, as neither Flint nor Perkins was a San Franciscan, they may have put the state's case before the city's.[30]

At any rate, the damage was quickly done. On the same day that Newlands spoke in Washington, May 2, Governor Pardee received confidential information to the effect that Congress would not guarantee San Francisco bonds. Pardee immediately transmitted the information to Phelan.[31] Phelan, however, continued to press for some government assistance. On May 4, he wired his friend, real estate dealer Thomas Magee, who was in Chicago, to go to Washington immediately to see Newlands about the bond matter. Herbert Law, the message said, was already at the capital, as was Franklin Lane.[32] Lane had served as city attorney for San Francisco, and now was beginning a term as Interstate Commerce Commissioner. Apparently, Phelan was directing some sort of campaign. Law, however, did not appear as scheduled before the Senate Finance Committee when it considered Newlands's resolution.[33] Phelan also tried to enlist the support of President Roosevelt. He sent the president a telegram predicting that unless government aid were made available, San Francisco would either be unable to borrow at all, or else would have to pay exhorbitant interest rates to eastern capitalists. But the pleas to Roosevelt brought no results. On May 7, the committee reported back to the Senate that it had unanimously agreed "that both the plans suggested are without the legitimate province of Congressional action." It recommended against appointment of a committee to consider other plans for national aid.[34]

The Senate's response disappointed Phelan, but it did not surprise him. He felt that Newlands had acted too quickly, that the "resolution was premature in that it raised a question for which the public mind was not prepared."[35] Though he continued for several months to press for a reopening of the matter and to find other ways in which government assistance might be enlisted, he also joined in the effort to attract private eastern capital. The most ambitious scheme was that which Newlands had outlined in his Senate resolution, a huge corporation making loans to persons for improvements on real estate in the burned district. Newlands had conveyed news of preliminary discussions about this plan to William Herrin, and Herrin revealed the general outlines to the press. As soon as it became clear that Newlands's effort in Congress would fail, the prospect of an influx of eastern capital was seized upon as a crucial sign that the world still had faith in San Francisco. At a meeting of the Finance Committee of the Citizens' Committee of Fifty, on May 3, Phelan announced that E. H. Harriman had agreed to supply San Francisco with $100 million, if the national government refused. Harriman was roundly cheered even though he said that he did not think the city would need outside help.[36]

Newlands went to New York from Washington and met with H. S. Black, president of the United States Realty Company, and several important bankers. Franklin K. Lane and Thomas Magee joined Newlands in attempting to organize the investment corporation or syndicate. Harriman, however, was the key. The other New Yorkers were awaiting his return from San Francisco before committing themselves to anything definite. He reached the metropolis on May 8 after a record-breaking transcontinental railroad trip. When reporters asked him about the syndicate, he replied that he knew nothing of it, although he felt certain that San Francisco could raise the money "if it could be shown that the city needed it." Harriman must have been somewhat disingenuous, for he had been in San Francisco when Herrin, who was his California lieutenant, broke the news of Newlands's preliminary conversations. After meeting on May 9 with Secretary of the Treasury Leslie Shaw and the president of the New York Chamber of Commerce, Harriman stated that he had no immediate plans for financial relief, nor could any such plans be formulated until the merchants and professional men of San Francisco had determined on an acceptable basis for such assistance.[37]

Despite Harriman's disclaimers, news about the organization of a vast syndicate to underwrite reconstruction continued to percolate. Lane and Magee sent back progress reports, promising that incorporation papers would soon be filed. Some of the details, especially the amount of capitalization, varied from day to day, but the outlines remained clear. In essence, the syndicate would emerge much as Newlands had first described it, a large stock company that issued bonds and then loaned money for rebuilding on the security of the real estate to be built upon. As Lane wrote to Phelan, any talk that the capitalists should assist San Francisco for sentimental reasons fell on deaf ears. As a business proposition, though, the Easterners were interested. Magee thought it essential that they take the lead. "Eastern confidence in San Francisco can be restored only by eastern financiers and eastern money," he telegraphed Walter Bartnett, who was then talking about setting up a similar syndicate based in San Francisco. "Let us welcome these financial kings without whom we cannot fully restore the city."[38]

There were problems, however. A writer in *Colliers' Magazine* remarked that the financial magnates were worried about the strength of the unions in San Francisco, and whether they would force up the construction costs of new buildings. Much depended on the attitude of Mayor Schmitz, on whether he would let his allegiance to the unions outweigh his interest in the city's welfare.[39] A more specific obstacle was the section of the California Constitution, adopted in 1879, that made the mortgagee of any property pay the taxes on that piece of land. The intent had been circumvented in practice; interest rates on loans were increased to cover the tax, and even a bit more. But out-of-state investors had always been wary of this arrangement, in part because they could not calculate exactly the return on their investment. Another clause in the same constitution taxed all stocks and bonds of corporations based outside of California. The joint effects of these measures made San Francisco real estate a desirable investment for Californians, but not for outsiders. Hence the fire hurt local fortunes more than it otherwise might have. Outside money was now urgently needed, and Phelan assured Magee that the mortgage tax provisions of the constitution would be repealed.[40] He did not seem to share the apprehensions of a local magazine that San Francisco might become too obligated "to one or more of the private interests of the country."[41]

While discussions continued in New York and Washington about how to finance the rebuilding of San Francisco, an organization to coordinate and oversee the reconstruction was being formed in the city. The Citizens' Committee of Fifty, nominally in charge of relief work, was clearly not compact enough to deal with the more complex tasks of rebuilding. At a meeting of the Citizens' Committee on April 30, attorney J. B. Reinstein moved that the mayor appoint a new subcommittee to be the Committee on Reconstruction of the city. It would consist of three engineers, three architects, three builders, three attorneys, and five members at large, with the mayor as ex officio chairman. The five at-large members would be the chairman of the Finance Committee, the presidents of the San Francisco Clearing House and the University of California, the superintendent of Golden Gate Park, and one representative citizen. The committee was to organize as quickly as possible and prepare a report that would include "a careful revision of the street plan, the widening and grading of certain streets, the creation of parks, parkways and reservoir sites, the creation of new streets and more convenient access between the lowlands and the hills districts, and such other matters as may come before them." When completed, the report was to be presented to the Board of Supervisors, who would consider it as an advisory document.[42]

Reinstein seems to have called for nothing less—and nothing more—than a reworking of the Burnham plan by a select committee. Others felt that the matter should be treated more broadly. Reinstein accepted the suggestion that the motion be put off to allow for consideration. On the following day, May 1, Abraham Ruef moved a substitute resolution. It called for the mayor to appoint a new committee of forty members to act in conjunction with a special committee of the Board of Supervisors in considering the general reconstruction of San Francisco and the changes in the laws that might be necessary. The committee would consider all the subjects Reinstein had proposed for it and would be, as Reinstein had suggested, merely advisory to the Board of Supervisors. The motion carried. Mayor Schmitz stated that he would announce his appointments shortly, and that they would include Benjamin Ide Wheeler, president of the University of California, John Galen Howard, professor of Architecture, and Daniel Burnham as advisory members.

The discussion that followed made it clear that there were legal as well as economic obstacles in San Francisco's path toward the City Beautiful. For example, the charter limited the bonded debt of the city to $15 per $100 of valuation. With a good part of the assessed property destroyed, this restriction would have to be removed if the city were to borrow on a large scale. Alterations in the city charter required approval of the state legislature, which was soon to meet in a special session to deal with the problems arising from the earthquake and fire. The rebuilding of the city thereby became a state issue. Similarly, Phelan noted that under present California law, leases could not be contracted for more than 50 years. He wanted this provision amended to permit leases to run for 99, so that a real estate owner without enough funds to build might find investors willing to put up a substantial building. Chicago had been rebuilt after its fire under such an arrangement. It was agreed that these and all other matters connected with rehabilitation should become the province of the new committee, thus broadening its scope considerably.[43]

On May 2, the membership of the new body, called both the Committee on Reconstruction and the Committee of Forty, was made public. Like the Citizens' Committee of Fifty that it superseded, the Committee of Forty was a misnomer, for it included more than the stated number of members, especially if one counts the ex officio and advisory personnel. In all, about 60 persons served; more than 60 percent of them had also been members of the Committee of Fifty.[44] The new committee was a smaller and more exclusive group, but most of the major interests of the city were directly represented, except perhaps manufacturers and retail merchants. Two members were connected with the United Railroads, two with the Southern Pacific, and two with the Western Pacific. Bankers, attorneys, real estate agents, builders, architects, and engineers filled most of the other positions. The presidents of the San Francisco Labor Council and the Building Trades Council had been appointed, as had the head of a carpenters' local, who was also a supervisor. Schmitz was chairman by virtue of his office; E. H. Harriman became vice-chairman, although he soon would leave the city. Burnham, Wheeler, and Howard joined several others, including Governor Pardee, as advisory members.

To an even greater extent than the Committee of Fifty, the Reconstruction Committee included most of the men who mattered in San Francisco. One who mattered very much, Abraham Ruef, was probably behind the appointments. Removed from center stage in the immediate aftermath of the earthquake, he had managed to reinstall himself at Schmitz's elbow. At the first meeting of the new committee, on May 3, he suggested that Schmitz select a group of five to draft a plan of organization; the mayor agreed, and left the task to Ruef. On the following day, after Ruef had read the list of subcommittees, Schmitz asked members to state their preferences. Although the mayor said it would take him a week to make up his mind, he returned on May 5 with all the subcommittees filled. Evidently Ruef worked fast. There were approximately 25 subcommittees, and Ruef was to serve on some of the most important, such as those on extending, widening, and grading the streets, and on amendments to the municipal charter.⁴⁵

Another sign of Ruef's return to power was the omission of Francis J. Heney, who had been a member of the Committee of Fifty, from the reconstruction committee. Phelan and Spreckels, two other political foes, were too prominent to be excluded. Spreckels, however, saw Ruef's fine hand in the reorganization. He allegedly said to Heney just after the appointments, "I see that they are getting ready to rob the dead; they are getting ready to take everything in sight; what they did before is not a marker to what they will take now."⁴⁶ Most likely his distrust of Ruef was widely shared, for projects bearing the endorsement of the boss were suspect. Another significant omission from the reconstruction committee was M. H. de Young, whose *Chronicle* had already begun seriously to question the wisdom of any change in the street plan.

The *Chronicle* opposed cutting new streets and widening existing ones on the grounds that the city's resources were now very meager. The newspaper reasoned that whatever changes were contemplated would cost more money than San Francisco could currently afford. To buy the land needed for new or wider streets, the city would have to increase the tax rate. Such an increase would deter Easterners from investing in San Francisco real estate or from opening new industries in the city. Since it was in the interest of all the people of San Francisco to encourage the influx of outside capital, any projects that raised the tax rate for primarily aesthetic purposes, for "mere beautification," were inimical to the good of the city.⁴⁷ Others agreed. The *Bulletin*, which had been Phelan's ally in supporting the Improvement Association, now argued that San Francisco could never become the Paris of America, that money spent to make the city into a beautiful tourist mecca would be a poor investment, especially at the present time. Even Mayor Schmitz, who at times seemed to regard the fire as San Francisco's golden opportunity, also spoke out against extravagance and in favor of caution.⁴⁸

Before the fire, the Burnham plans had been broadcast as the aesthetic salvation of San Francisco, though of course the economic benefits of a City Beautiful had not been ignored. Now the advocates of Burnham had to argue that the plans had a definite practical validity, that they made good sense in dollar terms, that the beautiful was the useful and the useful, in turn, was beautiful. The Berkeley architect John Galen Howard declared that "the plans should be carried out, not primarily because of the beauty of the effect to be created, but because of the conveniences involved in the arrangements, the provisions for taking care of traffic and for making each part of the city accessible." It was an old fallacy, wrote a supporter of Burnham, to suppose that there was an inconsistency between utility and beauty; at the highest level, they were identical.[49] No one was more vehement than architect Willis Polk in decrying the notion that the Burnham plan was visionary or extravagant. "The public ought to get rid of the idea," he explained,

> that we are working on a beauty plan. It is a business plan. Most people think that we will bring in a proposal for a city of parks and fountains and statues, like a second Paris. Our whole idea is for a city which will invite capital and make it safe for sound businessmen to stay here and rebuild San Francisco.[50]

Despite these and similar disclaimers, it was inevitable that in the public mind Burnham's name was linked with beautification and not commercial utility. In the Committee of Forty itself, there were originally three subcommittees dealing directly with matters relating to the street layout. The Committee on the Burnham Plans included Phelan, Howard, Polk, Herbert Law, and several others. Phelan and Polk were also members of the Committee on Parks, Reservoirs, Boulevards, and General Beautification. Finally, the Committee on Extending, Widening, and Grading the Streets and Restoring the Pavements had as members attorneys Ruef and W. H. Metson, engineer Edwin Duryea, real estate owner Herbert Law, and liquor wholesaler F. H. Hilbert.[51] The problems of having three committees with similar jurisdictions were soon recognized. On May 7 the park committee requested that it be consolidated with the Committee on the Burnham Plan, and that it be allowed to work with other committees, including the street committee. The committee promised always to give priority to utility and only turn to beautification at a later date. The amalgamation of the park committee and the Burnham plans committee was agreed to on May 8, but the street committee remained a separate unit. A week later "Autolycus" reported that a sort of competition existed between the two groups. On the beautification committee, he said, "Schmitz collected with a certain grim humor the men who are known as 'the dreamers,' " such as Phelan, Howard, and Polk. He filled the street committee with "hard-headed practical businessmen and lawyers, such as Herbert E. Law, William H. Metson, and Abe Ruef."[52] Even among friends of street changes, the marriage of beauty with utility seemed difficult to arrange.

In practice relations were harmonious. The task of altering the city's streets was obviously a difficult one. The destruction had been thorough enough to give to the planners the appearance at least of a free hand. Even before the committees were formed, Thomas Woodward, the city engineer, presented a detailed scheme for improvement of the burned district. The members of the subcommittee on streets had their own ideas of what changes were needed, and they thrashed these out in meetings open to the public. They soon learned that there were restrictions to their map redrawing. Some costly structures, like the Mills and the Kohl buildings on Montgomery Street, had survived, and the owners did not want to see them torn down to widen the roadway when another street might serve almost as well. Some owners of valuable but vacant lots were also leery of what the proposed changes would do to their real estate, although others expressed a willingness to go along. Patrick Calhoun of the United Railroad testified that the regrading of certain streets would aid the traction company in replacing cable cars with trolleys. The representatives of the Western Pacific prevailed upon the committee not to cut through the land that the company had acquired for a terminal. Abraham Ruef managed to save part of a lot he owned from being included in the proposed widening of Montgomery Avenue.[53] No doubt other interests also worked to shape the plan to suit themselves.

Another constraint on the street committee was the Burnham plan and the architect himself. Burnham had hastened home from Europe to Chicago, but he did not leave that city until May 11, despite urgings from Phelan to hurry.[54] When he did reach San Francisco, on May 14, he met with Phelan, Schmitz, Reuf, Polk, and others, and assisted the street and beautification committees.[55] Though he certainly gave a psychological boost to those working for street changes, he stressed that he was only present in an advisory capacity. He also made it clear that the plans under consideration were quite different from the Burnham *Report*. The *Report* had treated the whole city and had subordinated utility to beautification. Beauty and order had been elevated to socializing forces. The street committee, by contrast, focused on the burned district, north and south of Market Street, and had as a primary goal the opening and widening of streets to facilitate traffic and act as fire barriers. The Burnham plan served as a point of departure, but it was extensively modified, with Burnham's approval.[56]

On May 19 and 20, the street committee, with Burnham in

attendance, completed its labors. In final form, the plan it created called for the extension of several diagonals across Market Street, the widening of a number of streets in the downtown area and near the waterfront, the cutting of new avenues to scale Nob Hill at passable grades, and the opening of streets in the city hall section. There was no mention of a circular boulevard, of the great *places*, or of the perimeter of distribution, all so prominent in the Burnham *Report*. The extension of the Panhandle was put off. In the burned district itself, the new proposals departed from Burnham's original plans, but did seek to accomplish similar ends. There were fewer diagonals sweeping from one center to another, although more street widenings were suggested. Burnham was not at all miffed by these alterations, especially since his plans for a union railroad station had been retained.[57]

The committee decided that since not all these changes could be financed immediately, some would have to be put off for five and others for ten years. It indicated by a multicolor map what the order of progress should be, designating the ones for immediate action as "Class I." Two street widenings were to be paid for by the owners of property on those blocks, who would benefit directly from the enlargement. In order to forestall any building on property ultimately needed for the deferred projects, the committee recommended that the Board of Supervisors declare by ordinance the intent of the city to acquire that property within five years. All the purchases or condemnations of land were to be paid for by city bonds, but those bonds issued to cover the costs of the delayed projects would not be redeemable for five years.

The last meetings of the committee concluded in a spirit of confidence and self-satisfaction. Burnham judged the work to be excellent, all that he could have desired.[58] Benjamin Ide Wheeler wrote that the committee had overcome the original apprehensions about the costs of improvements, and that after May 17 the architects, the city government, and the larger financial interests were in complete accord for moving ahead with the altered plans. Phelan, Law, Willis Polk, all expressed their delight with the work and their confidence in its successful implementation. They stressed the fact that the plans as modified were both financially feasible and economically desirable. The special bond issue allowed the city to delay payments for some years. Meanwhile, wider streets, better grades, and new avenues would increase the value of real estate. When the bonds became due, they would easily be redeemed with-

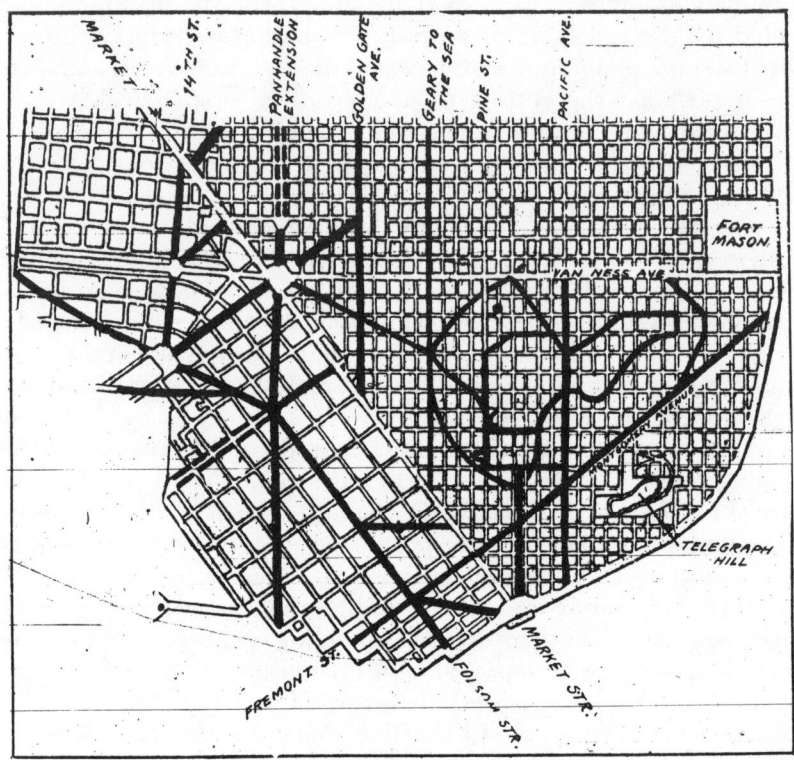

Street changes proposed by the Citizens' Committee. (*San Francisco Chronicle*, May 23, 1906)

out raising the tax rate, since the assessments would be so much higher. Also, wide thoroughfares would be an important deterrent to conflagrations, thus saving the city considerable money in insurance premiums. Whatever aesthetic benefits would accrue from the new street design were either incidental to it, or, as some said, inherent in the identity of beauty and utility. The aim of the street committee had been practicality, and its eyes had rested fixedly on commercial and financial necessities.[59]

The report of the street committee was presented on May 21 to the Committee on Reconstruction, which endorsed it enthusiastically. That very evening Abraham Ruef laid it before the Board of Supervisors for consideration. He asked that the officials express their approval and that they authorize a study of the costs of all the proposed improvements. Burnham assured the supervisors that the plan before them had nothing to do with his beautification proposals, but would relieve congestion and facilitate communication, benefiting people engaged in all sorts of business. Some disagreement was voiced by one Edgar Painter, who claimed to represent property owners whose land would be taken by the extension of Montgomery Avenue to Market Street. The proposal, said Painter, would leave many small, triangular lots not suitable for building, and would cost the city $1 million for no particular advantage. The supervisors disagreed and unanimously passed the resolution Ruef had introduced. In addition to a general approval of the plans and an authorization for a study of the costs, the resolution declared "that it is the intention of the board to proceed forthwith with the execution of the plans and improvements set forth in 'Class I' of said committee's recommendations so far as may be practicable and compatible with the city's financial conditions."[60]

Burnham left San Francisco immediately after the supervisors' meeting. He must have been delighted by the action of the board, for when he arrived in Chicago on May 26, he predicted that "within six months the new San Francisco with its wide driveways and handsome buildings will be well advanced. In a year's time it will not be easy to find a trace of the devastation left by the earthquake." The pride of San Francisco had been awakened, he felt, and he noted that "even the poorer people who lost their homes are preparing to build again on a more substantial and artistic scale." The old city hall, "an incongruous structure that could not be made to conform to any possible system of plans for the beautification of the city," would be taken down, and the new San Francisco would radiate from a new municipal center. With certainty and a high estimation of his own work, even after modification, Burnham declared that the "San Francisco of the future will be the most beautiful city on the continent with the possible exception of Washington."[61]

A week after the presentation of the street report to the Board of Supervisors, the committee on beautification delivered its own project to the reconstruction committee. The "dreamers" supported the work of the practical men on the street committee with whom they had cooperated. But like keepers of the true faith, they pushed for a greater commitment to the original Burnham plan. The great circular boulevard which Burnham had advocated should be kept in mind during the reconstruction of the waterfront, said this report. Property owners in the outlying districts should be encouraged to open up diagonal avenues by common agreement. The terraced roadways around California and Russian hills, envisioned by Burnham, might be achieved by cooperation of land owners. Other aspects of the original Burnham report were also retained. The beautification committee sought to remind San Francisco that a broad view was essential, one embodying future possibilities as well as current necessities. "The City of London," warned the committee,

> after its great fire, rejected the plans of Sir Christopher Wren, according to the history of that time, on account of the "jealousies among the people," and since then the City of London has not only regretted its failure to take advantage of the occasion, but has paid enormous sums to effect the very same results. There is no doubt but that the people of San Francisco, chastened by affliction and taking advantage of the present catastrophe, . . . will not only create out of the ruins a great and prosperous city, but also one which will be renowned for its beauty and its charms.[62]

In the face of opposition which was daily becoming more vocal and more organized, such confidence in the far-sightedness of San Franciscans was disarming, if not disingenuous.

8
The Defeat of Planning

Politics and Property Rights

Was the disaster really such a golden opportunity for San Francisco? Many thought not. They argued that the city must be rebuilt with haste or else it would lose even more ground to its rivals on the coast. Replanning meant delay and expense, and a stricken San Francisco could afford neither. M. H. de Young, publisher of the *San Francisco Chronicle*, led the opposition. He used the news pages and editorial columns of his paper to denounce the attempt at redesigning the street layout, and he organized fellow owners of downtown property to support his protests. Their antagonism was not simply theoretical; they also worried that a new street system might encourage a permanent relocation of the retail shopping district. Earthquake love barely survived the fire.

Discord pointed directly at one question planning advocates had refused to face: How to implement the plans? The city charter sharply constrained the government's authority over real estate. If old streets were to be widened and new ones created, the municipality would need augmented powers or the work would take forever. One person was willing to confront this problem—Abraham Ruef. He drafted an amendment to the state constitution giving the city increased authority over land use. He shepherded his project through the Committee on Reconstruction in San Francisco, and then through a special session of the state legislature in Sacramento.

He met bitter criticism at every step, for many suspected that he was trying to steal the very streets and parks of San Francisco. Ruef's activity made it clear that planning meant power, power meant government, government meant politics, and politics, of course, meant Ruef. The people who had brought Burnham to San Francisco had hoped to break out of this circle, and when they saw that they could not, they recoiled. James D. Phelan, the leading advocate of planning, sat on his hands while California voters defeated Ruef's cherished amendment. The fate of the planning movement was sealed; San Francisco would be rebuilt along the old lines.

Other cities laid waste by disaster have also inspired the hope that destruction might be opportunity in disguise, but these hopes have seldom been realized. For a number of reasons, devastation has not normally led to comprehensive planning. In San Francisco, a strong commitment to private property rights prevented the expansion of public authority. Without adequate power in the hands of the city government, a refashioned San Francisco depended on the unanimous voluntary agreement of property owners to accede to new plans. Prospects for such unanimity, it hardly needs saying, were slim.

As early as April 24, when the enthusiasm for a new San Francisco on "broader lines" was most intense, the *San Francisco Chronicle* dissented. The paper cautioned against official plans for adornment. Since public authorities would be preoccupied with other matters, initiative for changing the street plan would have to come from "associations of property owners, who in arranging for local changes for their mutual benefit can act in collaboration with a committee which will have in view the benefit of the entire city."[1]

The forecast proved in error. The Committee on Reconstruction, certainly at least a quasi-public body, moved energetically and speedily toward recasting the Burnham *Report* into an apparently practical model for a new and more efficient San Francisco. The *Chronicle* responded by arguing that the expenses necessary for any major reordering of the streets would be ruinous to the city in its present condition. High taxes would frighten away prospective investors and cause the city to stagnate. Without an accurate estimate of the cost of the proposed improvements, any major venture would be a blind leap, precarious at best, disastrous at worst. A policy of economy and retrenchment was a safer course to follow, given the great needs of the city and its depleted resources. The efforts of the street committee to convince San Francisco that it had abandoned beautification and adornment for efficiency and utility made little impression on the *Chronicle*, which continued to deride the parks and boulevards of the original Burnham plan after they had been eliminated from the revised version.[2]

The hostility of the *Chronicle* toward large-scale changes in the street plans, whether under the rubric of beautification or efficiency, was shared to a certain extent by other newspapers, especially the *Bulletin* and the *Call*. The *Bulletin*, which had supported the AIASF and Burnham in 1904 and 1905, now grew wary in the crisis following the fire. While it commented approvingly on some of the recommendations of the street committee, it argued that both economy and speed were more important than wide streets, and that nothing should be put in the way of those seeking to rebuild at once. Even the supposedly practical suggestions of the street committee were a hindrance, the paper said, because they cast doubt on future street lines and thus inhibited property owners from committing themselves to constructing substantial buildings. If those who owned the land needed for street widenings and extensions did not agree to part with it voluntarily, then protracted condemnation proceedings and court cases would hold up rebuilding for years. San Francisco needed to restore its commercial and industrial life at once and could not afford any substantial delay, no matter how noble or even beneficial the aims.[3] Comprehensive street changes would not merely discourage outside capital because of high taxes, but would also retard local reconstruction and the revival of commerce.

The members of the reconstruction committee, especially those concerned with new streets and beautification, could not have been blind to the strength of the arguments put forward by the newspapers. They were, by and large, practical men, businessmen of one sort or another, who were personally interested in the future prosperity of San Francisco, but somehow they took a more optimistic view of the conditions and needs of the city. They stressed the fact that they had departed in purpose and detail from Burnham's original plan, making utility their overriding objective. In their view, the city could not afford *not* to take advantage of the fire by changing its street pattern in the downtown area. They must have realized that alterations would delay rebuilding, that some commerce would be slow in getting started again, and that the costs of widening and extending the streets would have to be paid for by taxes at some future date. But they saw the proposed changes as an economic asset, making transportation more convenient, reducing the risks of large fires, increasing the city's attractiveness even if only in a functional sense, and establishing the confidence of the oustide world in a more fireproofed and better designed city. The natural advantages of the bay and the position of the city as the nation's leading Pacific port were not going to be lost by a moderate delay in restoring commerce. The costs of improvements could easily be met by the more rapid growth of a redesigned San Francisco.[4]

Both supporters and opponents of the new street plan argued economics, the opponents emphasizing the importance of immediate reconstruction, the supporters pointing to providential opportunities that must not be wasted. Why did they see things differently? Temperament is one possibility; another is how they estimated their own prospects in postfire San Francisco. The person who assumed leadership of the anti-street-change cause was thought by certain of his contemporaries to be motivated by selfish aims. M. H. de Young, publisher of the *Chronicle*, owned the newspaper and its large lot at Market and Kearny streets plus other property in the downtown area.[5] What made the property valuable was its position in the heart of the retail shopping district. The fire, destroying virtually all of this section, forced the relocation of retail trade to other parts of the city. First Fillmore Street in the Western Addition, then Van Ness Avenue became centers of retail activity. Merchants quickly secured whatever space they could, generally by leasing converted dwellings or by putting up temporary structures on vacant lots. Newspapers reported that the new locations were only temporary, that the retail district and other districts as well would certainly resettle in their old locations, once buildings were available.[6]

Though the *Chronicle* might write about "immutable laws of convenience in respect to the topographical features of the city,"[7] anyone familiar with the history of San Francisco and other cities must have realized that business districts had shifted before and would certainly shift again. In addition to the commercial and industrial areas, the fire had eliminated much of the residential section of the city, adding to the uncertainty. A weekly magazine pointed to the fluid condition of retail locations before the fire, with the wholesale center moving south of Market and the retail district moving westward. In the much more unstable circumstances after the destruction, the magazine argued, as few as "six plutocrats" might be able to determine the location of a major district if they all invested heavily in one area.⁸ To persons whose fortunes were tied to the value of property in the burned district, such speculation must have been unsettling.

In order to prevent any large-scale relocation of the downtown retail district, owners of real estate in that area met on May 7 to coordinate their efforts. The first meeting was held in the temporary offices of the *Chronicle* on Fillmore Street, the second meeting was called for the old *Chronicle* Building on Market, and the newspaper gave the activities considerable space. At the first session, the owners decided that they would not give preference in their new buildings to former tenants who had rushed to secure two-year leases on space in other locations. They envisioned the completion of steel frame structures within a year, and they were obviously trying to threaten or chastise tenants who exhibited doubt about the speedy recovery of the old retail section.⁹ On May 10 about 75 owners met and elected de Young as chairman of the Down Town Property Owners' Association. The meeting stressed the need for hasty reconstruction, possibly, as the *Bulletin* remarked, out of fear that the retail center might otherwise remain on Van Ness Avenue. Because it seemed to the owners that the insurance companies were being intentionally dilatory in paying claims, a committee was appointed to prod the underwriters. The watchword of the association was to rebuild at once. Meanwhile, editorials in the *Chronicle* exuded confidence that the retail shopping district would inevitably return to its old location, that the waterfront, the banks, the importance of Market Street, and the proximity of the section to East Bay patrons prevented any major shift westward, to Van Ness and its tributaries.¹⁰ If the somewhat worried activity of the association seemed at times to belie the placid assurance of the *Chronicle*, still they were complementary means to the same end, the maintenance of land values in the prefire retail district.

The grand design of the street committee, endorsed by the Committee on Reconstruction and the Board of Supervisors, clearly presented a formidable obstacle to those for whom immediate reconstruction seemed a necessity. At a meeting of the Down Town Property Owners' Association on May 22, just one day after the supervisors had approved the plan, de Young moved that the association oppose the proposals. It was unnecessary to widen the streets, he contended, and it was even worse to put off the matter for five years. Postponing a part of the new street program until the city had more funds had been, in the eyes of the would-be planners, a stroke of genius; to de Young and his associates, it was pure folly. They saw the delay as a cloud of uncertainty that would prevent any substantial reconstruction so long as there remained any doubt about which property would be appropriated for the widening. The association unanimously condemned this five-year provision. De Young then attacked the widening of Geary Street, especially the part facing Union Square on which he owned a large lot. He also had no use for the plans to enlarge some other streets, including Seventh and Folsom. The association passed his motion denouncing the report of the Committee of Forty and demanding that any street changes be accomplished immediately. At a second meeting a week later, de Young convinced the owners, some of whom felt the earlier resolution had been too extreme, that any changes in the streets would be a mistake, that it was better for the association totally to oppose the street committee than to support part of its recommendations.[11]

On May 26, a second group of real estate owners organized themselves as the Union-Square Property Owners' Association. The first meeting was held at the *Chronicle* Building, suggesting that de Young may have taken the initiative again. Although they do not seem to have passed any resolution, the Union Square owners, according to the *Chronicle*, were opposed to the widening of Powell and Geary streets.[12] Unlike the Down Town Association, which continued in existence for some time and took positions on other issues, the Union Square group seems to have faded away, perhaps by being absorbed into the other association. Probably de Young had breathed into it whatever life the organization had in an attempt to make opposition to street widening seem more widespread than it actually was. He may have wanted to avoid having all criticism of the new street plan traced to him, and thereby discounted.

Still, the *Chronicle* was not bashful in its attacks on the plans. A headline proclaimed the " 'Cobweb' Plan is Strongly Opposed: Business Men Don't Want It, and Lawyers, Including City Attorney, Say it Cannot Be Carried Out." And the editorials amassed new objections to buttress old ones. The first argument had been that the cost would be too high. Then the paper attacked the five-year postponement procedure, introduced, in all likelihood, to counter objections about the cost. It claimed that:

what property owners dread is the general unsettlement of values involved in these widening propositions. They will object to them in all cases where it cannot be clearly shown that property on the widened street will be suited to the same uses to which it has hitherto been put.[13]

The old plan had its faults, the editorial admitted, but business had accommodated itself to the imperfections. To change substantially the situation or width of existing streets would be to alter the location of different lines of business. The fear that owners in the former retail section had about losing their tenants to Van Ness and the Western Addition was elevated in the editorial to a general principle, upon which rested the fortunes of all owners of commercial property.

De Young did not mobilize all the opposition to the new plans. Other newspapers also urged economy and caution. According to the weekly *Argonaut*, because the publishers of the dailies were also large property owners and therefore large taxpayers, they pumped for utility and disparaged costly undertakings.[14] An historian of the San Francisco press saw the negative attitude of the newspapers resulting from the fact that the publishers acted "as spokesmen for downtown business and property interests primarily concerned with reaping the largest immediate yield from the smallest investment," rather than as "selfless utilities [motivated] by and for the public good."[15] But de Young was clearly the leader. He used his paper to attack the plans, and he organized a portion of the property owners to broaden the base of the opposition. The perceptive "Autolycus" accused him of raising false issues to secure selfish ends. According to "Autolycus," de Young's real antipathy was based on his fear that widening Geary Street would injure his own property, which lay on both sides of that thoroughfare. Instead of admitting as much, de Young attacked the high cost of widening, "an appeal to that niggardly and unprogressive spirit," that "Autolycus" thought would handicap all efforts for improvement.[16] Although he may have been accurate concerning de Young's motivation, "Autolycus" missed an important point. What de Young had done in the Down Town Property Owners' Association was to convince a powerful group of men that their interests were jeopardized by a plan that was supposedly intended to benefit the city as a whole. Apprehensive lest a delay in reconstruction lead to a massive relocation of the retail district, these property owners took a vocal stand against the street committee and worked to defeat its plans.

The Committee on Reconstruction had approved and the Board of Supervisors had "looked with favor" on the report of the street committee, and even had committed itself to implement some of the proposals, so far as practicable.[17] But formidable obstacles still stood between this favorable reception in principle and the actual accomplishment of any substantial changes. As de Young and others pointed out, securing the land necessary for widenings and extensions would be costly and time consuming. By law, the city could acquire land for municipal purposes only through donation, purchase from a willing owner, or condemnation and purchase from a reluctant one.[18] A property owner could appeal the purchase price decision in a condemnation suit to the state Supreme Court. The procedure might take considerable time and might also force the city to pay more for the condemned property than had been estimated. With so many property owners involved, some of whom were already manifesting reluctance willingly to part with their land, it was clear that a way of expediting this process had to be found if the street plan were to be realized.

The street committee apparently made no attempt at solving this dilemma, except to recommend that some improvements be put off for a while in order to reduce initial costs. If the proponents of widening tried to find a path around the condemnation procedure, they left no record of their efforts. The one person who recognized the problem and moved to alleviate it was Abraham Ruef. The means he chose were circuitous, to say the least. Among the most important subcommittees in the Committee of Forty was one concerned with a special session of the California legislature. Over some opposition from elsewhere in the state, San Francisco had convinced Governor Pardee that a special legislative session was necessary to deal with pressing problems arising from the earthquake and fire. The constitution of the state stipulated that during a special session the legislature could only act on those matters mentioned in the governor's official call to convene the session. Governor Pardee in effect asked the subcommittee in San Francisco to frame his call, and its final report formed almost verbatim the text of the governor's proclamation.[19]

The Subcommittee on the Special Session of the Legislature and State Legislation included some of the most distinguished legal minds, and some of the highest paid attorneys, in San Francisco. Tirey L. Ford served as chairman; the other four members were William F. Herrin, Gavin McNab, corporation attorney Garret McEnerney, and E. S. Heller, also a lawyer and the son-in-law of I. W. Hellman. Ruef was not a member, but he was chairman of the subcommittee on charter amendments and a member of the judiciary subcommittee, both of which met jointly with the subcommittee on state legislation, as did the subcommittee on municipal departments.[20]

These subcommittees discussed measures to alleviate some of the hardships brought about by the catastrophe and means to ensure that commercial and property relations would not be unduly upset. For example, the members considered, but ultimately rejected, proposing a change in the bankruptcy laws to prevent overanxious creditors from forcing their debtors into bankruptcy. They did recommend legislation to make it easier for owners of property whose records of ownership had been destroyed to secure new evidence of ownership. To aid San Francisco and other cities damaged by the quake to find capital to rebuild, the subcommittee suggested that counties, cities, school districts, and other bodies be permitted to issue bonds to run for 100 years, rather than 40 years as was currently the law. In order to raise needed revenue for the state, the subcommittees proposed some alterations in taxes on corporations and on inheritances.[21] In all, 32 specific topics requiring legislation, appropriations, or amendments to the state constitution were suggested by the subcommittees for inclusion in the governor's call.

The question of street widening was discussed on May 8, the third meeting of the subcommittees, and then neglected for almost two weeks while the subcommittees occupied themselves with other issues. On May 8, attorney William Metson suggested that the city of San Francisco be enabled, by amendments to the state constitution and the city charter, to deal in real estate. Metson's idea called for exempting from taxation those pieces of property fronting streets to be widened, provided that the owners gave to the city that portion necessary for enlarging the streets. In addition, the city should be allowed to condemn property for park purposes and resell it, even speculate in it. For example, if the city decided to extend the Panhandle, it might condemn not only the actual land required, but also the lots facing the extension. It could resell these lots, at a higher price, after the extension had been completed. The city could finance part of the changes in this way. Metson also suggested that the city be enabled to sell certain narrow alleys and streets to pay for widening neighboring streets. The existing law forbade the city to dispose of any officially dedicated street.[22]

Metson's suggestions were radical, calling for a significant enlargement of the powers and responsibilities of the city government. Ruef himself pointed to the dangers inherent in allowing cities to engage in real estate speculation. He suggested that it might work if the new powers could be limited to two years. Other committee members were also skeptical, and Metson's proposal was laid aside. There was no additional discussion of methods of street widening until May 18, when it was announced that Josiah Howell of the San Francisco Real Estate Board and R. H. Countryman were working on the subject.[23]

Ruef also must have been studying the problem. He was absent from several meetings and reappeared only on May 18. Three days later he presented his thoughts about a constitutional amendment that would allow San Francisco to acquire land for street purposes at a great savings. The idea was appealingly simple. Instead of the city having to purchase valuable property fronting on a thoroughfare it wanted to widen, it would condemn and acquire a strip at the rear of the lots, such as half way between the parallel streets of Montgomery and Sansome. The cost of this interior strip would be much lower than the frontage property. The city would then exchange an interior for an outside portion, and widen the street enough so that formerly interior property would now face the street. In a similar fashion, the city might trade some already existing back alleys it owned, such as Trinity Street behind Montgomery and Quincy Street behind Dupont, for property facing Montgomery and Dupont. The closing of the alley would permit widening of the main street without the city actually having to acquire additional property. In both cases, the owners of lots on the streets to be widened would be compensated by the increase in value of their land, in addition to what they would get for selling the back of their property.

Ruef also wanted the constitutional amendment to permit the city to sell or dispose of school property and other lots no longer necessary for the purposes for which they had originally been acquired. He gave as an example his own North Beach district, in which, before the fire, there had been five grammar schools. Only one was needed for the number of children in the area. If the city were allowed to dispose of four of the lots, either by sale or trade, it would gain some valuable resources to be used for street widening. The charter forbade the city from alienating any property it had acquired for street or other public purposes, and changes in the city charter had to be approved not only in a local election but also by the state legislature. Therefore Ruef argued that an amendment to the state constitution, conferring on San Francisco these new powers for a limited time and expressly voiding the prohibition in the city charter, would be the most expeditious means of proceeding.[24]

Ruef's colleagues appear to have responded positively to this aspect of his scheme, but they had reservations about a necessary corollary to the plan. As Ruef explained, the state constitution permitted utility companies that ran water mains, gas pipes, and electrical and telephone wires beneath the surface of city streets to tear up the roadway in order to install or repair their facilities whenever they chose, subject only to the provision that they restore the roadway when they were finished. This provision had been partially responsible for the perpetual disarray of San Francisco streets, since the utility companies operated at their own convenience and thought nothing of tearing up a newly laid road surface and keeping it open for weeks or months. Nor did they coordinate their operations with one another, so that a street might be opened, worked on, and finally restored by the gas company only to have the telephone company move in and repeat the process. The inconvenience was bad enough, but now that the city contemplated changing the street plan, a new problem arose. Ruef contended that unless the city were given some additional authority, it could not force the utility companies to move their pipes and wires to follow the altered street lines. Unless the companies were so compelled, their lines would run under private property and prevent excavations for new buildings. No property owner would trade some of his land for an equal amount of abandoned street property unless he could be assured that the utility conduits would be removed. So the possibility of widening streets by trades and exchanges of other property depended, Ruef said, on the ability of the city to move the utilities.[25]

Gavin McNab, a long-time political opponent of Ruef, disagreed. He saw the chief threat to the street widening proposal as coming not "from anybody's interest in the streets," which was legally a complex question, "but [from] the fear that a great many people have that there is going to be a rearrangment of the city, and the unsteadiness it gives to building operations." Though other members of the subcommittees were also wary, Ruef was instructed to prepare a draft of his amendment. He presented it on May 22, but the matter was continued for a day. On May 23, Ruef set forth his case in its entirety, and again McNab and others refused to be convinced that the city needed these new powers. They felt that in light of the seriousness of the amendment and the fact that it was such a new departure, to adopt it without further discussion would be premature. For two more days the subcommittees discussed Ruef's proposals, hearing objections and deciding on changes. Finally, on May 25, they approved an altered version of the proposed constitutional amendment that Ruef had first read on May 22.[26]

As originally introduced, Ruef's amendment gave to the Board of Supervisors and the mayor almost unrestrained power over the disposition of land currently held by the city or to be acquired by it during the two years for which the powers were to be granted. The Board of Supervisors, by a two-third vote of its members and approval by the mayor, could "acquire, purchase, condemn or accept donation of lands to be used for streets, parks, boulevards, reservoirs, or esplanades, or to be exchanged for land to be used for such purposes." More important, it could sell or exchange land now used "for such purposes for other lands to be used for the same or similar purposes." The same provisions applied to sites for public and municipal buildings; that is, the supervisors could sell or trade sites the city owned in order to acquire new sites. This portion of Ruef's amendment permitted two-thirds of the supervisors and the mayor to sell Golden Gate Park, for example, or the city hall lot, provided only that they used the proceeds to acquire park land or a municipal building site, or received such land in exchange. When McNab pointed out how sweeping was the grant of powers, and how much harm a dishonest Board of Supervisors might do, Ruef agreed to redraft the amendment so that all purchases and sales of city-owned land would be submitted to the voters for approval. Similar restrictions were placed on the powers of the supervisors over the utility companies. Ruef first proposed that two-thirds of the supervisors and the mayor might "change, widen, or extend the lines of [the] streets and the lines, routes, or terms of any privileges, or franchises for pipes, pipe lines, conduits, wires, tracks, or roadbeds now held or enjoyed by any person, firm, or corporation in or on any of its streets." A modification of this portion confined the powers to changing the routes of the lines and conduits; nothing in this section was to be "so construed as to confer upon the Board of Supervisors any power or authority, beyond that at this date possessed by it, to extend the term or time of existence, or condition, of any franchises."[27]

The restrictions that McNab and his colleagues had imposed on Ruef's amendment certainly curtailed, if they did not eliminate, the harm that a corrupt city government might do to the municipal property of San Francisco. For the *Chronicle*, however, the limitations were insufficient. Ruef's proposals were "revolutionary and hysterical," designed "to rip open the charter of this city and tear out of it a great batch of its most salutary restrictions on the power of the supervisors." The Committee of Forty should not have given them serious attention. Even in amended form, the newspaper con-

The Defeat of Planning

tended, the proposals would allow a crooked Board of Supervisors to condemn anyone's property and sell the city streets to corporations.[28] The *Chronicle* would probably have opposed any measure designed to implement a new street plan; that Ruef was the principal author of this particular measure, which gave novel opportunities for graft to a Board of Supervisors and a mayor already tainted by suspicions of corruption, made the *Chronicle*'s position stronger.

Later the *Chronicle* was to charge that Ruef had so dominated the joint subcommittees as to make them virtually his own, and had slipped the street widening amendment past an overworked Committee of Forty. But according to the omnipresent "Autolycus," the subcommittee on the special session of the state legislature was the one place where Ruef had been unable to overwhelm his colleagues. They paid particular attention to the street amendment and managed more or less to sanitize it so far as the possibilities for graft were concerned. "Even in its crippled and twisted condition," "Autolycus" felt that it might be able to provide the necessary means for a rebuilding plan. It eliminated the "iron-bound rigidity of the charter" where matters of real property were concerned. Acknowledging that "the prime assumption that a Supervisor is a rascal and a public enemy" was based on experience, he nevertheless felt that the amendment as revised was not a threat to the public interest. Still, he doubted it would pass the legislature. The distrust of politicians, so clearly expressed in the city charter of 1900, which actually had increased the authority of the mayor and the rest of the city government, was deeply rooted in all classes of San Franciscans. But if the city were to be rebuilt along "broader lines," if even parts of the revised Burnham plan were to be achieved, some increment in the authority of the city government was essential. The fact that Abraham Ruef, "the biggest man in San Francisco today," according to "Autolycus," was to be the indirect recipient of that authority must have increased the apprehensions of many who otherwise might have approved. Ruef's relationship to the city, "Autolycus" reported, was "something like a man with a black eye making love to a woman, and a pretty skittish woman at that."[29]

The fate of the new street program, then, was tied to Ruef's proposed constitutional amendment. Certainly Phelan and others from the Improvement Association, the original sponsors of the Burnham plan, would not voluntarily have chosen this means of making street replanning possible. Phelan had hoped that assistance from the federal government might supply the financial base on which a new San Francisco could be rebuilt. When that hope failed, he devoted himself to overseeing relief work and striving to have as much of the Burnham plan as possible incorporated into the revised version. Neither he nor most of the members of the subcommittee on extending, widening, and grading streets concerned themselves directly with the problem of implementation. Perhaps they assumed that no special method would be necessary, that public opinion would unite so strongly behind the street proposals that property owners would part voluntarily with those portions of their lots needed by the city. Perhaps they felt a method would be forthcoming from the city government once the proposals of the street subcommittee had been approved by the supervisors. Whatever the reason, their failure to answer the question of how the city might acquire and pay for the improvements they desired left open a serious lacuna that Abraham Ruef moved to fill.

Ruef had not been the first person to suggest that a constitutional amendment might solve the implementation problem. But he had adopted the idea, expanded it, supplied the first draft, and altered the text to suit objections. Other members of the joint subcommittees on the state legislature and related affairs were supposed to be working on the street problem, but they did not produce. Ruef had been an active member of the subcommittee on streets; that work, and his authorship of the proposed amendment made him, as "Autolycus" said, "the man to pull San Francisco out of her hole and bring about the rebuilding of the city on a reasonable and scientific plan."[30] Ruef's intimate connection with the plan was both a blessing and a burden. As boss of the Union Labor party, he controlled the San Francisco delegation in Sacramento and was a statewide influence in the Republican party as well. But his unsavory reputation, coupled with the potential for dishonesty inherent in his amendment, cast a shadow over the whole effort and provided ammunition to men like de Young, who opposed any alterations. Perhaps more of a handicap was the amendment itself, which granted new authority over public and private property to a body of men distrusted personally and for the offices they held. That the first contest over the amendment was to be in Sacramento rather than San Francisco, with state legislators rather than city voters as the judges, complicated the matter further.

A number of controversial proposals confronted the California legislature during the special session in June 1906. These included repeal of the mortgage tax provisions of the state constitution, extending the time for which a city or other agency could issue bonds from 40 to 100 years, and allowing amendments to the charters of San Jose and San Francisco made during the next two years to take effect without approval by the state legislature. But the street widening amendment, which became known as the Ruef amendment, aroused the most heated discussions and had the most tortuous legislative history. In the course of its consideration by the legislature, several groups in San Francisco sent delegates to the state capital to make clear their positions, and Ruef was kept busy answering the numerous, and sometimes conflicting, objections that were raised. He managed to steer the amendment through the committees and both houses, but not without having it modified to limit further the powers of the city government.

In an interview in the *Sacramento Evening Bee* on June 4, Ruef dismissed the *Chronicle*'s hostility to his amendment as based purely on de Young's ownership of a lot on Geary Street, facing Union Square, which would be trimmed if Geary were widened as planned. The same argument could not be applied to opposition arising from quite another source. An amorphous group of property owners and citizens complained that most of the legislation proposed by the Committee of Forty actually favored the corporations and did not meet the needs of the ordinary citizens of San Francisco. The leading representatives of this group were Walter Macarthur of the Seamen's Union, T. E. Zant, an organizer for the American Federation of Labor, E. P. E. Troy, a campaigner for municipal ownership, and Albert Johnson, brother of Hiram, an attorney with some reputation as a tribune for the people. Macarthur charged that the legislative session was intended merely to rubber-stamp certain acts that had already "been drawn up in the law offices of certain leading corporations," which he did not identify by name. Johnson was not so reticent. He pointed to the members of the subcommittee on the special session, who, he claimed, were closely connected with the United Railroads, the San Francisco Gas and Electric Company, the Southern Pacific, the Spring Valley Water Company, and other large business interests. The bills they proposed, he said, especially those changing the taxation of corporations and inheritances, benefited only the corporations. Johnson complained that when he and his friends had set these objections before Pardee, the governor had treated them with contempt. Pardee stated that the Committee of Forty represented the business community, to which Johnson replied that the rehabilitation of San Francisco did not depend upon the maintenance of existing privileges.[31]

To inform Sacramento, and especially those state legislators from outside San Francisco, of the true nature of the Committee of Forty, Macarthur, Johnson, Zant, and Troy hired a hall and held a public meeting on June 4. They reiterated all their charges, using the same vaguely populist rhetoric that pictured the corporations seeking to fool the legislature into enacting measures inimical to the good of the people. Johnson noted that the Committee of Forty and Governor Pardee had refused to insert in the call any provision for the construction of temporary quarters for the homeless. The omission, he asserted, was due to the opposition of landowners who wanted to raise rents by keeping the housing market tight. By contrast, he pointed to the St. Francis Hotel, which had been permitted to build a temporary hotel on Union Square to accommodate wealthy visitors to the city.[32]

This ostensibly radical group criticized the composition of the Committee of Forty and the subcommittee on the special session, the failure to provide any relief to small property owners or renters, and the proposals to increase state revenue by doubling corporation license taxes without regard to the size or assets of the corporation. They also attacked the Ruef amendment as dangerous, full of jokers, and designed to benefit certain property owners at the expense of all the taxpayers. Under its provisions, the public would have no control over franchises; the Southern Pacific might run a steam railroad through the residential parts of the Mission district. Legislators should not be stampeded into passing hasty, ill-conceived acts, advertised as a remedy for San Francisco's troubles, but designed in truth to aid large corporations and other special interests.

Another opposition group, consisting of property owners in the Mission district, echoed the theme that the Ruef amendment was special interest legislation. Spokesman Matt I. Sullivan attacked both the Ruef amendment and the revised Burnham plan as intended to benefit millionaire property owners in the downtown area north of Market Street. He predicted that the street widening program would cost about $40 million, with all taxpayers sharing the burden. Under present charter provisions, the area profiting from an improvement could be made into a special assessment district to meet the expense. Since, according to Sullivan, the proposed street changes focused predominantly in the north of Market section, owners of property in that area should pay for the improvements.

The Defeat of Planning

Sullivan expressed these objections on June 6 before the Assembly committee on constitutional amendments.[33]

At the same time, the Senate received a telegram from the Down Town Property Owners' Association, those very people whom Sullivan said would be the beneficiaries of the Ruef amendment. "It has been stated," the telegram read,

> that this bill is in the interest of the manufacturing, commercial, mercantile and property classes of this city. To our certain knowledge, we are positive the measure in question has excited general condemnation. The property classes of this city are opposed to any contemplated changes in the avenues and streets of the business district. It will prevent the quick rebuilding of this city and the rehabilitation of San Francisco's commercial supremacy. This act ties our hands in every direction....[34]

That Sullivan himself was one of the many signers of this telegram further complicates the question of who, in fact, was going to benefit.

Against this motley opposition, which seemed to come at him from the left, the right, and the Mission district, Ruef utilized all of his considerable political ability. When Sullivan or Johnson appeared before the Assembly to voice a criticism of the amendment, Ruef was on hand to counter the arguments. He gave interviews to the press; he placated legislators from other parts of the state; he kept a tight hold on the San Francisco delegation. The *Bulletin* remarked that he seemed to have no other business in town, so avidly did he attend to the passage of the amendment.[35] All his skills were necessary to keep the measure from failing; its movement from Assembly to committee and back was fraught with danger, and several times there were majority votes against passage. But somehow, through compromise and probably through exerting his influence, Ruef managed to win the motions to reconsider. The original text was introduced on June 2. As amended on June 8 in the Assembly and the Senate, the amendment gave the supervisors the right to sell and exchange land the city then owned or would acquire in the future only upon authorization by a majority of voters at a special election. No existing public park or square, either whole or in part, could be sold or exchanged. The changes of the routes of street railways and of the conduits, wires, and pipes of the utility companies could be done only in cases where street widenings, extensions, or closings had made such alterations necessary. An original provision giving the supervisors the authority to prevent the utility companies from digging up the streets was stricken out.[36] The companies, in other words, would neither be at the mercy of a hostile Board of Supervisors, nor would they be able to get additional concessions from a friendly one.[37] On June 11, the Assembly passed the altered amendment by a vote of 56 to 7, and the Senate followed suit.[38]

The entire issue had become so complicated that opinions differed on whether the amendment, as finally adopted, was a victory for Ruef or a setback. The *Bulletin* felt that after the initial alterations in the Assembly, the heart of the measure had been virtually stricken out, leaving the supervisors with restricted and harmless powers. This analysis assumed that the true purpose of the measure had not been to aid in enacting the revised Burnham plans, but rather to put the Board of Supervisors in a position from which they might personally profit through crooked dealings. The *Bulletin* did not shrink from these implications; "if the proposed amendment," it declared, "were ever written into the constitution, a place on the Board of Supervisors would be worth a million dollars a year to a boodler."[39] Fortunately, the legislature had not fallen for Ruef's deceptive language and his seemingly cogent explanations. In the form in which it went to the governor, according to the *Bulletin*, the amendment was fairly acceptable, although the paper still had reservations about the extent of the powers granted to the supervisors.

"Autolycus" disagreed. He felt that Ruef had made an impressive fight and had won, "although he and his amendment came out a little disfigured." Ruef's strength lay in his great command of municipal affairs and San Francisco conditions; he had used this knowledge to convince legislators of the need for the amendment. Now that the issue was before the people, "Autolycus" advised them to vote for ratification. "It is true," he admitted,

> that it puts large powers in the hands of the San Francisco Board of Supervisors, and that means Ruef. But if we are to get anything done at all we must entrust power to somebody. I confess that I would rather trust Ruef than any other politician in San Francisco. He will, of course, take care of himself and his people in the process, but he will not be any worse in this regard than the others. Moreover he will use his power in a broad-minded and enlightened manner because he is really a big man.[40]

The legislature's action put Ruef's amendment on the November ballot and left the question up to the voters of the state of California. The fate of street improvements hung in the balance, for without passage of the amendment, there seemed to be no practical way to accomplish any large-scale changes.[41] Conditions in San

Francisco, however, developed during the months between the legislative session in June and the November elections in such a way as to becloud the issue, so that the vote on the amendment was no longer a statewide referendum on San Francisco street plans.

First, some of the pressure for street widening of the most utilitarian sort was eased by a relocation of the wholesale section. Before the fire, the center of wholesaling had been in the area between Montgomery and Market streets and the bay. Some firms had been leaving this location and settling south of Market Street nearer to the railroad depot. After the fire destroyed their old warehouses, wholesale merchants decided to abandon their former congested section and move to land owned by the Southern Pacific in the vicinity of the railroad tracks. The center of this new district was bounded by Sixth and Seventh, Irwin and Sixteenth streets. In July, warehouses went up. A leading merchant told the *Bulletin* that the apparent failure of the street improvement plans, which would have relieved some of the crowding in the old sections, had been a determining factor in the decision to move. The wholesalers were also upset with the property owners from whom they had leased their lots. These men had not only opposed sacrificing any of their property for wider streets, but were also demanding the same rent for bare lots as they had for lots with buildings before the fire. The new district had better freight facilities, more room, and was being leased by the Southern Pacific at reasonable rates. Rather than contend with their old landlords, the merchants had pulled out and resettled.[42] Thus, a group that might have been organized to work for street improvement no longer had a major stake in the issue, and would take no part in any political conflict concerning it.

Second, there appeared sometime in early October a revision of the street plans that had been adopted by the Committee of Forty and the Board of Supervisors. A major objection to the plans was that they included no accurate and detailed estimate of the cost of proposed improvements. To meet this criticism, Walter Bartnett engaged former city engineer Marsden Manson to do a study of the plans, both to determine the cost and to evaluate their significance for the industrial and commercial development of the port of San Francisco. In Manson's view, the economic future of the city depended on improving the waterfront, with better wharves, warehousing facilities, and efficient transportation to link ships, railroad cars, and local factories.[43] Therefore, while he included in his report an estimate of the cost of each change proposed by the Committee of

Forty, he also took the opportunity to present his own version of what needed to be done and the costs he thought the city must assume.

Manson's proposals shifted the emphasis of street change from the area north of Market Street, primarily a retail and wholesaling shopping district, to the section south of Market extending to the bay, where manufacturing, warehousing, and shipping were concentrated. He estimated that the most crucial improvements, those which should be carried out immediately, would cost about $6.3 million. The interest on bonds necessary to finance this work would be minor; if the tax roll of the city totalled $500 million, property assessed at $5,000 would have to pay only $3.15 per year for these changes, which, Manson argued, would quickly increase the value of the property affected. So obvious were the advantages of the improvements that Manson was confident "that a broad and generous spirit will actuate property holders in view of the benefits which will accrue to them by opening these fire avenues and highways, and that normal values for rights of way will be accepted."[44]

The pamphlet in which Manson's report was printed included letters of endorsement from Mayor Schmitz, the San Francisco Real Estate Board, the Potrero Commercial and Manufacturers' Association, and Walter Bartnett. The Real Estate Board commended Manson for producing a plan from which all vestiges of beautification or adornment had been expunged, leaving only "those improvements which are of strict commercial value and which will immediately aid in the reconstruction of the city from a business standpoint."[45] Only Bartnett included a plea for the passage of the street widening amendment and other constitutional changes essential to the carrying out of any general plan.[46] But Manson's work may actually have helped to lessen support for the street amendment. He had scaled down the expected costs and had demonstrated, in a very businesslike fashion, that the improvements would benefit both the city as a whole and those whose land would be needed for wider streets. Of course the advocates of widening had always maintained as much; they, however, had not had the figures. What Manson did was to complete the transformation of the Burnham plan from a grand vision for adornment and social order to a street map for a more efficient waterfront district. At the same time, he seemed to reduce the need for granting any new and dangerous powers to the city government. The cash benefits of improvement would be so obvious that the established practices of eminent domain would suffice to produce the land necessary for new streets.

Walter Bartnett did not agree. Of all the major spokesmen for street change, he emerged as the one most devoted to the Ruef amendment. On October 22, he wrote to Phelan and Tirey Ford urging them to become active in a campaign of support for all the proposed amendments affecting rebuilding, including the most controversial Ruef amendment, Number 11 on the ballot. "Unless concerted action is taken now," he warned, "the City will be built up on the old lines and perhaps under the old laws."[47] Phelan agreed, at least to the extent of suggesting a meeting in the following few days "to promote concert of action in the matter of the plan."[48] But his role should have been something more than acquiescent. As Herbert Law wrote to him,

the city naturally looks forward to you, Mr. Phelan, to carry this great project to success. It is the work of a Napoleon—far-reaching in its importance and value to the city. . . . It was inaugurated by you, followed up constantly and earnestly by you, and it should be by you carried to its utmost success.[49]

Yet, if his papers are a true gauge, Phelan was loath at this time to don the mantle of Napoleon.

One does not have to search far to find the cause of his reluctance. In October 1906, Francis Heney, Fremont Older, Walter J. Burns, District Attorney William H. Langdon, financier Rudolph Spreckels and, to a lesser extent, James D. Phelan, decided to bring into the open the fact that they intended to prosecute Abraham Ruef and Eugene Schmitz for graft. On Saturday, October 20, Langdon announced that a newly impaneled grand jury would begin an official investigation.[50] At such a juncture, it would have been virtually impossible for Phelan openly to advocate the passage of a constitutional amendment, known by Ruef's name, that would have given the boss, at least until his conviction, opportunities for graft on an unprecedented scale. Not everyone shared Phelan's reluctance. The *San Francisco Real Estate Circular*, published by Phelan's friend Thomas Magee, argued that the powers granted by the amendment were quite necessary, regardless of who occupied the supervisors' chairs, and that an aroused city could easily oversee the actions of the current administration and prevent any double-dealing. It was simply a question, the *Circular* felt, of now or never.[51] But Phelan, it seems certain, could not go along. He did not make a highly visible entrance into the campaign, through statements to the press or speeches either for or against passage of the amendment, but he did indirectly endorse an advertisement in a Stockton paper urging San Francisco's sister cities to defeat Amendment Number 11.[52]

On November 6, 38,802 San Franciscans went to the polls to elect a governor, state legislators, congressmen and other officials, and to pass on a number of constitutional amendments, including four that had been proposed during the special session of the legislature. The street widening amendment was badly defeated in the city, with only 4,128 affirmative votes against 7,940 negative ones.[53] The apathy or lack of understanding on the question is even more remarkable than the almost two-to-one margin against the measure. Only one-third of those who went to the polls bothered to vote on this seemingly crucial issue, and the largest vote cast on any amendment question numbered only 13,161. The state as a whole rejected the Ruef amendment by a somewhat smaller majority than had San Francisco, 35,649 voting for adoption against 58,042 opposed.[54] Clearly the proponents of street widening had not mounted the kind of informational campaign needed to educate the voters on so complex a matter. Most likely, they were occupied with other concerns, personal and civic, and did not have a great deal of time to devote to the question. Also, as we have seen, the situation in San Francisco had changed since the legislative session, making the amendment appear both less necessary and more drastic. So they more or less let their opponents like de Young and the *Chronicle* use the widespread suspicion of citizens toward increasing the authority of local government to kill the measure.[55]

Despite the defeat of the street widening amendment, interest in modernizing the street system of San Francisco did not disappear. In fact, in the months after election, discussion shifted back from the limited and commercial emphasis of Manson's proposals or those of the Committee of Forty to the original Burnham plan and the ideals it embodied. The directors of the Merchants' Association, for example, passed a resolution urging the Committee of Forty to continue its work of preparing an estimate of the costs of executing its version of the Burnham plans. "The Association recognizes the utilitarian value of Mr. Burnham's work," the resolution read, "and the necessity of having his scheme carried out as a whole in the course of time." Though it could now make only a modest start, the city should do nothing that might later prove an obstacle to the completion of Burnham's work. "School children should be taught to look at it as the agreed program for the future growth of their city," the directors declared, "and public sentiment should oppose projects that conflict with its essential requirements."[56]

Willis Polk, the local architect who worked with Burnham on the plan and other projects, argued in an article called "The City Beautiful," that the aims of the Burnham plan had never been fully understood. "Adornment" through statues, monuments, fountains, or parks had always been secondary; the thrust of the plan was to design a more efficient—and therefore more grand and beautiful—city for the future. Though the necessities of getting things moving again militated against undertaking any major aspects of the plan, Polk was confident that after a temporary city had been completed, the mere economic benefits to be gained would induce the city to adopt Burnham's suggestions.[57] The Committee of Forty continued its work; it published a pamphlet to inform the citizens that maps were being made as a basis for assessing the costs of improvements.[58] In 1907, Bartnett renewed his efforts on behalf of the plans and worked hard to get Burnham himself to come to San Francisco and head the undertaking.[59] But this loyalty to the Burnham plan was not enough to transform it from an ideal into a reality. When the street widening amendment met defeat, the reconstruction of San Francisco along the old lines was virtually assured.

San Francisco did not take advantage of the disaster to reform and modernize its basic plan. Have other cities suffering from similar destruction been any more successful? The record is mixed. As we have seen, those San Franciscans favoring adoption of the revised Burnham plan pointed to London's experience after the 1666 fire as something to avoid. In their view, London was foolish to reject Christopher Wren's design for a refashioned city. But Wren's plan was not the sole option facing London. Other designers, including Jon Evelyn, Robert Hooke, and Valentine Knight, also presented King Charles II with models for a new city. While none of these plans was accepted, London did manage to widen some of its major streets and even create a few new ones.[60] San Francisco could do neither. Had the advocates of planning pointed to these more modest accomplishments, instead of trying to use the rejection of Wren's vision as a warning, they might have had more success. In 1906, after all, the City of London was the financial capital of the world, Christopher Wren notwithstanding.

In the years since the San Francisco fire, a large number of cities have been confronted with the challenges and opportunities which destruction on a large scale offers. Advances in the technology of war mean that cities no longer need wait for natural or accidental catastrophes to clear away the residue of the past. The intensive bombing of urban areas during World War II was particularly effective in this respect. While the bombs were still falling, planners offered optimistic forecasts about the new and purified cities to emerge with the peace. In some cases, they actually started on the plans themselves.[61] But in the construction of destroyed cities, continuity and persistence outweighed innovation. After the war, almost every heavily bombed city in Europe and Japan rebuilt on the same site it had previously occupied. Moreover, the internal structure of these cities remained largely unchanged. Only in rare instances was the central district relocated. Business firms tended to return to their old sites. The prewar pattern of land values reemerged. Rather than offering a clean slate to the planners, destruction imposed severe constraints on radical changes. Even in the most heavily bombed cities, some improvements remained. The buildings that could be restored, the foundations of structures that had been leveled, and the underground utilities were all too precious, in the bleak days after the war, to be torn down in the name of progress. Both national and city governments had to satisfy extraordinary needs with scant resources and were unable to underwrite an expensive redesign. As they had in San Francisco, businessmen opposed delay. In both Western Europe and Japan, the widely dispersed ownership of land militated against comprehensive planning. Finally, there were strong emotional attachments to the city and neighborhood that argued for a restoration of the prewar structure. A sociologist looking at Western European cities ten years after the war believed that "affection for the visible heritage of a long, rich, and proud past, the historical monuments, churches, and treasured buildings, is widespread and has been intensified by destruction."[62] Even in Eastern Europe and the Soviet Union, where private ownership of real estate was not such an obstacle to new design, sentiment could help ensure the replication of large parts of cities like Leningrad and Warsaw.[63]

While the overall pattern of reconstruction was one of continuity, there were still a number of cities in which street plans were modified and a few in which more extensive changes were accomplished. In Bristol and Kiel, the city centers were moved to new sites, and in a number of cities the central areas were substantially expanded according to plans. Widening downtown streets was common, especially in places where streets had retained their medieval dimensions. New thoroughfares were also cut. These changes may not have been adequate for the unanticipated increase in automotive traffic, but they did help to modernize the central areas and permit them to cope at some level with the internal combustion engine. Rotterdam, Stalingrad (now Volgograd), Le Havre, and Plymouth were four cities in which large segments were replanned. No doubt more thorough investigation would turn up additional examples. Replanning was not out of the question in the postwar reconstruction, but it was extraordinarily difficult, probably even more so than in normal times. The experience of San Francisco after the earthquake and fire was not unique; disaster seems more likely to beget substantial continuity in urban form, rather than radical innovation.

What may distinguish San Francisco from these European cities is not so much the outcome of the planning efforts as the reason why planning lost out. In all cases, the economic imperative of getting things back to normal was a powerful deterrent. In European cities, a sentimental attachment to the city that was destroyed operated in the same direction as the economic calculus, in some places probably with greater intensity. This emotional tie was not present in San Francisco, despite all the nostalgia for "the city that was." In 1906, San Francisco was only a half-century old. Even James Duval Phelan, who so valued that European sentimental attachment and hoped to instill it in his fellow San Franciscans, was the son of a migrant to the city. For most of the people in San Francisco, there is every reason to assume that they were at least as mobile as those "men in motion" whom recent historical research has shown flowing into and out of American cities with incredible rapidity.[64] When they could afford it, these people treated urban property as a commodity rather than a revered heritage. Still, San Francisco proved to be at least as inhospitable an environment as the destroyed cities of Europe when it came to implementing new plans. Why? One possible answer is that what San Franciscans lacked in reverence for the past they more than made up for in their attachment to the ideal of private property and the implications that this ideal had for social and political organization.

A reading of numerous and diverse sources makes it clear that a large majority of articulate San Franciscans believed the private ownership of property and the ability to dispose of it as one wanted were crucial to the maintenance of social order. Part of the philosophy behind the relief programs was predicated on this belief. This is not to say that some absolute state of laissez-faire prevailed in the city. The municipality regulated, if it did not own, all public utilities, and it enforced building codes and issued licenses restricting the freedom of home owners and businessmen. But these exceptions merely qualify; they do not invalidate. By contrast, the imposition of an extensive planning project on the real estate of the city, in which future economic advantage had been influenced by an architect, a committee of experts, or an engineer, rather than by astute or fortuitous private individuals, this project to be implemented by the coercive actions of public and political officials—such an undertaking represented a danger to the prevailing system of values and rewards. Put more formally, the enactment of any large-scale plan in the city by any means other than the voluntary compliance of almost all property owners directly affected would have meant the transference to government of functions that the private market had been fulfilling.

Most of the vocal advocates of planning were reluctant to support such a transfer. Phelan, for example, thought for some time after the disaster that the street changes could be accomplished through cooperation, that is, without the enlargement of governmental power. As late as October 1906, he was writing that the revised Burnham plan could be secured through normal channels. Enlightened self-interest would be sufficient, and even the most obdurate would be willing to see the city progress "so long as they will rise with it."[65] But in fact the most obdurate would not go along voluntarily, and there was no real campaign to coerce them. The street amendment received only lukewarm support at best from most of those who favored the new street plan in the abstract. After it met defeat, no serious alternative was presented. Even on more limited issues, none of which involved anything so total, novel, or risky as the street amendment, a similar respect for property rights prevailed, preventing alterations in the prefire city. A few examples will demonstrate that this respect was powerful enough to protect the poor as well as rich, Chinese as well as Caucasian.

The first instance centered around an attempt on the part of the Citizens' Committee to move Chinatown. In the nineteenth century, the Chinese in San Francisco had settled most densely in a small section of the city bounded by Kearny, California, Stockton streets and Broadway.[66] The area became a mecca for tourists who flocked to see the strange ways of the celestials, their temples, restaurants, shops, gambling parlors, and opium dens.[67] But the presence of a large number of Chinese near the heart of San Francisco upset some of the local whites, who found the intense congestion of the area a potential health hazard and resented the Orientals for less defensible reasons.⁶⁸ Chinatown also abutted the downtown retail and financial district, on land that otherwise might have been devoted to these profitable uses. In 1905, local businessmen formed a company to purchase the real estate in Chinatown. The Chinese would be resettled, presumably voluntarily, in a new oriental city, complete with modern sanitation, just south of San Francisco on the bay at Hunter's Point. The company intended to demolish the old Chinatown and replace it with new retail stores, fashionable boarding houses, and fine residences. It would widen the streets and treat the whole district harmoniously. A writer estimated that the value of the land would increase from $6 million to $25 million if the project were completed. One commentator on the subject linked the plans for a new Chinatown with the formation of the AIASF as the two projects testifying to the birth of a new civic spirit in San Francisco.⁶⁹

The fire completely destroyed historic Chinatown, and most of the Chinese left the city to find shelter in neighboring towns, particularly Oakland. Those who remained, numbering perhaps in the hundreds, were shunted from one relief location to another. First they were housed at the foot of Van Ness Avenue, near the bay. Phelan and others, fearing that it would be difficult to dislodge them once established in a new location, objected to this site. On April 28, the Chinese were uprooted and taken first to Fort Mason, then to the golf links on the Presidio. It was felt by those who wanted to establish a new Chinatown at Hunter's Point or elsewhere that housing the Chinese on government property would prevent a permanent settlement. Their stay on the golf course lasted one day. When nearby residents complained that summer breezes would carry the noxious oriental odors into their houses, the Chinese were forced once again to break camp, this time to be settled on the military parade grounds above Fort Point.⁷⁰ During these migrations, the Citizens' Committee appointed Ruef, Phelan, Jeremiah Deneen, Doctor James Ward, and Reverend Thomas Filben as a committee to secure a permanent location for the rebuilt Chinatown.

Several obstacles confronted Ruef and his colleagues in their attempt to find a new place for Chinatown. First and most important, the land that the Chinese had formerly occupied was owned largely by Caucasians who had been receiving high rentals from the oriental businessmen and residents, due partially to overcrowding. These property owners would not willingly sacrifice their lucrative holdings in exchange for the assurance that moving Chinatown would benefit the city. Second, the Chinese quarter was a major tourist attraction and brought a good deal of money into the city.

Third, it was widely believed that the presence of the Chinese in San Francisco was responsible for the city's preeminence in trade with China. If the Chinese left the city en masse, for Oakland, Los Angeles, or Seattle, some feared that the oriental trade would go with them. Fourth, merchants and official spokesmen for the Chinese adamantly refused to resettle in San Francisco anywhere but on the old site. They especially resisted the attempt to locate them at Hunter's Point or elsewhere far from the main lines of trade.

Despite the difficulties, the committee on Chinatown sought to find a new site and to persuade the Chinese to accept it. They continually stressed that they did not want to drive the Chinese from San Francisco, and that the new location would be convenient and more sanitary than the old. Meetings were held between the committee and representatives of the Chinese Six Companies and the Chinese consulate. Realizing that Hunter's Point was out of the question, Ruef sought to interest them in the area to the south and east of Telegraph Hill, within the section bounded by Sansome, Front, Pacific streets, and the bay. But diplomacy and promises of a new and glorious city were to no avail. The Chinese wanted their old location, and a number of landlords in the area wanted them back. On May 9, 1906, Caucasian property owners organized the Dupont Street Improvement Club to secure the rebuilding of Chinatown on the old site. The Chinese themselves emphasized their determination by sending representatives of the largest commercial firms to call on the mayor of Oakland. They discussed the possibilities of establishing an oriental district in the East Bay city, and promised that they would settle in Oakland or elsewhere rather than move to Hunter's Point or any location in San Francisco other than their former quarters.[71]

This threat was not lost on Ruef. On June 16, he asked that his committee be discharged, having obviously failed in its purpose. The Chinese did not want to be moved, and no other neighborhood wanted them. Moreover, he added, they had the Constitution on their side, meaning presumably that neither they nor their landlords could be deprived of their property without due process of law.[72] So the Chinese returned, as secure in their property rights—including the right to rent at high rates from Caucasian landlords—as anyone else in the city.

The *Chronicle*, for one, had never thought that the attempt to remove them would be successful. "Both Chinese and other property owners in the old Chinatown," an editorial affirmed, "have legal

The Defeat of Planning

rights which there is no intention anywhere to attempt to infringe. The Chinese can return to their old locations if they and other property owners so desire and nothing can prevent them." The newspaper placed its hopes for improving the area on building regulations and street widenings that would make it more sanitary, and not be "such a blot on our civilization and a menace to public health as the old Chinatown has constituted during the past years."[73] But dreams of a new and more beautiful oriental city were not to be realized immediately. With the same absence of concern for aesthetics and safety that marked the construction of the rest of San Francisco, Chinatown was rebuilt with hastily constructed buildings on narrow streets.[74] Plans were formulated by the Chinese Merchants' Association and the Merchants' Association of San Francisco to reconstruct Chinatown according to an "Oriental plan of architecture."[75] As elsewhere in the city, the original diagnosis for surgery was rescinded in favor of a prescription for cosmetics.

A second incident illustrating a respect for property rights concerned the attempt by the Committee of Forty to extend the fire limits. The fire limits defined an area within the city in which certain types of construction, mostly wooden frame, were prohibited. The Board of Supervisors adjusted the fire limits from time to time, to incorporate new areas in which costly steel frame, concrete, or brick structures were common. Inflammable frame buildings already standing did not have to be torn down, but no new ones might be put up. The purpose of fire limits was to protect the more substantial buildings from the threat of conflagration and thus reduce fire insurance premiums. If the premiums were too high, the argument ran, capitalists would not invest large sums in modern buildings and the city would stagnate.

The subcommittee on building laws of the Committee of Forty, meeting jointly with a committee of supervisors, decided to recommend that the fire limits be extended. The new district they proposed would roughly follow the lines of the fire itself, with some exceptions for Russian and Nob hills and in the vicinity of the railroad tracks to the south of Market Street: 90 blocks, 60 north of Market and 30 on the south side, would be added to the old boundaries, increasing the size of the district by about 50 percent. The committee acted on the assumption that these additions were likely to become areas of wholesale and retail trade and that incorporating them within the fire limits right away would curtail the construction of inflammable structures. Arguments were made to the committee that such an extension would be a blow to the poorer landowners who would not have the resources to build in brick. Supervisor Gallagher, however, responded that a brick building conforming with the mandates of the law need only cost 10 to 12 percent more than a wooden one of similar size. Insurance underwriters told the committee that if frame buildings were permitted within the fire limits, the rates on all buildings would be doubled. To this news there was no rebuttal; the committee voted for the proposed extensions. It soon modified its position somewhat, acceding to requests from owners of planing mills within the new boundaries to make some accommodations permitting them to rebuild structures they could afford.[76]

The major source of opposition to the new fire limits came not from manufacturers but from small homeowners in the area south of Market Street and east of Tenth. Rightly fearing that the new regulations would prevent them from rebuilding, they quickly organized to protest the move. An executive committee called a mass meeting on May 27 for property owners affected by the changes. Many of these people were Irish-Americans, and Catholic priests took prominent parts in the organization, acting as spokesmen for their parishioners. At the rally, the Reverend T. P. Mulligan voiced the widely shared sentiment that extending the fire limits benefited the wealthy and was a blow at the poor. "Better a city of shacks owned by the people," he proclaimed, "than a city of skyscrapers owned by Eastern capitalists. The extension of the fire limits will mean our ruin.... Frame buildings are our safeguard." The protestors decided to call themselves the Property Holders' Protective Association, and agreed to attend the meeting of the Board of Supervisors on the following day. They selected Garrett McEnerney, corporation attorney and a member of the Committee of Forty, to represent them.[77]

In addressing the supervisors, McEnerney spoke for the Archbishop of San Francisco as well as the property owners. He argued that the existing fire limits were already too broad. Many homeowners would be prevented from rebuilding because their lots fell within the existing boundaries. The law said that the limits could not be contracted. Therefore he pleaded for no changes at all, asserting that any extension would amount to a virtual confiscation of the property of small landowners. McEnerney was joined by spokesmen for property owners in two areas north of Market, both of whom made objections similar to his. Father Mulligan and another priest also made pleas, reminding the Union Labor Party supervisors that enlarging the fire limits would be committing an outrage on the people who had elected them.

The supervisors, however, were not moved by the arguments or hisses from the audience, and seemed determined to pass the ordinance as it came to them from the Committee of Forty. But Mayor Schmitz, who arrived late, changed matters around. He told the supervisors:

> I am the appointer of the Committee of Forty and under no circumstances will I criticize or repudiate their acts. However, as I said to the subcommittee, that as the business men had been permitted to erect temporary shacks, the small householders should be permitted to do likewise. I do not think the fire limits should be extended until the small property owners have been given an opportunity to sell their property or rebuild. I would recommend that the fire limits not be extended.

The supervisors followed his lead and voted unanimously to reject the recommendations of a committee on which seven of them had served.[78]

Several months later the *Chronicle* claimed that the small property owners and priests had been an unwitting front for speculators who owned most of the property in the district. These speculators wanted to erect flimsy firetraps with which they could extort high rents from the poor. They had used "the voices of clergymen and other sentimentalists who know little of business and were easily deceived," to pressure the supervisors into a stupid decision. The decision was foolish, the *Chronicle* had maintained, because it meant higher insurance rates and because the reconstruction of frame houses prevented the area from becoming high-grade industrial property on which manufacturing establishments would have been built.[79]

There was more than a little irony involved in the *Chronicle*'s tacit demand that small property owners sacrifice their holdings to a general good, while at the same time leading the campaign against the Burnham plan. The weekly *Argonaut* saw the relationship, if not the irony, when it commented that property owners, rich and poor, had come forward to oppose changes in the street lines and in the fire limits. It would be unjust, the *Argonaut* contended, to prevent the thousands of small property owners south of Market from rebuilding on their lots. At the same time, property owners in the business district north of Market should have some assurance that their buildings would not be destroyed by a conflagration originating in the frame homes.[80]

This was indeed a dilemma, the origins of which lay in the rights of property owners, large and small, against the claims of some diffuse and therefore weak public interest. A solution, if one could be found, would have to respect the rights of property, north and south of Market. The construction of a superior fire-fighting system, with auxiliary mains, 10,000-gallon cisterns, and pumping stations on the bay, provided a partial answer, although the impetus for such a development would have been there no matter how wide the fire limits.

The city government was unable to overcome the particular needs and desires of property owners, and private efforts worked no better. After the fire, a number of wealthy men owning valuable lots on Montgomery Street indicated a desire to have the street widened. Andrew McCreery, millionaire owner of both the northeast and southwest corners of Montgomery and Pine, told the *Chronicle* that he favored broadening Montgomery and was willing to pay his share of the cost. I. W. Hellman informed the directors of the Wells-Fargo Nevada National Bank that only if Montgomery Street were widened about twenty feet by the property owners would he recommend rebuilding the bank on the old site. Hellman's plan called for property owners on the east side of the street to give up twenty feet to the city, ten as a donation, the other ten to be paid for by their neighbors on the west side. But not everyone was so generous. The frame of the Mills Building had survived the fire, and a spokesman for D. O. Mills told the subcommittee on streets that any widening of Montgomery Street would make it too costly to renovate the building.[81]

By August, with the fate of Montgomery Street still undecided, the property owners met to reach a decision, one way or the other, so the rebuilding could commence. The meeting agreed that only existing legal forms could be relied on, meaning that they had little confidence in the Ruef amendment to be voted on in November. Under the Brooman Act, which authorized the city to raise money for street widening, an assessment district had to be created; those property owners who benefited from the changes would be assessed to pay damages to those whose property was confiscated. The owners admitted that a few persons opposed to widening could effectively prevent a change by contesting any condemnation proceedings in the courts. The long delay, during which no construction could take place, would make the project too costly for all.[82]

Despite the calls for immediate action, it was only at the end of October that the issue was resolved. On October 25, the Montgomery Street Property Owners' Association met to vote on the question. Owners of 942 feet of street frontage favored widening; only W. Wilson, who owned 34 feet, opposed. Those in favor included representative of the Union Trust Company, the Wells-Fargo Nevada National Bank, the Italian-American Bank, the Pacific Mutual Life Insurance Company, the Mills Estate, Umbsen and Company Realtors, and other names of note. They were supported by the Merchants' Association. Yet Wilson won the day. The meeting refused even to wait for the vote on the Ruef amendment, nor did it petition the Board of Supervisors to establish an assessment district to appraise damages and benefits.[83] It was voluntary compliance or nothing, and here, as elsewhere, nothing prevailed.

Clearly, the property owners discussed in these examples were armed with legal rights or political influence, and did not have to rely merely on popular support of the desirability of private property. Just as the high value that Europeans placed on restoring locations hallowed by tradition helps to explain their conservative approach to rebuilding, so the value of private ownership and control of real property helps to explain the case of San Francisco. The very limited efforts by the proponents of planning to find some means by which they could get their desired results stemmed in part from their adherence to a set of values that contradicted, and ultimately overwhelmed, their hopes for a refashioned city. I have argued that the city planning movement in San Francisco was largely an effort to build a community of mutually supportive and accommodating citizens out of a disorganized mass. A principal weakness in the logic of this reform was that while planning might create community, only a community already existing would be able to make and abide by a plan. The only other alternative was centralized authority in the manner of Napoleon III, who could enforce decisions without having to be constantly accountable. In Daniel Burnham, San Francisco had found its Haussmann, but Napoleon was another matter altogether. So, without the unity of affection and purpose of the idealized community, without the dictatorial power of an autocrat, San Franciscans settled for the classical liberal and urban version of order, namely the marketplace and the values of private property and individual acquisitiveness and responsibility on which it is based. Given the open and transitory nature of San Francisco society, any other version of order seems either utopian or arbitrary.

Conclusion
Planning and Politics

The Search for Authority

In the three or four years after the earthquake and fire San Francisco was rebuilt. It was a great undertaking in which commonplace deeds of thousands of individuals became awesome when considered in the aggregate. Marsden Manson calculated that from the moment in April 1906, when the fire had extinguished itself, to the end of December 1907, one new structure was erected every 104 minutes, and that for each elapsed minute, $103 was spent on rebuilding.[1] There were occasional complaints that reconstruction was not moving fast enough, but most people considered the work a marvel.[2] This rebuilding, however, was almost wholly the work of people and firms pursuing their own interests.[3] The "broader lines" that had excited so much confident discussion in the days following the disaster were ignored. There was no great influx of eastern capital to finance the construction of a new city.[4] The City Beautiful remained a pious hope at least until 1912, when voters finally authorized bonds for a new civic center.[5] The disaster accelerated San Francisco's decline relative to other cities in the state, especially to its own suburbs.[6]

People on the scene had no difficulty in explaining the triumph of individual initiative over centralized planning. They saw the American system of democracy and free enterprise, which included the right of invididuals to own and dispose of property as they wished, as inimical to any vast and unified undertaking such as

Conclusion: Planning and Politics

comprehensive planning. John Carrère, an architect who had worked with Burnham on the Cleveland plan, made this point shortly after the fire in a letter to Senator Newlands. Carrère commended the senator for suggesting that the municipal government of San Francisco be suspended for a number of years, to be replaced by a "committee of five broad-minded men of executive ability and high integrity." The architect thought that the actual rebuilding should be directed in the same manner, "by a competent commission of, say, five experts acting under the direction of the governing committee but otherwise having full authority to plan, and a veto power which would prevent anything from being done which would not meet with their approval." Otherwise, it would be impossible to coordinate all the necessary aims and activities. The commission should have control over "not only the development of every feature of the burnt area but also of the entire city," to influence for the future what it could not achieve at the moment. For this enterprise, Carrère concluded, the fitting example was the work of Haussmann in Paris, executed under the aegis of Napoleon III.[7]

Carrère's suggestion revealed the central dilemma of planning: to build an imperial city, one needed a hand free from the constraints of petty, short-sighted, and individualistic demands.[8] In place of the emperor, Carrère chose a nonpartisan commission of experts. Others searched for their supreme authority elsewhere. An editorial in the *American Monthly Review of Reviews* urged San Franciscans to seize the opportunity presented by Burnham. It offered E. H. Harriman and the Southern Pacific, aided by other large industrial and transportation interests, as the proper agents for San Francisco's reconstruction. After all, the magazine noted, "it was concentrated imperial authority that made the modern Paris, and the same is true of the modern Vienna. It will take concentrated industrial and corporate power to make the modern San Francisco what it ought to be."[9] Six months later, "Autolycus" bemoaned the lack of a great man in the city. Only Harriman had the magnitude necessary to oversee the rebuilding. "I believe," wrote "Autolycus," "it would pay us to give him the town."[10]

Few San Franciscans were willing to follow this advice. As the *Argonaut* pointed out, the improvements in Paris and Berlin were made under the semi-oligarchic rules of Napoleon III and Bismarck. By contrast, the magazine knew "of no city in a country governed by constitutional methods, such as is ours, where sweeping improvements have been made in city streets and squares." The history of London after 1666 confirmed this fact, and so would the record of San Francisco.[11] The *Argonaut* was right. On the fifth anniversary of the fire, Joseph Redding observed that "there is no city of olden times renowned for the beauty of its public buildings and its scope and landscape plan, but what their design and fulfillment were due to some one individual who was in supreme control." In Athens it had been Pericles, in Rome, Servius Tullius and Aurelian, and in Paris, the inevitable Napoleon III. For almost all American cities, this unitary control was out of the question; it collided too directly with the ideals of representative democracy. Thus the only way for San Francisco to realize its potential beauty was for the leading men, the members of the Down Town Association to whom Redding spoke, to educate the public about the practical benefits to be attained through municipal adornment. Convince the ordinary citizen, Redding stressed, that the influx of visitors will more than pay for the cost of beautification, and the way lies open.[12]

Redding's advice was stale. Phelan had made these points a decade before, and neither Burnham's impressive designs nor the 1906 disaster had been powerful enough to make people overcome their suspicions of city government or alter their individualistic attitudes toward real property. Redding's own audience, composed of property owners in the downtown area, had given sufficient testimony on that account.[13]

The most interesting response to the actual possibilities of planning, as opposed to rhetorical idealizations of it, came from Phelan himself. He had been its foremost advocate, and the person most responsible for bringing Daniel Burnham to San Francisco. Yet when presented with an opportunity for realizing the revised Burnham plan, Phelan hesitated and then drew back. Having never directly concerned himself with the question of enactment, he could not support Abraham Ruef's solution to the problem. It was Ruef who came to personify civic concern in the crucial months from June through November, 1906, while Phelan stood aside and let private interests reassert themselves. But Ruef was hardly the embodiment of the public interest. At the same time that he was pushing his amendment in San Francisco and Sacramento, he was selling out the city to the United Railroads, the Home Telephone Company, and the Bay City Water Company.[14] All the skeptics had been right; to trust Ruef and his supervisors with any more power would have been disastrous.

Ruef's behavior was central to the problem that confronted

Conclusion: Planning and Politics

Phelan, one for which he could find no satisfactory solution. His failure should not be surprising, for the dilemma he faced was perennial, rooted in the very nature of urban social and political life.

It surfaced in San Francisco as a consequence of the city's pattern of growth. Having boomed spectacularly from the discovery of gold until around 1880, its advance since then had been sluggish, especially when contrasted to the progress of other cities on the coast. Though still the regional metropolis in 1900, it faced a genuine challenge for the first time. An affront to local pride, the challenge was also a threat to the city's continued prosperity, since it was difficult to see any middle ground between getting bigger and stagnating. San Francisco's growth depended on its providing an environment that would attract new enterprises and expand existing ones. The beauty of the site made it the natural center for a lucrative tourist trade, but it could only realize the full potential of that trade if it had buildings, parks, and public spaces worthy of its location. Its appeal to prospective residents also depended on its physical charms and on its ability to offer a desirable social environment.

To improve its economic, social, and physical environment, San Francisco needed direction; it needed effective public policy. The conditions of modern urban life had spun webs of interdependencies among those who lived and worked in large cities. Some of these interdependencies were efficiently handled by market transactions between employer and worker, seller and customer, or lender and borrower. There were also the unanticipated and unseen consequences that the actions of individuals might have on persons at some remove from the marketplace exchange. Decisions regarding land use and other environmental questions like pollution were obvious examples. Less apparent but equally important were corporate and labor policies that might precipitate a general strike and affect the entire economy of the city, not merely the wages and hours of the workers involved. In the words of Charles Tilly, "The concentration of people and their activities in big, busy, complicated centers made most people vulnerable to the decisions of many other people, some of them far away. As collective creations, cities impose collective risks and collective responsibilities."[15]

Needs do not automatically find fulfillment. How were these collective responsibilities to be met? The hallmark of a new and bustling city like San Francisco was not homogeneity but diversity. It had grown by attracting and accommodating all sorts of people doing thousands of different things, sharing very little except a desire to succeed in one way or another. How were these individuals to be made to see that they in fact had collective responsibilities? How were they to be brought to agree on what these responsibilities were, and how they should be handled?

Phelan was responding to questions like these, though not to this formulation of them, when he turned to city planning as his solution. On the practical level, the Burnham plan offered a series of proposals intended to create a physical environment that would make San Francisco attractive to businesses, tourists, and residents. It would make the city efficient, beautiful, and therefore prosperous. Its message on these points was clear: beauty pays. Just as important, however, the plan was intended to create an environment that would transform the diverse and frequently divisive urban society of San Francisco into some sort of community in which a common set of values and desires harmonized the previously discordant elements. The plan offered a cultural solution to the question of how collective responsibilities were to be handled; it promised to socialize San Franciscans to agree on what those responsibilities were, and, presumably, on who was to be in charge of dealing with them.

There was a defect in this approach. The plan might indeed have worked over time to create a community of like-minded and affectively tied persons who were convinced that the planners should be entrusted with making important decisions affecting everyone's life. Authority is not much of a threat if everyone agrees on what they want and trusts that those in power know how to get it. The difficulty, of course, was how to get agreement in the absence of a common set of values and desires and without abundant trust in those in power. If the socializing influence of a planned environment was a necessary precondition for the acceptance of planning as a process, then one was caught in a vicious circle with only one way out: power. If people were not to agree voluntarily to abide by the dictates of a plan, then they could be forced to do so by the coercive power of the government.

A coercive approach created its own problems. First, constitutional and legislative prohibitions severely limited the actual coercive power of the city government in San Francisco. The city could seize property under the doctrine of eminent domain, but the procedure was cumbersome and expensive. It was to get around this difficulty that Ruef drafted his amendment and pushed for its adoption. Yet he had little support from the erstwhile advocates of planning. Their

Conclusion: Planning and Politics

reluctance stemmed from a second problem connected with coercive planning, namely that the coercive powers of the city government would be subject to popular, meaning electoral, direction. The community, that is the cultural, approach to planning sought to avoid the political dimensions of the question by assuming a unanimity of values and desires that would have sanctioned authority without politics. But the coercive approach put governmental authority, meaning politics, back in the center of things, where it was bound to threaten the planners. A political contest might put the wrong people into office. If government were granted augmented coercive power over property, what would guarantee that it would use that power correctly? The Union Labor Party gave ample testimony to how even limited power could be used for corrupt purposes. And if the party had actually been the representative of organized labor, rather than the instrument of Ruef's ambitions, then the danger it posed to established interests would have been much more alarming.

Political control of planning was not the only threat, perhaps not even the most important. Planning meant restricting the rights of individuals to use their property as they saw fit. That might be justified if there were widespread agreement that the restrictions would lead to some higher community good. But in the absence of such an agreement—without, in other words, a community already in existence—all these restrictions might do would be to undermine the workings of individual responsibility. In the aftermath of the earthquake and fire, the administrators of relief and rehabilitation feared that a prolonged reliance on public enterprise that supplied food or housing would sap the energies of relief recipients and "pauperize" them. To avoid permanent demoralization, people had to be put back on their feet quickly and made to reassume responsibility for their own welfare. As some San Franciscans saw it, private property rights were an essential ingredient of social stability. To grant the government extensive coercive power over these rights would menace the foundations of a social order built on the interlocking of private wants. "Exchange," as Charles Lindblom has pointed out, "is not merely a method for reshuffling the possession of things, [but] a method of controlling behavior and of organizing cooperation among men."[16] If a temporary operation like relief and rehabilitation could be seen to threaten this order, how frightening the dangers inherent in comprehensive planning of the entire city must have been. So, Phelan may have thought, better to leave the

Burnham plan as an inspiring ideal at which to aim than to try to enact it by a political process that might weaken the very basis of social stability.

There was one final contradiction in Phelan's vision of a new San Francisco. He confused community with empire. He sought to overcome the divisiveness and heterogeneity of a modern city through a unifying affection and interdependence, to transform a society into some kind of community. But the goal of this transformation was prosperity through growth, and growth meant newcomers in abundance, who would inevitably put strains on whatever community might be achieved. It was not San Francisco that swelled in this period, but its rival to the south. And Los Angeles, despite a population drawn from much more homogeneous sources than was San Francisco's, emerged from its era of expansion as a "fragmented metropolis."[17] By contrast, San Francisco remained smaller yet more diverse. Its modernization has been, up to the present, gradual and partial. The city shows its age as well as its youth; its imperial future has never dawned.

Appendix
Tables 1–10

Table 1
Population of West Coast Cities, 1850–1900

	1850	1860	1870	1880	1890	1900
San Francisco	34,776[a]	56,802	149,473	233,959	298,997	342,782
Los Angeles	1,610	4,385	5,728	11,183	50,395	102,479
Oakland	—	1,543	10,500	34,555	48,682	66,960
Sacramento	6,820	13,785	16,283	21,420	26,386	29,282
Portland	821	2,874	8,293	17,577	46,385	90,426
Seattle	—	—	1,107	3,533	42,837	80,671

SOURCE: U.S., Department of Commerce and Labor, Bureau of Statistics, *Statistical Abstract of the United States: 1911* (Washington: Government Printing Office, 1912), pp. 55–56; U.S., Census Office, *Abstract of the Twelfth Census of the United States: 1900* (Washington: Government Printing Office, 1902), p. 101; U.S., Census Office, *Tenth Census of the United States: 1880. Census Reports. 19. Social Statistics of Cities, Pt. 2* (Washington: Government Printing Office, 1887), pp. 769, 789, 829.

[a]The returns for 1850 for San Francisco were destroyed by fire. The figure given is that reported in the California census of 1852.

Table 2
Population of California, Oregon, and Washington, 1860–1900, with Comparisons to San Francisco

	1860	1870	1880	1890	1900
California	379,994	560,247	864,694	1,213,398	1,485,053
S.F. as percent of Cal.	14.9%	26.7%	27.1%	24.6%	23.1%
Oregon	52,465	90,923	174,768	317,704	413,536
Washington	11,594	23,955	75,116	357,232	518,103
Tristate total	444,053	675,125	1,114,578	1,888,334	2,416,692
S.F. as percent of tri-state total	12.8%	22.1%	21.0%	15.8%	14.2%

SOURCE: U.S., Department of Commerce and Labor, Bureau of Statistics, *Statistical Abstract of the United States: 1911* (Washington: Government Printing Office, 1912), pp. 40–42.

Table 3
Manufacturing in San Francisco, California, Oregon, and Washington, 1860–1900

	1860		
	Capital invested (times 1,000)	Number of hands	Value added by manufacture[a] (times 1,000)
San Francisco[b]	$ 2,100	1,549	$ 4,442
California[b]	11,037	6,610	12,344
Oregon	1,337	978	1,546
Washington	1,296	872	905
Tristate total	13,670	8,460	14,795
S.F. as percent of Cal.	19%	23%	36%
S.F. as percent of tristate total	15%	18%	30%

SOURCE: U.S., Census Office, *Eighth Census of the United States: 1860. 3. Manufactures in 1860* (Washington: Government Printing Office, 1865), pp. 29, 36, 492, 673.

[a]Value added by manufacture is derived by substracting cost of raw materials from value of products.

[b]For San Francisco and California, the totals given above are exclusive of gold mining.

Table 3 continued

	1870		
	Capital invested (times 1,000)	Number of hands	Value added by manufacture[a] (times 1,000)
San Francisco	$21,171	12,377	$17,354
California	39,728	25,392	31,244
Oregon	4,377	2,884	3,457
Washington	1,894	1,026	1,416
Tristate total	45,999	29,302	36,117
S.F. as percent of Cal.	53%	49%	56%
S.F. as percent of tristate total	46%	42%	48%

SOURCE: U.S., Census Office, *Ninth Census of the United States: 1870. Census Reports. 3. The Statistics of the Wealth and Industry of the United States* (Washington: Government Printing Office, 1872), pp. 496, 560, 579.

[a]Value added by manufacture is derived by subtracting cost of materials from value of products.

	1880		
	Capital invested (times 1,000)	Number of hands	Value added by manufacture[a] (times 1,000)
San Francisco	$35,368	28,442	$29,846
California	61,244	43,693	43,611
Oregon	6,312	3,473	3,977
Washington	3,202	1,147	1,283
Tristate total	70,758	48,313	48,871
S.F. as percent of Cal.	58%	65%	68%
S.F. as percent of tristate total	50%	59%	61%

SOURCE: U.S., Census Office, *Tenth Census of the United States: 1880. Census Reports. 2. Manufactures* (Washington: Government Printing Office, 1883), pp. 5, 435.

[a]Value added by manufacture is derived by subtracting cost of materials from value of products.

Table 3 continued

	1890		
	Capital invested (times 1,000)	Number of hands	Value added by manufacture[a] (X 1,000)
San Francisco	$ 74,834	41,764	$ 56,969
California	146,797	72,696	93,160
Oregon	32,122	16,760	19,638
Washington	34,370	18,677	21,851
Tristate total	213,289	108,133	134,649
S.F. as percent of Cal.	51%	57%	61%
S.F. as percent of tristate total	35%	39%	42%

SOURCE: U.S., Census Office, *Abstract of the Twelfth Census of the United States: 1900* (Washington: Government Printing Office, 1902), pp. 331, 333, 359.

[a]Value added by manufacture is derived by subtracting cost of materials from value of products.

	1900		
	Capital invested (times 1,000)	Number of hands	Value added by manufacture[a] (times 1,000)
San Francisco	$ 80,103	41,978	$ 53,576
California	205,395	91,047	114,749
Oregon	33,422	17,236	19,893
Washington	52,650	33,806	37,696
Tristate total	291,467	142,089	172,338
S.F. as percent of Cal.	39%	46%	47%
S.F. as percent of tristate total	27%	30%	31%

SOURCE: U.S., Census Office, *Abstract of the Twelfth Census of the United States: 1900* (Washington: Government Printing Office, 1902), pp. 331, 333, 359.

[a]Value added by manufacture is derived by subtracting cost of materials from value of products.

Table 4
Manufacturing in San Francisco, Los Angeles, Oakland, Portland, Seattle, 1870–1900

	1870		
	Capital invested (times 1,000)	Number of hands	Value added by manufacture[a] (times 1,000)
San Francisco	$21,170	12,377	$17,354
Los Angeles (County)	649	621	430
Oakland (Alameda County)	446	648	619
Portland (Multnomah County)	1,574	1,142	1,401
Seattle (Kings County)	110	123	164
	1880		
San Francisco	$35,368	28,442	$29,846
Los Angeles	942	706	657
Oakland	1,371	1,397	1,168
Portland	1,958	1,148	1,300
Seattle	401	174	216
	1890		
San Francisco	$74,834	48,446	$56,969
Los Angeles	6,811	4,957	4,880
Oakland	6,629	4,438	4,425
Portland	16,864	9,731	12,620
Seattle	4,758	4,048	5,425
	1900		
San Francisco	$80,103	41,978	$53,576
Los Angeles	11,743	8,044	10,725
Oakland	6,365	4,012	4,896
Portland	13,332	8,572	10,139
Seattle	10,132	8,480	16,241

SOURCE: U.S., Census Office, *Ninth Census of the United States: 1870. Census Reports. 3. The Statistics of the Wealth and Industry of the United States* (Washington: Government Printing Office, 1872), pp. 496, 560, 579; U.S., Census Office, *Tenth Census of the United States: 1880. Census Reports. 2. Manufactures* (Washington: Government Printing Office, 1883), pp. 91, 92, 165, 186, 380; U.S., Census Office, *Eleventh Census of the United States: 1890. Census Reports. 12. Manufacturing Industries. Pt. 2. Statistics of Cities* (Washington: Government Printing Office, 1895), pp. 304–07, 410–13, 462–65, 530–33, 546–49; U.S., Census Office, *Twelfth Census of the United States: 1900. Census Reports. 8. Manufactures. Pt. 2. States and Territories* (Washington: Government Printing Office), pp. 46–49, 52–53, 738–39, 932–33.

[a]Value added by manufacture is derived from subtracting cost of raw material from value of products.

Table 5
Foreign Trade, San Francisco and Pacific Coast, 1860–1901[a]

A. Merchandise Imports in millions of current dollars

	1860	1865	1870	1875	1880	1885	1890	1895	1900	1901
San Francisco	$7.4	$15.8	$16.0	$24.7	$35.2	$35.0	$48.8	$36.3	$47.9	$35.2
Pacific Coast	7.4	15.9	16.2	25.2	35.7	36.0	51.0	40.3	58.9	48.2
Seattle (Washington)	—	0.012	0.035	0.025	0.0175	0.24	0.31	2.2	7.1	6.7
S.F. as percent of Pacific Coast	100%	99%	99%	98%	99%	97%	96%	90%	81%	73%

B. Merchandise Exports (Domestic and Reexports) in millions of current dollars

	1860	1865	1870	1875	1880	1885	1890	1895	1900	1901
San Francisco	$4.9	$10.0	$14.0	$24.1	$32.4	$38.1	$36.9	$24.9	$40.4	$34.6
Pacific Coast	5.0	10.9	14.6	27.3	38.9	47.9	45.4	36.1	70.2	69.5
Seattle (Washington)	—	0.632	0.428	0.395	0.361	3.2	3.3	5.8	17.9	20.7
S.F. as percent of Pacific Coast	98%	92%	96%	88%	83%	80%	81%	69%	58%	50%

SOURCE: U.S., Department of Commerce, Bureau of Foreign and Domestic Commerce, *Statistical Abstract of the United States: 1923* (Washington: Government Printing Office, 1924), pp. 821, 822, 825.

[a]The customs district of San Francisco probably included other ports on San Francisco Bay. I have not been able to find a list of the ports making up the customs district for these years in the volumes of the *Foreign Commerce and Navigation of the United States*. Years are fiscal years ending June 30.

Table 6
Population of the Commuter District Compared with San Francisco

	1860	1870	1880	1890	1900
San Francisco	56,802	149,473	233,959	298,997	342,782
Commuter district	2,003	23,644	66,870	104,680	150,202
Commuter district as percent of S.F.	3.5%	16%	29%	35%	44%

SOURCE: Bion J. Arnold, *Report on the Improvement and Development of the Transportation Facilities of San Francisco* (San Francisco: Hicks-Judd, 1913), Appendix, Table 2.

Table 7
Foreign Born Population as Percent of Total Population for Far Western Cities, New York, and Boston, 1870–1900

	1870	1880	1890	1900
San Francisco	49.3%	44.6%	42.4%	34.1%
Los Angeles	35.0	28.7	25.3	19.5
Oakland	—	31.9	29.9	25.8
Portland	31.1	35.9	37.4	28.6
Seattle	—	—	31.9	27.3
Denver	23.9	24.4	23.9	18.9
New York	44.5	39.7	42.2	37.0
Boston	35.1	31.6	35.3	35.1

SOURCE: U.S., Department of Commerce and Labor, Bureau of Statistics, *Statistical Abstract of the United States: 1911* (Washington: Government Printing Office, 1912), pp. 66–67.

Table 8
Population Having at least One Foreign Born Parent as Percent of Total Population for Far Western Cities, New York, and Boston, 1890 and 1900

	1890	1900
San Francisco	78.2%	75.2%
Los Angeles	48.1	45.2
Oakland	60.9	61.6
Portland	58.2	57.0
Seattle	52.7	51.4
Denver	45.8	47.2
New York	80.5	76.9
Boston	68.0	72.2

SOURCE: U.S., Census Office, *Eleventh Census of the United States: 1890. Census Reports 1. Population* (Washington: Government Printing Office, 1895), p. 704: U.S., Census Office, *Twelfth Census of the United States: 1900. Census Reports. 1. Population* (Washington: Government Printing Office, 1901), pp. clxxxvii–ix.

Table 9
Largest Immigrant Groups by Country of Origin in San Francisco, 1870–1900

Country of Origin	1870	1880	1890	1900
British America	2,367	3,860	4,371	5,199
France	3,547	4,160	4,663	4,870
Germany	13,602	19,928	26,422	35,194
Ireland	25,864	30,721	30,718	15,963
Italy	1,622	2,491	5,212	7,508
Sweden	780	1,737	3,594	5,248
China	11,703	21,213	24,613	10,762

SOURCE: U.S., Census Office, *Ninth Census of the United States: 1870. Census Reports. 1. Population* (Washington: Government Printing Office, 1872), pp. 386–91; U.S., Census Office, *Tenth Census of the United States: 1880. Census Reports. 1. Population* (Washington: Government Printing Office, 1883), pp. 538–41; U.S., Census Office, *Eleventh Census of the United States: 1890. Census Reports. 1. Population* (Washington: Government Printing Office, 1895), pp. 670–73; U.S., Census Office, *Twelfth Census of the United States: 1900. Census Reports. 1. Population* (Washington, Government Printing Office, 1901), pp. 738–39.

Table 10
Manufacturing in San Francisco, 1899 and 1904

	1899		1904	
	Number	Percent of California	Number	Percent of California
Number of manufacturing establishments	1,748	35%	2,251	33%
Capital invested (× 1,000)	$69,643	40	$100,362	36
Wage earners	32,555	42	38,429	38
Value added by manufacture (× 1,000)	$41,488	45	$61,842	41

SOURCE: U.S. Bureau of the Census, *Manufactures, 1905. Pt. 2. States and Territories* (Washington: Government Printing Office, 1907), p. 63.

Notes

Introduction

1. See especially Lewis Mumford, *Sticks and Stones: A Study of American Architecture and Civilization*, 2nd ed. rev. (New York: Dover Publications, 1955), ch. 6, "The Imperial Facade."
2. Charles Tilly, *An Urban World* (Boston: Little, Brown, 1974), p. 2.

Chapter 1

1. James Bryce, *The American Commonwealth*, 2nd ed. rev., 2 vols. (London and New York: Macmillan, 1891), 2:388. For his 1910 revision of *The American Commonwealth*, Bryce changed the sentence to read: "San Francisco dwarfed the other cities; for in those days Los Angeles had not risen to importance . . . " (*The American Commonwealth*, new ed. rev., 2 vols. [New York: Macmillan, 1913], 2:429).
2. Robert Greenlaugh Albion, *The Rise of New York Port: 1815–1860* (New York: Scribner's, 1939), pp. 392–93; Roger Lotchin, *San Francisco, 1846–1856: From Hamlet to City* (New York: Oxford University Press, 1974), p. 45.
3. John S. Hittell, *A History of the City of San Francisco and Incidentally of the State of California* (San Francisco: A. L. Bancroft, 1878), p. 130.
4. Walton E. Bean, *California: An Interpretative History*, 2nd ed. (New York: McGraw-Hill, 1973), ch. 10. Population figures are on p. 197. The term "warehouse for the diggings" is taken from James E. Vance, Jr., *Geography and Urban Evolution in the San Francisco Bay Area* (Berkeley: Institute of Governmental Studies, University of California, 1964), p. 17. "In-

stant City" is imaginatively defined in Gunther Barth, *Instant Cities: Urbanization and the Rise of San Francisco and Denver* (New York: Oxford University Press, 1975).

5. Beverly Duncan and Stanley Lieberson, *Metropolis and Region in Transition* (Beverly Hills: Sage Publications, 1970); David Ward, *Cities and Immigrants: A Geography of Change in Nineteenth Century America* (New York: Oxford University Press, 1971), pp. 19–46; Allan R. Pred, *Urban Growth and the Circulation of Information: The United States System of Cities, 1790–1840* (Cambridge: Harvard University Press, 1973); Eric E. Lampard, "The Evolving System of Cities in the United States: Urbanization and Economic Development," in Harvey Perloff and Lowden Wingo, Jr., eds., *Issues in Urban Economics* (Baltimore: Johns Hopkins University Press, 1968), pp. 81–139; Charles N. Glaab, "Historical Perspectives on Urban Development Schemes," in Leo F. Schnore, ed., *Social Science and the City: A Survey of Urban Research* (New York: Praeger, 1968), pp. 197–219.

6. Lotchin, *San Francisco*, pp. 44–45, 77; Albion, *The Rise of New York Port*, pp. 354–72; Earl Pomeroy, *The Pacific Slope: A History of California, Oregon, Washington, Idaho, Utah, and Nevada* (New York: Knopf, 1965), pp. 122–23.

7. Hittell, *History of the City of San Francisco*, pp. 241–42.

8. Gunther Barth, "Metropolism and Urban Elites in the Far West," in Frederic Cople Jaher, ed., *The Age of Industrialism in America: Essays in Social Structure and Cultural Values* (New York: Free Press, 1968), pp. 158–87.

9. On migration, see Pomeroy, *Pacific Slope*, p. 42; Bean, *California*, pp. 115–16. For the superiority of San Francisco Bay, see Vance, *Geography and Urban Evolution*, pp. 13–14. I am not concerned here with the question of why the major city on the bay developed at San Francisco (Yerba Buena Cove) rather than some other hamlet. Vance, *Geography*; Hittell, *History of San Francisco*; and Lotchin, *San Francisco*, handle that question well. Lotchin is especially interesting on the importance of the technology of water transportation.

10. Richard C. Wade, *The Urban Frontier: The Rise of Western Cities, 1790–1830* (Cambridge: Harvard University Press, 1959).

11. Duncan and Lieberson, *Metropolis and Region in Transition*, pp. 52–54. The authors consider the largest cities to include all those with populations equal to or greater than New Orleans's; Pomeroy, *Pacific Slope*, p. 122; Vance, *Geography and Urban Evolution*, p. 17; Lotchin, *San Francisco*, chs. 1, 3. Martyn Bowden, "Growth of the Central District in Large Cities," in Leo F. Schnore, ed., *The New Urban History: Quantitative Explorations by American Historians* (Princeton: Princeton University Press, 1975), pp. 75–109, discusses the early appearance of specialized districts for these commercial functions, and contrasts the speed with which these functions sorted themselves out in San Francisco to the more gradual evolution of districts in London and Atlantic Coast cities.

12. Bean, *California*, p. 122; Lotchin, *San Francisco*, pp. 79–82; Gerald D. Nash, "Stages of California's Economic Growth, 1870–1970: An Interpretation," *California Historical Quarterly* 51 (Winter 1972): 318–19.

13. Wilbur R. Thompson, *A Preface to Urban Economics* (Baltimore: Johns Hopkins University Press, 1965), p. 14.

14. Pomeroy, *Pacific Slope*, pp. 86–89; Lotchin, *San Francisco*, pp. 347–49. The *New York Tribune* listed American millionaires as of 1892; it included 192 Californians of which 156, or 81 percent, lived in San Francisco. The list referred to estates as well as individuals. The *New York World Almanac and Encyclopedia 1902* also printed an "American Millionaires" list; of 110 Californians, 99, or 90 percent, lived in San Francisco. See Sidney Ratner, ed., *New Light on the History of Great American Fortunes: American Millionaires of 1892 and 1902* (New York: Augustus M. Kelley, 1953).

15. The term *circular and cumulative process* is from Gunnar Myrdal. It is quoted by Allan R. Pred in *The Spatial Dynamics of United States Urban-Industrial Growth, 1880–1914: Interpretative and Theoretical Essays* (Cambridge: M.I.T. Press, 1966), pp. 25–26.

16. James E. Vance, Jr., *The Merchant's World: The Geography of Wholesaling* (Englewood Cliffs, N.J.: Prentice-Hall, 1970), p. 149; Pred, *Urban Growth*, p. 202.

17. Vance, *Merchant's World*, pp. 92–93; U.S., Census Office, *Twelfth Census of the United States: 1900. Special Reports. Occupations at the Twelfth Census* (Washington: Government Printing Office, 1904), pp. 590, 686, 720.

18. Blake McKelvey, *The Urbanization of America, 1860–1915* (New Brunswick: Rutgers University Press, 1963), p. 45; Ward, *Cities and Immigrants*, pp. 39–44; Duncan and Lieberson, *Metropolis and Region in Transition*, ch. 4; Pred, *Spatial Dynamics*, pp. 16–18; Harvey S. Perloff, et al., *Regions, Resources and Economic Growth* (Baltimore: Johns Hopkins University Press, 1960), pp. 183, 157, 182; Pomeroy, *Pacific Slope*, pp. 113–15, 187.

19. Pred, *Spatial Dynamics*, ch. 2; Thompson, *Preface to Urban Economics*, pp. 21, 24.

20. Pred, *Spatial Dynamics*, pp. 72–73.

21. Alexander Saxton, *The Indispensable Enemy: Labor and the Anti-Chinese Movement in California* (Berkeley and Los Angeles: University of California Press, 1971), pp. 3–7, 171.

22. The "industrial profile" is taken from Duncan and Lieberson, *Metropolis and Region in Transition*, ch. 5. They use occupational data for 1900, and couple San Francisco with New Orleans as the only major cities in which "the sole manufacturing speciality was a direct outgrowth of the center's role as a regional metropolis" (pp. 85–86). Vance, *Geography and Urban Evolution*, pp. 26–27, discusses the importance of mining equipment and agricultural machinery. I investigated manufacturing in San Francisco in the *Census of Manufactures* for 1905, which used data collected for the year 1904. Using an index that summed the rank order of industries in numbers of persons employed, capital invested, and value added by manufacture, I found the eight largest industries to be: (1) Printing and publishing; (2) Foundry and machine shop products; (3) Canning and preserving; copper, tin, and sheet metal products; liquors, malt (all tied); (6) Clothing, men's; bread and bakery products (tied); (8) Lumber and timber products. U.S., Bureau of the Census, *Manufactures, 1905. Part II. States and Territories* (Washington: Government Printing Office, 1907), pp. 74–79.

23. Pomeroy, *Pacific Slope*, ch. 4–5; Charles N. Glaab and A. Theodore Brown, *A History of Urban America* (New York: Macmillan, 1967), pp. 121–23.

24. Brian J. L. Berry, "City Size and Economic Development,"

Economic Development and Cultural Change 9 (July 1961): 573–88.

25. Thompson, *Preface to Urban Economics*, pp. 39–43.

26. William Baumol, "Macroeconomics of Unbalanced Growth: The Anatomy of Urban Crisis," *American Economic Review* 57 (June 1967): 415–26.

27. Richard Meier, *A Communications Theory of Urban Growth* (Cambridge: M.I.T. Press, 1962), p. 36.

28. Kenneth T. Jackson, "Metropolitan Government Versus Political Autonomy: Politics on the Crabgrass Frontier," in Kenneth T. Jackson and Stanley K. Schultz, eds., *Cities in American History*, (New York: Knopf, 1972), pp. 442–62.

29. Mel Scott, *The San Francisco Bay Area: A Metropolis in Perspective* (Berkeley and Los Angeles: University of California Press, 1959), p. 43.

30. Barth, "Metropolism and Urban Elites," p. 164. Thompson, *Preface to Urban Economics*, pp. 56–57, has some interesting remarks about urban land and especially about hills.

31. Scott, *San Francisco Bay Area*, p. 63.

32. Glaab and Brown, *History of Urban America*, pp. 150–52; Vance, *Geography and Urban Evolution*, pp. 48–54.

33. Pred, *Spatial Dynamics*, pp. 55–56; Ward, *Cities and Immigrants*, ch. 3; Sam Bass Warner, Jr., *Streetcar Suburbs: The Process of Growth in Boston, 1870–1900* (Cambridge: Harvard University Press and M.I.T. Press, 1962).

34. Vance, *Geography and Urban Evolution*, pp. 8, 55; Scott, *San Francisco Bay Area*, pp. 84–85.

35. See Appendix, Table 6.

36. Scott, *San Francisco Bay Area*, pp. 85, 167; Bion J. Arnold, *Report on the Improvement and Development of the Transportation Facilities of San Francisco* (San Francisco: Hicks-Judd, 1913), pp. 3–5; *Merchants' Association Review* 10 (December 1905): 4; San Francisco, Transportation Technical Committee, *History of Public Transit in San Francisco, 1850–1948* (San Francisco, 1948), p. 32; Walton Bean, *Boss Ruef's San Francisco: The Story of the Union Labor Party, Big Business, and the Graft Prosecution* (Berkeley and Los Angeles: University of California Press, 1952), pp. 112–13.

37. Lucile Eaves, *A History of California Labor Legislation* (Berkeley: The University Press, 1910), p. 6, as quoted in Robert K. L. Knight, *Industrial Relations in the San Francisco Bay Area, 1900–1918* (Berkeley and Los Angeles: University of California Press, 1960), p. 4.

38. Pomeroy, *Pacific Slope*, pp. 179–81; Grace Heilman Stimson, *Rise of the Labor Movement in Los Angeles* (Berkeley and Los Angeles: University of California Press, 1955); Knight, *Industrial Relations*, ch. 1.

39. Thompson, *Preface to Urban Economics*, pp. 25–26.

40. Alfred D. Chandler, Jr., "The Beginnings of 'Big Business' in American Industry," *Business History Review* 33 (Spring 1959): 1–31.

41. Bryce, *The American Commonwealth*, 1: 606–8; Thomas C. Cochran, "The Paradox of American Economic Growth," *Journal of American History* 71 (March 1975): 935.

42. Fred I. Greenstein, "The Changing Pattern of Urban Party Politics," *Annals of the American Academy of Political and Social Science* 353 (May 1964): 7. See also Bruce M. Stave, ed., *Urban Bosses, Machines, and Progressive*

Reformers (Lexington: D.C. Heath, 1972); Blaine A. Brownell and Warren E. Stickel, eds., *Bosses and Reformers: Urban Politics in America, 1880–1920* (Boston: Houghton Mifflin, 1973); Alexander B. Callow, Jr., ed., *The City Boss in America: An Interpretative Reader* (New York: Oxford University Press, 1976).

    43. Frank Mann Stewart, *A Half Century of Municipal Reform: The History of the National Municipal League* (Berkeley and Los Angeles: University of California Press, 1950); James Weinstein, "Organized Business and the City Commission and Manager Movement," *Journal of Southern History* 28 (May 1962): 166–82; Samuel P. Hays, "The Politics of Reform in Municipal Government in the Progressive Era," *Pacific Northwest Quarterly* 55 (October 1964): 157–69; Robert Wiebe, *The Search for Order: 1877–1920* (New York: Hill and Wang, 1967); John D. Buenker, *Urban Liberalism and Progressive Reform* (New York: Scribners, 1973), ch. 1.

    44. Alexander Callow, Jr., "San Francisco's Blind Boss," *Pacific Historical Review* 25 (August 1956): 261–62.

    45. Ibid., 261–79. On Buckley's methods and those of his opponents, see William A. Bullough, "Hannibal Versus the Blind Boss: The 'Junta,' Chris Buckley, and the Democratic Reform Politics in San Francisco," *Pacific Historical Review* 46 (May 1977): 181–206.

    46. U.S., Census Office, *Twelfth Census of the United States, 1900. Reports 1. Population. Part I* (Washington: United States Census Office, 1902), p. 710. For detailed population figures, see Appendix, Tables 7–9.

    47. David Shannon, ed., *Beatrice Webb's American Diary: 1898* (Madison: University of Wisconsin Press, 1963), p. 141.

    48. San Francisco Chamber of Commerce, *Fifty-fifth Annual Report of the Chamber of Commerce of San Francisco* (San Francisco, 1905), p. 46. See also the *Annual Reports* from 1899 to 1907 for additional evidence of the Chamber's promotional efforts.

    49. No effort will be made here to review the literature on progressivism, other than to indicate a debt to the great suggestiveness of Robert Wiebe's *The Search for Order*.

Chapter 2

    1. Robert E. L. Knight, *Industrial Relations in the San Francisco Bay Area, 1900–1918* (Berkeley and Los Angeles: University of California Press, 1960), ch. 1.

    2. Ibid., p. 36; Thomas Walker Page, "The San Francisco Labor Movement in 1901," *Political Science Quarterly* 17 (December 1902): 664.

    3. William Magee, "San Francisco's Future," *Sunset Magazine* 17 (September 1906): 238; *San Francisco Bulletin*, January 7, February 2, April 14, 1906; *San Francisco Real Estate Circular* 40 (April-June 1906).

    4. See Appendix, Table 10.

    5. U.S., Bureau of the Census, *Manufactures, 1905. Part II, States and Territories* (Washington: Government Printing Office, 1907), p. 63; Bion J. Arnold, *Report on the Improvement and Development of the Transportation Facilities of San Francisco* (San Francisco: Hicks-Judd, 1913), Table 4.

    6. John P. Young, *San Francisco: A History of the Pacific Coast Metropolis*, 2 vols. (San Francisco: S. J. Clarke, [1912]), 2:740.

    7. Ibid., p. 687.

8. Knight, *Industrial Relations*, pp. 97, 41–43.
9. Frederick Lynne Ryan, "Industrial Relations in the San Francisco Building Trades" (Ph.D. diss., University of California, Berkeley, 1930), pp. 37–43.
10. Ibid., ch. 3; Knight, *Industrial Relations*, pp. 34, 37.
11. Ryan, "Industrial Relations," pp. 184–85; Knight, *Industrial Relations*, pp. 55–56, 122.
12. Bernard Cornelius Cronin, *Father Yorke and the Labor Movement in San Francisco, 1900–1912* (Washington: Catholic University of America Press, 1943), pp. 40–41.
13. Knight, *Industrial Relations*, p. 130.
14. Page, "Labor Movement," p. 666; Knight, *Industrial Relations*, pp. 107, 109, 122. See also Marc Karson, *American Labor Unions and Politics, 1900–1918* (Carbondale: Southern Illinois University Press, 1958), ch. 9.
15. Knight, *Industrial Relations*, p. 133.
16. Ibid., pp. 124, 131.
17. "Annual Report of the President, December 14, 1904," in Commonwealth Club of California, *Transactions* 1 (January 2, 1905): 2.
18. Commonwealth Club, *Transactions* 1 (April 1, 1905): 1–15, 22–24, 26–31.
19. Walter Macarthur, "San Francisco: A Climax in Civics" typewritten manuscript, ca. 1906, Bancroft Library, University of California, Berkeley, pp. 4–7; Knight, *Industrial Relations*, pp. 28–29, 32.
20. Knight, *Industrial Relations*, pp. 62–71; Page, "Labor Movement," pp. 670–72.
21. Page, "Labor Movement," pp. 668–69; Knight, *Industrial Relations*, pp. 66–67.
22. Page, "Labor Movement," pp. 674–75.
23. Ibid., pp. 677–87; Knight, *Industrial Relations*, pp. 72–86.
24. Knight, *Industrial Relations*, pp. 88, 101.
25. Ibid., ch. 4.
26. Ibid., pp. 84–85; Walton Bean, *Boss Ruef's San Francisco: The Story of the Union Labor Party, Big Business, and the Graft Prosecution* (Berkeley and Los Angeles: University of California Press, 1952), p. 23.
27. For Ruef's early years, see Bean, *Boss Ruef's San Francisco*, ch. 1; for a brief biography see Walton Bean, "Ruef, Abraham," in Robert Livingston Schuyler, ed., *Dictionary of American Biography*, vol. 22 (New York: Scribner, 1958), 587–88.
28. Abraham Ruef, "The Road I Traveled. An Autobiographical Account of My Career from University to Prison. With an Intimate Recital of the Corrupt Alliance Between Big Business and Politics in San Francisco" (*San Francisco Bulletin*, April 6 and May 21–September 5, 1912), June 25, 1912. Hereafter cited as Ruef, *Bulletin*, date.
29. Ibid., June 26–27, 1912.
30. Ibid., June 28, 1912.
31. Ibid.; Bean, *Boss Ruef's San Francisco*, ch. 1.
32. Bean, *Boss Ruef's San Francisco*, p. 18; Knight, *Industrial Relations*, p. 93.
33. Ruef, *Bulletin*, June 29, 1912.
34. Ibid., July 1, 1912.

Notes

35. Ibid.; Bean, *Boss Ruef's San Francisco*, pp. 19–20; Macarthur, "Climax in Civics," pp. 14–16.

36. *San Francisco Chronicle*, November 7, 1901; Ruef, *Bulletin*, July 1, 1912; Bean, *Boss Ruef's San Francisco*, ch. 2.

37. Eugene E. Schmitz, "The San Francisco Elections," *Independent* 53 (December 5, 1901): 2867.

38. Ruef, *Bulletin*, July 2, 1912.

39. Cronin, *Father Yorke*, p. 137; Knight, *Industrial Relations*, pp. 119–20; Bean, *Boss Ruef's San Francisco*, pp. 108–10; Ruef, *Bulletin*, July 5, 1912.

40. Ruef, *Bulletin*, July 5, 1912; Bean, *Boss Ruef San Francisco*, p. 110.

41. Ruef, *Bulletin*, July 5, 1912.

42. Knight, *Industrial Relations*, p. 121.

43. Ruef, *Bulletin*, July 10, 1912.

44. Ibid., July 6, 1912; Bean, *Boss Ruef's San Francisco*, pp. 29–30, 113–14.

45. Ruef, *Bulletin*, July 17, 1912; Bean, *Boss Ruef's San Francisco*, pp. 38–39. Schmitz won 26,016 votes compared to 19,621 for Crocker and 12,578 for Lane. *Chronicle*, November 5, 1903; San Francisco. Board of Supervisors, *San Francisco Municipal Reports 1903–4* (San Francisco, 1905), pp. 232–33.

46. Ruef, *Bulletin*, July 3, 1912.

47. Blake McKelvey, *The Urbanization of America, 1860–1915* (New Brunswick: Rutgers University Press, 1963), pp. 109, 113; Charles N. Glaab and A. Theodore Brown, *A History of Urban America* (New York: Macmillan, 1967), pp. 213–15.

48. Ruef, *Bulletin*, July 8, 1912.

49. San Francisco, Auditor's Office, *Statement Showing Taxation and Bonded Debts of the City and County of San Francisco, compiled by the direction of the Auditor, S. W. Horton* (San Francisco [1906]).

50. *Chronicle*, October 12, 15, 1904; *Bulletin*, October 14, 1904.

51. Ruef, *Bulletin*, July 8. 1912.

52. Ibid.; Edward Joseph Rowell, "The Union Labor Party of San Francisco, 1901–1911," (Ph.D. diss., University of California, Berkeley, 1938), p. 119.

53. Knight, *Industrial Relations*, p. 162.

54. Ruef, *Bulletin*, July 22, 23, 1912; Bean, *Boss Ruef's San Francisco*, p. 60; Rowell, "Union Labor Party," pp. 90–93.

55. Ruef, *Bulletin*, July 22, 23, 1912.

56. Macarthur, "Climax in Civics," p. 27.

57. Bean, *Boss Ruef's San Francisco*, chs. 4–5.

58. Macarthur, "Climax in Civics," p. 27; Bean, *Boss Ruef's San Francisco*, p. 68; George Mowry, *The California Progressives* (Berkeley and Los Angeles: University of California Press, 1951), p. 32.

59. Macarthur, "Climax in Civics," p. 30; Ruef, *Bulletin*, July 22, 1912; Knight, *Industrial Relations*, p. 140.

60. *Town Talk*, November 11, 1905, p. 16. See also Macarthur, "Climax in Civics," p. 2.

61. *Chronicle*, November 5, 1903, November 8, 1905.

62. Ruef, *Bulletin*, July 24–29, 1912; Bean, *Boss Ruef's San Francisco*, ch. 7.

63. *Town Talk*, January 13, 1906, p. 9.
64. Bean, *Boss Ruef's San Francisco*, pp. 84–85.
65. "Autolycus," *Stockton Evening Mail*, June 9, 1906. "Autolycus" was the pseudonym of an extremely knowledgeable and perceptive San Franciscan who wrote a weekly letter on San Francisco affairs for the *Stockton Evening Mail*. I have not been able to identify him. Hereafter citations to him will read "Autolycus," *Evening Mail*, date of paper.
66. *Town Talk*, November 11, 1905, p. 16.
67. Ruef, *Bulletin*, July 30, 1912; Bean, *Boss Ruef's San Francisco*, pp. 83–85.
68. Ruef, *Bulletin*, July 31–August 28, 1912; Bean, *Boss Ruef's San Francisco*, chs. 7–8, 11.
69. James D. Phelan, speech at a banquet of the Merchants' Association, November, 1904, quoted in *Merchants' Association Review* 9 (December 1904): 6.
70. See Bean, *Boss Ruef's San Francisco*, ch. 4, for details of the French restaurant extortion, and the "municipal crib."
71. This picture of bosses and machines is drawn from Robert K. Merton, *Social Theory and Social Structure*, rev. and enl. ed. (Glencoe: Free Press, 1957), "Manifest and Latent Functions," especially pp. 70–82. James P. Walsh, "Abe Ruef Was No Boss: Machine Politics, Reform and San Francisco," *California Historical Quarterly* 51 (Spring 1972): 3–16, argues that Ruef did not fit the accepted definition of a boss. I disagree.
72. Knight, *Industrial Relations*, pp. 144, 172; Rowell, "Union Labor Party," p. 127.
73. Knight, *Industrial Relations*, pp. 145, 151, 374.
74. *Bulletin*, July 24, 1906; Bean, *Boss Ruef's San Francisco*, pp. 128–30.
75. "Autolycus," *Evening Mail*, July 21, 1906.

Chapter 3

1. For details about the elder Phelan's downtown property, see Martyn John Bowden, "The Dynamics of City Growth: An Historical Geography of the San Francisco Central District, 1850–1931," 2 vols. (Ph.D. diss., University of California, Berkeley, 1967), 1:375–76.
2. "Biography of James Phelan," galley proof, Bancroft Library, University of California, Berkeley.
3. There are several biographical sketches of Phelan in typescript in the James D. Phelan Papers, Bancroft Library. I assume they were written by Phelan, or at his direction, for various biographical directories. The information used here is compiled from them.
4. Ibid.; Roy Swanstrom, "Reform Administration of James D. Phelan, Mayor of San Francisco, 1897–1902" (Master's thesis, University of California, Berkeley, 1949), p. 74.
5. The charter he spoke about was not the one adopted during his administration, but it had some of the same provisions.
6. James D. Phelan, "Municipal Conditions and the New Charter," *Overland Monthly*, 2d. ser. 17 (July 1896): 104–11.
7. James D. Phelan, *The New San Francisco* (Address delivered Sep-

Notes

tember 1, 1896, at the opening of the Mechanics Institute Fair, [San Francisco, 1896]), p. 5.

8. Ibid., p. 6.

9. See, for example, the promotional booklet *San Francisco: The Imperial City* (San Francisco: Mercantile Illustrating Co., 1899), which predicted that the city would dominate the trade of the Pacific, (p. 20), and the *Annual Reports of the Chamber of Commerce of San Francisco* referred to in ch. 1, note 48, above.

10. Phelan, *The New San Francisco*, p. 12.

11. Ibid., pp. 8, 12.

12. Ibid., p. 13.

13. George H. Fitch, "San Francisco's Mayor," *Harper's Weekly* 64 (December 30, 1899): 1333.

14. James D. Phelan, "Municipal Conditions and the New Charter," pp. 109–12; Walter Macarthur, "San Francisco: A Climax in Civics," typewritten manuscript, ca. 1906, Bancroft Library, pp. 31–33; William Issel, "Class and Ethnic Conflict in San Francisco Political History: The Reform Charter of 1898," *Labor History* 18 (Summer 1977), pp. 341–59; San Francisco. Board of Supervisors, *Charter of the City and County of San Francisco in effect January 8, 1900* (San Francisco: Bender-Chaquette, 1907); Kendric Charles Babcock, "San Francisco: The Charter of 1900," *Annals of the American Academy of Political and Social Science* 19 (January 1902): 151; "Acquisition of Municipal Monopolies under the new San Francisco Charter," *Municipal Affairs* 3 (June 1899): 362.

15. Swanstrom, "Reform Administration of James D. Phelan," p. 74.

16. James D. Phelan, *Addresses* (San Francisco: Cubery, 1902). pp. 39–43.

17. See note 3 above. This information is included in the typescript dated February, 1925, p. 3, and in another without date, p. 9; James D. Phelan, "The Growth of Municipal Art in California," *For California* (June 1904), in Phelan Papers, Scrapbook No. 17.

18. [James D. Phelan], *The Mayor's Message to the Board of Supervisors, of the City and County of San Francisco, 1897, 1899, 1900* (n.p., n.d.), "Message of January 3, 1899," p. 11; James D. Phelan, as quoted in Fitch, "San Francisco's Mayor," p. 1333; typescript biography, 1925, p. 3, Phelan Papers.

19. James D. Phelan, "Valedictory to the Board of Supervisors, January, 1902," in Phelan, *Addresses*, p. 76; [Phelan], *Mayor's Message*, "Message of January 3, 1899," p. 10.

20. "Democratic Municipal Platform," in [Phelan], *Mayor's Message*, p. 31.

21. Ibid., "Message of January 4, 1897," p. 7; "Message of January 3, 1899," p. 5.

22. A. J. Cleary, "The Municipal Engineering Works of San Francisco," *Engineering News* 73 (February 18, 1915): 305; Oscar Lewis, *The History of San Francisco* (Chicago: S. J. Clarke, 1931), p. 391.

23. J. H. Stallard, "The Municipal Government of San Francisco," *Overland Monthly*, 2nd. ser. 19 (March 1897): 287–88; Philip King Brown, M.D., in Commonwealth Club of California, *Transactions* 1 (May 1905): 1–5.

24. Harold Kirker, *California's Architectural Frontier: Style and Tradition*

in the Nineteenth Century (San Marino, California: Huntington Library, 1960), p. 97; John P. Young, *San Francisco: A History of the Pacific Coast Metropolis*, 2 vols. (San Francisco: S. J. Clarke, [1912]), 2:572.

25. Lamberta Margaretta Voget, "The Waterfront of San Francisco, 1863–1930: A History of its Administration by the State of California" (Ph.D. diss., University of California, Berkeley, 1943), pp. 20–21. The state assumed control largely because of the corruption of city officials and the rapacity of private interests and because of the need to build a seawall which local resources were insufficient to do.

26. John F. Quinn, in Commonwealth Club of California, *Transactions* 1 (January 1906): 13–14; *Argonaut*, November 24, 1906, p. 249.

27. Young, *San Francisco*, 2:709, 712; Swanstrom, "Reform Administration of James D. Phelan," pp. 13–14, 77; Lewis, *The History of San Francisco*, p. 391.

28. [Phelan], *Mayor's Message*, "Message of January 8, 1900," p. 9. The "dollar limit" was written into the new charter. Construction projects, however, like school buildings and sewers, could be financed by bonds, not current taxes; successful operation of revenue-producing utilities could be self-supporting.

29. Ibid., "Message of January 4, 1897," p. 7; Phelan, "Municipal Conditions and the New Charter," p. 112.

30. Fitch, "San Francisco's Mayor," p. 1333; Phelan, "Municipal Art in California."

31. B. J. S. Cahill, "The Bond Issue and the Burnham Plan—A Study in 'Panhandling,' " *Architect and Engineer* 7 (June 1909): 65–72, implies but never explicitly states that Phelan pushed his route for the Panhandle because he would personally profit from it. My research into the block books for the area did not disclose any property in the immediate vicinity of the proposed route owned by either Phelan or his sister and brother-in-law, Alice and Frank Sullivan.

32. *Town Talk*, March 31, 1906, p. 18.

33. James D. Phelan, Speech at the banquet of the Merchants' Association, November, 1904, in *Merchant's Association Review* 9 (December 1904): 6.

34. See the quotation from the "Democratic Municipal Platform," in [Phelan], *Mayor's Message*, "Message of January 3, 1899," p. 31, which begins "When a city realizes that its future is secure. . . . "

35. John W. Reps, *The Making of Urban America: A History of City Planning in the United States* (Princeton: Princeton University Press, 1965), pp. 496–501; Mel Scott, *American City Planning Since 1890* (Berkeley and Los Angeles: University of California Press, 1969), pp. 31–37. See also Montgomery Schuyler, "Last Words About the World's Fair," *Architectural Record* 3 (January-March 1894): 271–301, reprinted in Schuyler, *American Architecture and Other Writings*, ed. William H. Jordy and Ralph Coe, abr. William H. Jordy (New York: Antheneum, 1964), pp. 275–93, which stresses "unity," "magnitude," and "illusion" as the three components of the fair's success.

36. Both quotes are in Reps, *Making of Urban America*, pp. 497–98.

37. Frederick L. Ford, "City Making," *Chautauquan* 47 (June 1907): 66.

38. John Burchard and Albert Bush-Brown, *The Architecture of America:*

A Social and Cultural History (Boston: Little, Brown, 1961), pp. 275–76; Charles Mulford Robinson, "New Dreams for Cities," *Architectural Record* 17 (May 1905): 413–14.

39. George Kriehn, "The City Beautiful," *Municipal Affairs* 3 (1899): 595–97; Charles Mulford Robinson, "Making the City Beautiful," *Current Literature* 31 (August 1901): 139–43; Andrew Crawford Wright, "Recent Park Development," *Chautauquan* 47 (June 1907): 31–41. See also Roy Lubove, *The Urban Community: Housing and Planning in the Progressive Era* (Englewood Cliffs, N.J.: Prentice-Hall, 1967), pp. 1–13, for the connection between nature and the city as seen by these early planners.

40. Burchard and Bush-Brown, *Architecture of America*, p. 276; Christopher Tunnard and Henry Hope Reed, *American Skyline* (New York: New American Library, 1956), pp. 139–41; Jane Jacobs, *The Death and Life of Great American Cities* (New York: Random House, 1961), p. 24.

41. Kriehn, "The City Beautiful," pp. 594–99; Clinton Rogers Woodruff, "Value of Beauty as a Municipal Asset Is Proving A Factor in the Advance of Civic Art," *Craftsman* 9 (1905–06): 540; Charles H. Caffin, "The Beautifying of Cities," *World's Work* 3 (November 1901): 1430.

42. Blake McKelvey, *The Urbanization of America, 1860–1915* (New Brunswick: Rutgers University Press, 1963), chs. 7–8.

43. Burchard and Bush-Brown, *Architecture in America*, p. 275; Lubove, *The Urban Community*, p. 2.

44. Herbert Croly, " 'Civic Improvements,' The Case of New York," *Architectural Record* 21 (May 1907): 352.

45. Woodruff, "Value of Beauty," p. 541; Caffin, "The Beautifying of Cities," pp. 1429–35.

46. Clinton Rogers Woodruff, "The National Impulse for Civic Improvement," *Chautauquan* 47 (June 1907): 28; also Lubovz, *Urban Community*, p. 10.

47. Kriehn, "The City Beautiful," p. 598; Woodruff, "National Impulse," pp. 28–30.

48. Frederick M. Mann, "Architecture and Civic Progress," *Chautauquan* 47 (June 1907): 74–80.

49. Robinson, "Making the City Beautiful," p. 139.

50. Quoted in Tunnard and Reed, *American Skyline*, p. 153. The words themselves have been attributed by Burnham's son to Willis Polk, Burnham's associate in San Francisco. See Henry H. Saylor, " 'Make No Little Plan,' Daniel Burnham Thought It But Did He Say It?" *Journal of the American Institute of Architects* 27 (1957): 95–99. Certainly the sentiment was Burnham's.

51. Croly, " 'Civic Improvements,' " p. 347; Charles Mulford Robinson, " 'Civic Improvements,' A Reply," *Architectural Record* 22 (July 1907): 118.

52. Kriehn, "The City Beautiful," pp. 599–600.

53. Louis Sullivan, *Autobiography of an Idea* (New York: Dover Publications, 1956), p. 323.

54. Patrick Geddes, *Cities in Evolution* (London: Williams & Norgate, 1915), p. 254.

55. Lewis Mumford, *Sticks and Stones: A Study of American Architecture*

(New York: Dover Publications, 1955), ch. 6. Thomas S. Hines borrowed Mumford's title for his article, "The Imperial Facade: Daniel H. Burnham and American Architectural Planning in the Philippines," *Pacific Historical Review* 41 (February 1972): 33–53.

56. Burchard and Bush-Brown, *Architecture of America*, p. 273. Others to see the building and planning aesthetic as "imperial" include Scott, *American City Planning*, p. 36, and Michael T. Klare, "The Architecture of Imperial America," *Science and Society* 33 (Summer-Fall 1969): 257–84. Robert Goodman, *After the Planners* (New York: Simon and Schuster, 1971), makes similar points and then lumps the architecture of the Third Reich and current American architectural and planning tastes in a category called "The Architecture of Repression," pp. 92–116. I think some of Goodman's judgments are silly, but I agree with him on recognizing the importance of the intended awesomeness of these designs.

57. Lewis Mumford, *The City in History* (New York: Harcourt, Brace & World, 1961), p. 152.

58. Quoted from the *Journal of William Loughton Smith*, in Reps, *Making of Urban America*, p. 248. Smith was a visitor to the site for the federal city and talked there with L'Enfant. Reps also notes that L'Enfant's background and training had been in Versailles and Paris, where he was influenced by baroque design (p. 252).

Chapter 4

1. The best treatment of Burnham's career is by Thomas S. Hines, *Burnham of Chicago: Architect and Planner* (New York: Oxford University Press, 1974).

2. *San Francisco Bulletin*, January 4, 1904. Local news was usually carried on an interior page in this newspaper.

3. Ibid., January 7, 1904. See also Mel Scott, *The San Francisco Bay Area: A Metropolis in Perspective* (Berkeley and Los Angeles: University of California Press, 1959), pp. 97–98. I am indebted to Scott for this reference to the *Bulletin* articles although I disagree with him on their meaning.

4. *Bulletin*, January 8, 1904.

5. Ibid., January 9, 1904.

6. *San Francisco Call*, January 13, 1904; *Bulletin*, January 14, 1904.

7. *San Francisco Chronicle*, January 16, 1904.

8. Burnham to Phelan, May 11, 1903, Burnham Papers, Burnham Library of Architecture, The Art Institute of Chicago. There was a previous telegram to Phelan on May 9, 1903, in which Burnham promised Phelan a response after he, Burnham, had seen his San Francisco associate Willis Polk. The Burnham-Phelan correspondence must be reconstituted from Burnham's papers alone, as Phelan's were lost in the 1906 fire.

9. Burnham to Willis Polk, October 20, 1903; Burnham to Polk, November 12, 1903, Burnham Papers. Hines, *Burnham of Chicago*, pp. 177–78, has a slightly different chronology for this interchange between Burnham, Phelan, and Polk. Still, it is clear that Phelan had contacted Burnham a number of months before the inception of the AIASF.

10. The list of founding members is in Daniel Hudson Burnham, assisted by Edward H. Bennett, *Report on a Plan for San Francisco* (San

Francisco: City of San Francisco, 1905), p. 7. The rest of the paragraph is based on information in city directories for the years 1875, 1880, 1885, 1890, 1895, 1897, 1900, 1904, *Langley's San Francisco Directory for the Year Commencing 1875–1897* (San Francisco: J. B. Painter, 1875–1897). In 1900, it became Crocker-Langley's *San Francisco Directory* (San Francisco: H. S. Crocker, 1900). For Hopkins's relation to Burnham, see Burnham to E. W. Hopkins, March 1, 1902, Burnham Papers.

11. AIASF, untitled printed bulletin, c. 1904; Board of Directors, AIASF, untitled mimeograph notice, 1904; both in Phelan Papers, Scrapbook No. 17, Bancroft Library, University of California, Berkeley.

12. *Call*, May 4, 5, 1904; *Bulletin*, May 5, 1904; *Chronicle*, May 7, 1904; Scott, *San Francisco*, pp. 99–100.

13. Scott, *San Francisco*, p. 100; Burnham to Phelan, July 20, 1904, Burnham Papers.

14. Charles Moore, *Daniel H. Burnham: Architect, Planner of Cities*, 2 vols. (Boston: Houghton Mifflin, 1921) 1:234–36, states that Burnham did meet Phelan and others several times. His evidence was Burnham's diaries. Unfortunately, the diaries in the Burnham Papers in the Art Institute are blank for these days. Professor Thomas Hines informed me that Moore had access to Burnham's pocket diaries which the architect used when on trips, some of which are not in the Burnham papers. Hines, *Burnham of Chicago*, is silent on this question. On Burnham in the Philippines, see Hines, *Burnham of Chicago*, ch. 10.

15. *Chronicle*, February 20, 1905; Scott, *San Francisco*, p. 100; *First Annual Report of the President of the Association for the Improvement and Adornment of San Francisco* (San Francisco, 1905), p. 3; Burnham Diaries, May 1–11, 1905, Burnham Papers; *First Annual Report*, p. 4. The exact words are Phelan's.

16. *New York Tribune*, January 30, 1905.

17. San Francisco. Board of Supervisors, *San Francisco Municipal Reports, 1904–5* (San Francisco, 1907), p. 609.

18. *Chronicle*, September 28, 1905; Burnham to Eugene E. Schmidt [*sic*], September 14, 1905, Burnham Papers.

19. Burnham, *Report*, pp. 40, 41.
20. Ibid., pp. 43, 42.
21. Ibid., p. 44.
22. Scott, *San Francisco*, p. 104.
23. Burnham, *Report*, p. 36.
24. San Francisco Board of Supervisors, *San Francisco Municipal Reports, 1908–9* (San Francisco, 1909), p. 496.
25. Ibid.; Scott, *San Francisco*, pp. 19, 24.
26. Burnham, *Report*, pp. 68–70.
27. Ibid., p. 53.
28. Ibid., p. 34.
29. Ibid., p. 53.
30. Ibid., pp. 36, 70, 80–85.
31. Ibid., pp. 69, 70, 73.
32. Ibid., pp. 86, 73–74.
33. Ibid., pp. 79–80.
34. Ibid., pp. 67, 53.

35. Ibid., pp. 67, 68.
36. Ibid., p. 144.
37. The *Report* contains a list of "Small Parks and Playgrounds, Approximate Areas," which does locate twelve new sites. But the list appears on p. 191, after Burnham and Bennett have signed their names to the *Report* (p. 184). Thus it seems possible that they may not be responsible for the suggested location of the small parks and playgrounds.
38. Ibid., pp. 111–13.
39. For a discussion of the importance of seeing the total city, see Kevin Lynch, *The Image of the City* (Cambridge: M.I.T. Press, 1960), and Anselm Strauss, *Images of the American City* (Glencoe: Free Press, 1961).
40. "From the Hill Tops," *Wasp* 53 (June 3, 1905): 16.
41. Burnham, *Report*, pp. 114, 131, 145, and the drawing following p. 146, showing suggested architectural treatment.
42. Ibid., pp. 191, 114–68, 145.
43. Ibid., pp. 146, 167. For population density computed by assembly districts, see "Report of William Barclay Parsons on the Future of Street Railway Development in this City," *Merchants' Association Review* 10 (December 1905): 3–4.
44. Burnham, *Report*, p. 191.
45. Ibid., pp. 154–55.
46. Ibid., p. 157.
47. Ibid., p. 158.
48. Ibid., p. 167.
49. Ibid., pp. 156, 158.
50. Ibid., pp. 43, 86, 181–83.
51. Ibid., pp. 179–83.
52. Ibid., p. 35.
53. John W. Reps, *The Making of Urban America: A History of City Planning in the United States* (Princeton: Princeton University Press, 1965), p. 516; Herbert Croly, "The Promised City of San Francisco," *Architectural Record* 19 (June 1906): 433. This article was written before the fire, though it did not appear until afterwards.
54. Reps, *Making of Urban America*, p. 519; Hines, *Burnham*, ch. 14.
55. Scott, *San Francisco*, pp. 106–07.
56. Burnham, *Report*, pp. 145, 41, 88, 113, 158.
57. Ibid., pp. 88, 43.
58. For a detailed study of the groupings of major functions in the Central District see Martyn John Bowden, "The Dynamics of City Growth: An Historical Geography of the San Francisco Central District, 1850–1931" (Ph.D. diss., University of California, Berkeley, 1967).
59. Sam B. Warner, Jr., *Streetcar Suburbs: The Process of Growth in Boston, 1870–1900* (Cambridge: Harvard University Press and M.I.T. Press, 1962), p. 4. For a discussion and critique of this version of segregation see Jane Jacobs, *The Death and Life of Great American Cities* (New York: Random House, 1961), esp. chs. 8, 12.
60. Burnham, *Report*, pp. 112, 145.
61. David H. Pinkney, *Napoleon III and the Rebuilding of Paris* (Princeton: Princeton University Press, 1958), p. 189.

Chapter 5

1. James D. Phelan, "Historical Sketch of San Francisco...," in Daniel Hudson Burnham assisted by Edward H. Bennett, *Report on a Plan for San Francisco* (San Francisco: City of San Francisco, 1905), pp. 193–209.
2. Ibid., p. 208.
3. Ibid., p. 209.
4. See above, ch. 2; *San Francisco Bulletin*, October 14, 1904.
5. San Francisco. Board of Supervisors, *San Francisco Municipal Reports 1904–5* (San Francisco, 1907), p. 293. Block #67 was bounded by Polk Street on the east, Fulton Street on the north, Van Ness Avenue on the west, and Grove Street on the south.
6. The three meetings were held on December 16 and 23, 1904, and March 6, 1905. They are covered in the *San Francisco Examiner*, December 17, 24, 1904; *San Francisco Call*, December 24, 1904; *Examiner*, March 7, 1905; *San Francisco Bulletin*, March 7, 1905; Board of Supervisors, *Municipal Reports 1904–5*, p. 293. See also B. J. S. Cahill, "The Bond Issue and the Burnham Plan—A Study in Panhandling," *Architect and Engineer* 7 (June 1909): 68.
7. *Town Talk*, March 18, 1905, in Phelan Papers, Scrapbook No. 17, Bancroft Library, University of California, Berkeley.
8. See above, ch. 3. Theodore Bonnet, editor of *Town Talk*, later published a book called *The Regenerators* (San Francisco: Pacific Printing Co., 1911), attacking the graft prosecution, of which Phelan was a prominent advocate.
9. *Edwards Abstracts from Records* (San Francisco: Edwards Publishing Co., December 16, 1904); "San Francisco Manuscript Block Books," [ca. 1868–1915], vol. 9, Bancroft Library.
10. Cahill, "Bond Issue," pp. 68–69.
11. Charles Moore, *Daniel H. Burnham: Architect, Planner of Cities*, 2 vols. (Boston: Houghton Mifflin, 1921), 1:243–44, is uncertain when Burnham left San Francisco in March 1905. From Burnham's diaries it is possible to learn that he departed after March 2, but soon enough to arrive in Chicago on March 9. Thus he probably left on either March 6 or 7; Cahill, "Bond Issue," pp. 66–67.
12. B. J. S. Cahill, "A Plan to Beautify Market Street," *California Architect and Building News* 20 (October 1899): 110–19. See Mel Scott, *The San Francisco Bay Area: A Metropolis in Perspective* (Berkeley and Los Angeles: University of California Press, 1959), p. 102, for an illustration from this plan, with Cahill's signature in the lower left corner.
13. Burnham, *Report*, p. 68. Whatever land is left in the block is bisected by a new thoroughfare, the continuation of Eleventh Street to Gough and Fulton (p. 70). See also the map on pp. 99–102.
14. *Bulletin*, March 8, 1905.
15. Board of Supervisors, *Municipal Reports 1904–5*, p. 610. Moore, *Burnham*, 2:4, quotes a letter from Willis Polk to the effect that the Burnham plan was presented to the city government on April 17, 1906. Polk was in error, and others have erred by following him. John W. Reps, *The Making of Urban America: A History of City Planning in the United States* (Princeton:

Princeton University Press, 1965), pp. 514–16, is even further off the mark when he explains the failure of the plan to gain adoption as due to the fact that the plan was not presented until May 21, 1906, that is, until after the earthquake and fire. A plan was presented in May 1906, by Burnham and others, but it was a drastic modification of the earlier plan which correctly is known as *the* Burnham plan.

16. *Merchants' Association Review* 10 (October 1905): 3–4; *Bulletin*, February 27, 1906, March 15, 1906, March 25, 1906.

17. *San Francisco Chronicle*, March 4, 1906.

18. Charles A. Keeler, "Municipal Art in American Cities," *Craftsman* 8 (August 1905): 584–602; Herbert E. Law, "The San Francisco of the Future as Planned by Daniel H. Burnham, Builder of Cities," *Craftsman* 9 (January 1906): 511–21; for additional examples see *American Builders Review* 3 (February 1906): 49–78, and Eleanore F. Lewys, "A Dream of a Fair City," *Overland Monthly*, 2nd ser. 67 (March 1906): 276–88.

19. Herbert Croly, "The Promised City of San Francisco," *Architectural Record* 19 (June 1906): 426–36.

20. AIASF, untitled circular, Phelan Papers, Scrapbook No. 17.

21. Martin Kelly, "Martin Kelly's Story," *Bulletin*, September 24, 1917.

22. Ibid., September 22, 1917.

23. Walton Bean, "Boss Ruef's San Francisco: The Story of the Union Labor Party, Big Business, and the Graft Prosecution," typescript, 1951, Bancroft Library, pp. 141–44. This is a longer and more fully annotated version of the published work.

24. *Merchants' Association Review* 10 (January 1906): 9; excerpts from C. E. Grunsky's report to the Board of Public Works, October 25, 1901, in San Francisco. Board of Supervisors, *Municipal Reports 1901–2* (San Francisco, 1903), p. 190.

25. *Moody's Manual of Railroads and Corporate Securities, Seventh Annual Number, 1906* (New York: Moody Manual Co., 1906), pp. 1242–45; Walton Bean, *Boss Ruef's San Francisco: The Story of the Union Labor Party, Big Business, and the Graft Prosecution* (Berkeley and Los Angeles: University of California Press, 1952), pp. 109–10.

26. *Moody's Manual, 1906*, pp. 1243–44.

27. Bean, *Boss Ruef's San Francisco*, p. 115.

28. "San Francisco Manuscript Block Books," vol. 6 fifty vara block #75, #96, #141, #142; Hicks-Judd, *San Francisco Block Book* (San Francisco: Hicks-Judd Co., October 1906), p. 39. See also *Chronicle*, September 26, 1905; Bean, *Boss Ruef's San Francisco*, pp. 115–16.

29. Fremont Older, *My Own Story* (New York: Macmillan 1962), pp. 77–79; Bean, *Boss Ruef's San Francisco*, p. 116.

30. *Merchants' Association Review* 10 (December 1905): 12; (January 1906): 26; (September 1905): 1.

31. Daniel Hudson Burnham to Edward W. Bennett, August 10, 1905, Burnham Papers, Burnham Library of Architecture, Art Institute of Chicago.

32. *Merchants' Association Review* 10 (December 1905): 5.

33. See the testimony of Phelan, In the Superior Court of the State of California in and for the City and County of San Francisco, Department No.

11, Honorable William P. Lawlor, Judge, *The People of the State of California vs. Patrick Calhoun, Defendant No. 1436, XIX*, Trial, p. 2739, in A. A. Moore and Stanley Moore Papers, Bancroft Library.

34. *Merchants' Association Review* 10 (December 1905): 7, 9, 10.
35. Ibid., p. 11.
36. Ibid., (January 1906): 2.
37. Ibid., p. 5. The mention of "bondholders who live six thousand miles away," referred to the investment banking firm of Ladenburg, Thalmann and Company, which had financed acquisition of the street railroads and which represented interests in New York, Holland, Germany, and other European countries. Ernst Thalmann was president of the United Railways Investment Company. (*Moody's Manual*, 1906, p. 1243).
38. *Merchants' Association Review* 10 (January 1906): 5–7.
39. Ibid., (February 1906): 1.
40. Ibid., p. 1; *Chronicle*, February 13, 1906; Bean, *Boss Ruef's San Francisco*, p. 116.
41. *Bulletin*, February 8, 1906; see also for the following dates: January 10, 30, 31, February 10, 20, 27, 1906; etc. For the *Chronicle* see January 1, February 9, 1906.
42. *Bulletin*, March 16, 1906, and other dates.
43. Ibid., February 8, 1906.
44. *Chronicle*, March 15, 1906.
45. *Bulletin*, March 15, 1906.
46. Ibid., March 21, 1906; *Chronicle*, March 21, 1906.
47. *Chronicle*, March 22, 1906.
48. Ibid., February 13, 1906.
49. See Bean, *Boss Ruef's San Francisco*, chs. 6, 9; Phelan's testimony in *People vs. Calhoun*, pp. 2862–82.
50. *Chronicle*, March 22, 23, 1906.
51. Ibid., December 15, 1905, contains a story about a proposed new road. Phelan denied under oath that he knew of any such road in 1905, *People vs. Calhoun* pp. 2817–19.
52. *Chronicle*, March 23, 1906; *Bulletin*, March 23, 1906.
53. *Bulletin*, March 24, 1906.
54. Ibid., March 23 and April 10, 1906; *Examiner*, March 31, 1906.
55. *Bulletin*, April 3, 1906.
56. *Chronicle*, April 18, 1906. This edition was printed before the earthquake and fire.
57. *Bulletin*, April 10, 14, 1906; see also *Chronicle*, April 6, 15, 1906.
58. Abraham Ruef, "The Road I Traveled," *Bulletin*, August 22, 23, 24, 1912; Bean, *Boss Ruef's San Francisco*, pp. 117, 130.
59. *Merchants' Association Review* 10 (December 1905): 4. See also *Bulletin*, January 4, 15, 1906.
60. *Bulletin*, February 8, 1906.
61. *Chronicle*, March 25, April 16, 1906. In light of the news appearing in the *Chronicle*, perhaps the caucus should be called semi-secret.
62. *Argonaut*, April 14, 1906, p. 234; *Town Talk*, March 31, 1906, p. 4.
63. *Chronicle*, March 18, 24, 25, 1906.
64. See above, note 41.

65. Quoted in the *Chronicle*, March 25, 1906.

66. Ruef, "The Road I Traveled," August 22, 1912; Bean, *Boss Ruef's San Francisco*, pp. 115–16.

67. *Bulletin*, March 15, 1906.

68. The board elected in 1903 included a physician, a dentist, two attorneys, a stockholder, a journalist, a wholesale grocer, a retail grocer, two wine and liquor dealers, a partner in a dairy, a painting contractor, a salesman for a coffee importer, the cashier of a shipping company, and one blue-collar worker, who was foreman at a sand and sawdust company. San Francisco. Board of Supervisors, *Municipal Reports 1903–4* (San Francisco, 1905), p. 467, for the list of supervisors. Occupations were found in *San Francisco City Directory* for 1900, 1903, and 1905.

69. Bean, *Boss Ruef's San Francisco*, p. 116.

70. See above, ch. 2. The holdovers from those elected in 1903 included the dentist, the wholesale grocer, and the painting contractor, who, by the way, did not wittingly accept bribes. Those who took office for the first time in 1906 included a hackman, a machine operator, a carpenter, an electrician, a blacksmith who owned a fur store, a bakery wagon driver, a pressman, a piano polisher, a retail clerk, a saloon keeper, a grocer, and a furniture dealer. Several of the workingmen were also union officials. Bean, *Boss Ruef's San Francisco*, ch. 7.

71. Bean, *Boss Ruef's San Francisco*, ch. 4.

72. Quoted in Older, *My Own Story*, p. 83.

Chapter 6

1. John P. Young, *San Francisco: A History of the Pacific Coast Metropolis*, 2 vols (San Francisco: S. J. Clarke, [1912]) 1:468. Also, the 1868 quake was along the Hayward Fault, a branch of the San Andreas. Damage was more extensive in Oakland.

2. S. Albert Reed, *The San Francisco Conflagration of April, 1906: Special Report to the National Board of Fire Underwriters Committee of Twenty* ([New York, 1906]), p. 5.

3. *Report of the Sub-Committee on Statistics to the Chairman and Committee on Reconstruction* (San Francisco, April 24, 1907), p. 6.

4. Ibid., pp. 1–4; William Bronson, *The Earth Shook, the Sky Burned* (Garden City: Doubleday, 1959), p. 84.

5. E. W. Bennett to Sir Edward Grey, Great Britain Consulate General Papers, May 4, 1906 (microfilm in library of California Historical Society); *Report of Sub-Committee on Statistics*, p. 16. Bronson, *Earth Shook*, p. 83, guesses at more than 450 fatalities; Robert W. Kates and David Pijawka, "From Rubble to Monument: The Pace of Reconstruction," in J. Eugene Haas, Robert W. Kates, and Martyn T. Bowden, eds., *Reconstruction Following Disaster* (Cambridge: M.I.T. Press, 1977) p. 4, put the figure at 550, but cite no source.

6. *Report of the Sub-Committee on Statistics*, p. 4; John Castillo Kennedy, *The Great Earthquake and Fire; San Francisco, 1906* (New York: Morrow, 1963) puts the figure at $450 million.

7. Here again, one must estimate the extent of the destruction. Bron-

son, *Earth Shook*, p. 83, says 250,000 persons out of a population of 400,000 lost their homes; Kates and Pijawka, "From Rubble to Monument", p. 4, claim 220,000.

8. *New York Times*, April 20, 1906; *Oakland Enquirer*, April 18, 1906, in Bronson, *Earth Shook*, p. 47.

9. Printed letter from I. W. Hellman to Harrison Grey Otis and others, April 21, 1906, I. W. Hellman Papers, California Historical Society, San Francisco.

10. See photograph of the broadside in Bronson, *Earth Shook*, p. 45.

11. Young, *San Francisco*, 2:832; Bronson, *Earth Shook*, pp. 51, 74.

12. Young, *San Francisco*, 2:858.

13. There are several lists of the Citizens' Committee of Fifty. The most complete, which includes 133 names, appears in San Francisco, Board of Supervisors, *San Francisco Municipal Reports, 1906–7*, (San Francisco, 1908), pp. 755–56. Other lists, which contain several names omitted from the *Municipal Report*, are in Young, *San Francisco*, 2:838, and in *The Greater San Francisco Directory: Business Edition, 1906* (San Francisco: Greater San Francisco Association, 1906). American National Red Cross, *Sixth Annual Report* (Washington: Government Printing Office, 1911), pp. 153–54, prints a list of the original fifty names.

14. See Young, *San Francisco*, 2:828, for a list of subcommittees.

15. *San Francisco Relief Survey* (New York: Survey Associates, 1913), p. 33 (hereafter cited as *SFRS*).

16. Ibid., p. 9.

17. *San Francisco Bulletin*, April 24, 25, 1906; *SFRS*, pp. 11, 377–78.

18. *Bulletin*, April 24, 1906.

19. Ibid., April 25, 1906; Board of Supervisors, *Municipal Reports, 1906–7*, p. 766.

20. *SFRS*, p. 111, 10.

21. *Bulletin*, April 25, 1906. On the same day, the *Bulletin* carried another story which said that the transportation committee urged all who could to leave the city. Obviously the new policy had not permeated all levels of the organization.

22. The total leaving the city, under the auspices of various branches of the relief organization, from April 26, 1906, through June 1908, was only 4,876 (*SFRS*, p. 67, Table 14).

23. *SFRS*, p. 59.

24. Edward T. Devine, "Relief of the Stricken City," *Review of Reviews* 23 (June 1906): 684.

25. See the pamphlet by W. D. Sohier and Jacob Furth, *Report to the Massachusetts Association for the Relief of California* (San Francisco, 1906); *SFRS*, p. 99–100.

26. See the printed circular, "To the Executive Committee and Board of Directors, San Francisco Relief and Red Cross Funds, Inc." in Allan Pollok Papers, Bancroft Library, University of California, Berkeley. No date is given on the circular, but external circumstances suggest it was written in December 1906, or January 1907.

27. General A. W. Greely to James D. Phelan, June 15, 1906, in *SFRS*, pp. 387–90.

28. "Autolycus," *Stockton Evening Mail*, June 16, 23, 1906.

29. *SFRS*, pp. 25–27; minutes of a meeting of the Finance Committee, July 16, 1906, in Phelan Papers, carton 19, Bancroft Library, University of California, Berkeley.

30. John G. Jurgens to James D. Phelan, June 2, 1906, in Pollok Papers.

31. "Autolycus," *Evening Mail*, July 14, 1906. During and shortly after the fire, stores of food and other necessities were commandeered from merchants by the military and others for use in supplying the refugees. Those people who had their goods taken filed claims to be reimbursed, and many of them were. But each claim involved an investigation and delay, leading to charges of favoritism. For evidence that favors were asked for, if not granted, see Pollok Papers. Pollok was a member of the Finance Committee and the recipient of numerous requests, including one from Congressman Julius Kahn, May 21, 1906, asking for jobs for Kahn's brother and brother-in-law.

32. Committee of Friends of Refugees, "Refugees Attention," (broadside, [July 31, 1906]), Bancroft Library.

33. "Autolycus," *Evening Mail*, August 11, 1906; *Chronicle*, August 1, 1906.

34. One exception is the strange and partially incomprehensible pamphlet by Mrs. Mary Kelly, *Shame of the Relief* (San Francisco, 1908), in the form of an affidavit. Mrs. Kelly testified that she was maltreated because of her opposition to the Finance Committee and the corporation. Some of her statements sound convincing; others are hard to follow. See Sohier and Furth, *Report to Massachusetts*, for several references to refugee discontent.

35. *Chronicle*, July 14, 1906. See also the same paper, July 15, for a tongue-in-cheek account of General Greely driving the cooks and servant girls back to their former employers.

36. *Town Talk*, October 13, 1906, p. 10; Edward Devine to James D. Phelan, July 10, 1906, in *SFRS*, p. 397.

37. *SFRS*, pp. vii, viii. See also Phelan's letter to members of the Committee on Special Relief and Rehabilitation, June 29, 1906, Phelan Papers.

38. *SFRS*, p. 107.

39. "Autolycus," *Evening Mail*, January 26, 1907, chided the relief fund in January 1907, for sitting on idle money when people were in need of coal and food. The corporation refused to supply these necessities, he charged, because it would hurt private business. See also *SFRS*, p. 93, for evidence that the army encouraged retail drug stores by closing its free dispensaries in neighborhoods in which stores were later opened.

40. "Autolycus," *Evening Mail*, June 16, 1906.

41. Ibid., June 23, 1906; *Argonaut*, June 30, 1906, p. 3.

42. *SFRS*, p. 39. See a description of the rations allotted by the army, p. 381. There are scores of photographs showing San Franciscans cooking in the streets. For two examples, see ibid., opposite p. 40, and Young, *San Francisco*, vol. 2, opposite p. 802; *SFRS*, p. 43, Table 6.

43. *SFRS*, p. 44.

44. Ibid., pp. 44–47.

45. Ibid., pp. 49, 50, 54, Chart I.

46. S. B. McNear to James D. Phelan, n.d., in Pollok Papers.

47. Allan Pollok to Horace Davis, May 26, 1906, Pollok Papers; "Autolycus," *Evening Mail*, July 16, 1906; Allan Pollok to S. B. McNear, May 29, 1906, Pollok Papers; Red Cross, *Sixth Annual Report*, p. 66, which contains a barrel by barrel accounting of the sale of the flour.

48. William C. Edgar, telegram to Edward Devine, June 3, 1906, in Pollok Papers.

49. See Allan Pollok to S. B. McNear, June 25, 1906, Pollok Papers; "Autolycus," *Evening Mail*, June 16, 1906.

50. *SFRS*, p. 153, Table 33.

51. For a more detailed breakdown on the size of the various grants, see *SFRS*, p. 165, Table 45.

52. *SFRS*, pp. 167, 168, Table 47.

53. Ibid., pp. 171–73.

54. Ibid., p. 173.

55. Ibid., pp. 174–75, 184, Table 56; p. 185.

56. Ibid., p. 186, Table 57; pp. 187–208.

57. Ibid., p. 220, Table 64; Red Cross, *Sixth Annual Report*, pp. 53, 89.

58. *SFRS*, pp. 218–19.

59. Edward Devine, "The Housing Problem in San Francisco," *Political Science Quarterly* 21 (December 1906): 600–01.

60. "The Work of Rehabilitation in San Francisco," *Charities* 16 (June 16, 1906): 372.

61. Devine, "Housing Problem," p. 602.

62. Edward Devine to James D. Phelan, "Recommendations submitted to the Finance Committee, July 10, 1906," in *SFRS*, Appendix 6, pp. 394–95.

63. Ibid., pp. 396–97.

64. Devine, "Housing Problem," pp. 606–07.

65. *SFRS*, pp. 239–52.

66. Ibid., p. 220, Table 64, and pp. 253–57.

67. Ibid., pp. 258–76.

68. *Chronicle*, August 18, 1906; Devine, "Housing Problem," p. 607; *SFRS*, pp. 217–18.

69. *SFRS*, pp. 221, 81–85.

70. Ibid., p. 226, Table 68.

71. Ibid., p. 228, Table 70.

72. Ibid., pp. 230, 222.

73. Winnifred Mears, "How San Francisco Spent the Relief Fund," *The World Today* 13 (November 1907): 1097; Red Cross, *Sixth Annual Report*, p. 49.

74. James D. Phelan, "San Francisco—The Victory of Humanity," *The Red Cross Courier* 5 (April 15, 1926): 7.

75. *SFRS*, pp. 230–33.

76. Katherine G. Felton to Mrs. Mary E. Hart, October 8, 1907, in Phelan Papers, Associated Charities of San Francisco folder.

77. See comment in *SFRS*, p. 233.

78. *SFRS*, pp. 237–38.

79. I would like here to acknowledge a debt to the late Christopher M. Douty, whose dissertation, "The Economics of Localized Disaster: An Em-

pirical Analysis of the 1906 Earthquake and Fire in San Francisco," (Stanford, 1970) contains an extraordinarily thorough study of relief, rehabilitation, and the economics of recovery. I only learned of this work several years after completing the first version of this book, when a colleague referred me to an article by Douty, "Disaster and Charity: Some Aspects of Cooperative Economic Behavior," *American Economic Review* 62 (September 1972): 59–92, which mentioned Douty's thesis. As a footnote sadly revealed, the article was published posthumously, Douty having died in 1970 at the age of 33. He and I worked on related topics, during the same years, at neighboring universities. We often extracted identical quotations from common sources. Yet somehow we never met, which I deeply regret. I have benefited from reading his dissertation.

Chapter 7

1. Henry Adams to Charles Milnes Gaskell, April 23, 1906, in Worthington C. Ford, ed., *Letters of Henry Adams, 1892–1918* (Boston: Houghton Mifflin, 1938), p. 469.
2. "Comment," *Harper's Weekly*, May 5, 1906, pp. 617, 616.
3. *New York Times*, April 20, 1906.
4. See, for example, editorials in the *San Francisco Bulletin*, April 24, 25, 1906; an interview with capitalist D. O. Mills, *San Francisco Chronicle*, April 28, 1906, and the daily and weekly press.
5. William James to Henry James and William James, Jr., May 9, 1906, in Henry James, ed., *The Letters of William James*, 2 vols. (Boston: Little, Brown, 1926), 2:251. See also William James, "On Some Mental Effects of the Earthquake," in James, *Memories and Studies* (New York: Greenwood Press, 1968), pp. 209–26.
6. I. W. Hellman to Jackson A. Graves, April 26, 1906, Hellman Papers, California Historical Society, San Francisco; Ray Stannard Baker, "A Test of Men: The San Francisco Disaster as a Barometer of Human Nature," *The American Magazine* 62 (November 1906): 81.
7. Jean Jules Jusserand, *Proceedings on the Occasion of the Presentation of the Gold Medal to the City of San Francisco by the Republic of France at the Hands of Her Ambassador His Excellency Jean Jules Jusserand* (San Francisco, Stanley-Taylor, 1909).
8. *Bulletin*, April 26, 1906.
9. Ibid., May 6, 1906.
10. *Chronicle*, May 3, 1906.
11. William F. Herrin, "The Builders," *Overland Monthly*, 2nd ser. 47 (August 1906): 13.
12. *Bulletin*, April 23, 1906; *Chronicle*, April 22, 1906.
13. Clinton Rogers Woodruff to James D. Phelan, June 6, 1906, Phelan Papers, Bancroft Library, University of California, Berkeley; I. W. Hellman to Jackson A. Graves, April 26, 1906, Hellman Papers; *Bulletin*, April 30, 1906.
14. See *Bulletin*, April 28, 1906; *Argonaut*, April 28, 1906; "D. O. Mills on San Francisco's Future," *Leslie's Weekly*, May 10, 1906, p. 455.
15. See the comments by Herbert Law, *Bulletin*, May 20, 1906; by E. H.

Harriman, *Chronicle*, May 7, 1906; Benjamin Ide Wheeler, "The Future of San Francisco," *Century Magazine* 72 (August 1906): 630; *San Francisco Examiner*, April 22, 1906.

16. Charles Moore, *Daniel H. Burnham: Architect, Planner of Cities*, 2 vols. (Boston: Houghton Mifflin, 1921), 2:2, says that the telegram came from Ernest Graham. Other sources say it was Schmitz who sent the wire.

17. Ethelbert D. Burrows, "San Francisco: Yesterday, Today and Tomorrow," *New San Francisco Magazine* 1 (May 1906): 22.

18. *Examiner*, April 23, 1906.

19. *Chronicle*, April 27, 1906; *Bulletin*, April 27, 1906.

20. *Bulletin*, April 29, 1906.

21. Ibid., May 1, 1906; *Times*, May 1, 1906; *Stockton Evening Mail*, May 5, 1906.

22. *Bulletin*, April 25, 1906; *Times*, April 25, 1906.

23. U.S., Congress, Senate, *Congressional Record*, 59th Cong., 1st sess., 1906, 40, pt. 7:6245.

24. See ibid.; "Autolycus," *Evening Mail*, May 26, 1906, says that the word *earthquake* was more or less banished from committee meetings.

25. Daniel H. Burnham to Eugene Schmitz, May 1, 1906, Burnham Papers, Burnham Library of Architecture, The Art Institute of Chicago.

26. John P. Young, *San Francisco: A History of the Pacific Coast Metropolis*, 2 vols. (San Francisco: S. J. Clarke, [1912]), 2:506–07. For a brief account of Newlands's career, see Arthur B. Darling, "Newlands, Francis Griffith," in Dumas Malone, ed., *Dictionary of American Biography* vol. 13 (New York: Scribners, 1934), pp. 462–63.

27. Senate, *Congressional Record*, p. 6244.

28. Ibid., p. 6245.

29. Ibid., p. 6247.

30. Ibid., p. 6248. California had a standing claim to be paid 5 percent of the proceeds that had come to the federal government from the sale of public lands in the state. After the earthquake, attempts were made to have this claim acted upon. See a letter from Governor George Pardee to President Theodore Roosevelt, May 8, 1906, George Pardee Papers, Bancroft Library.

31. George Pardee to James D. Phelan, May 2, 1906, Pardee Papers.

32. James D. Phelan to Thomas Magee, May 4, 1906, Phelan Papers.

33. *Bulletin*, May 4, 1906.

34. James D. Phelan to Theodore Roosevelt, May 4, 1906, Phelan Papers; Senate, *Congressional Record*, p. 6435.

35. James D. Phelan to Thomas Magee, May 23, 1906, Phelan Papers; *Bulletin*, May 3, 1906.

36. *Bulletin*, May 1, May 3, 1906. See also the editorial in the *Bulletin*, May 4, 1906, praising Harriman for his "public-spirited action."

37. *Chronicle*, May 8, 9, 10, 1906.

38. Franklin K. Lane to James D. Phelan, May 11, 1906, Phelan Papers; Thomas Magee to Walter Bartnett, May 12, 1906, in Phelan Papers. For news about the incipient formation of the corporation, see *Chronicle*, May 12, 1906; *Bulletin*, May 16, 1906.

39. Frederick Palmer, "San Francisco Rising Again," *Collier's* 37 (May 19, 1906): 20.

40. James D. Phelan, "The Future of San Francisco," *Out West* 24 (June 1906):537; James D. Phelan to Thomas Magee, May 17, 1906, Phelan Papers.

41. Editorial, *The New San Francisco* 1 (May 1906): 40.

42. Typescript of meeting of the Citizens' Committee of Fifty, April 30, 1906, Phelan Papers; *Bulletin*, April 30, 1906.

43. Typescript of meeting of Citizens' Committee of Fifty, May 1, 1906, Phelan Papers; *Bulletin*, May 1, 1906.

44. See the lists in *The Greater San Francisco Directory: Business Edition, 1906*, (San Francisco: Greater San Francisco Association, 1906); typescript of meeting of Citizens' Committee of Fifty, May 2, 1906, Phelan Papers; *Architect and Engineer* 5 (May 1906); also the daily press.

45. *Bulletin*, May 3, 4, 5, 1906; see the discussion in Walton Bean, *Boss Ruef's San Francisco: The Story of the Union Labor Party, Big Business and the Graft Prosecution* (Berkeley and Los Angeles: University of California Press, 1952), pp. 121–27. The subcommittees and their members are listed in the *Bulletin*, May 5, 1906, the *Greater San Francisco Directory*, and San Francisco. Board of Supervisors, *San Francisco Municipal Reports, 1906–7* (San Francisco, 1908), p. 768. The number of subcommittees varied from list to list because of several consolidations.

46. Speech by Francis Heney, April, 1907, in *Merchants' Association Review* 11 (May 1907): 8.

47. See both the editorials and the news articles in the *Chronicle* for May and June 1906, especially May 7, 18, and June 10.

48. *Bulletin*, May 3, 5, 1906.

49. Ibid., May 5, 1906; Samuel E. Moffett and C. F. Gould, "An Ideal San Francisco: Some Preliminary Sketches of the Burnham Civic Plan," *Collier's* 37 (May 12, 1906): 14.

50. *Bulletin*, May 17, 1906.

51. Ibid., May 5, 1906.

52. *Chronicle*, May 8, 9, 1906; "Autolycus," *Evening Mail*, May 19, 1906.

53. *Chronicle*, April 27, May 8, 11, 19, 1906; *Bulletin* May 3, 12, 14, 1906; "Autolycus," *Evening Mail*, June 2, 1906.

54. James D. Phelan to Daniel Burnham, May 2, 1906, Phelan Papers; *Bulletin*, May 11, 1906.

55. Daniel Burnham, Diary, May 14–18, Burnham Papers.

56. *Bulletin*, May 17, 1906; *Chronicle*, May 17, 1906.

57. See *Bulletin*, May 20, 21, 1906; *Evening Mail,* May 21, 106; Board of Supervisors, *Municipal Reports, 1906–7*, pp. 788–93, for the plans in detail and a discussion of the meeting itself.

58. Board of Supervisors, *Municipal Reports, 1906–7*, pp. 788–93. It is interesting to note that Napoleon III had presented Haussmann a map of Paris with the proposed street changes drawn in four colors, "the colors indicating the relative urgency he attached to each project" (David H. Pinkney, *Napoleon III and the Rebuilding of Paris* [Princeton: Princeton University Press, 1958], p. 25).

59. Wheeler, "The Future of San Francisco," p. 632; *Bulletin*, May 20, 21, 1906.

60. *Chronicle*, May 22, 1906; *Bulletin*, May 22, 1906.
61. Interview with Daniel Burnham, *Bulletin*, May 26, 1906.
62. *Chronicle*, May 29, 1906.

Chapter 8

1. *San Francisco Chronicle*, April 24, 1906.
2. Ibid., May 15, 16, 23, 1906.
3. *San Francisco Bulletin*, May 5, 24, 27, 29, 1906.
4. For a succinct statement of most of these ideas, see Earle Walcott, "Calamity's Opportunity," *Sunset* 17 (August 1906): 151–58.
5. Hicks-Judd Company, *The San Francisco Block Book* (San Francisco: Hicks-Judd, October 1906), pp. 28, 40.
6. Frank W. Aitken and Edward Hilton, *A History of the Earthquake and Fire in San Francisco* (San Francisco: E. Hilton, 1906), pp. 183–84; *Bulletin*, May 14, 1906; *Chronicle*, May 19, 1906; *Bulletin*, April 26, 1906; *Chronicle*, April 28, May 3, 1906.
7. *Chronicle*, April 28, 1906.
8. *Argonaut*, May 5, 1906.
9. *Chronicle*, May 8, 1906. Additional evidence that de Young was the leader of the movement is supplied by an invitation, dated May 8, 1906, sent to I. W. Hellman and others, asking him to attend the second meeting of the group. The text begins, "Mr. M. H. de Young and other large owners of down-town properties . . . ," Hellman Papers, California Historical Society, San Francisco.
10. *Bulletin*, May 10, 1906; *Chronicle*, May 11, 12, 20, 1906.
11. *Chronicle*, May 23, 30, 1906. See also the report in the *Argonaut*, June 9, 1906, p. 2, in which de Young is credited with convincing people who had favored street widening and new diagonals that all changes were to be opposed.
12. *Chronicle*, May 27, 1906.
13. Ibid., May 26, 1906.
14. *Argonaut*, May 19, 1906, pp. 1–2.
15. Emerson L. Daggett, "Introduction," in Russell Quinn, *The San Francisco Press and the Fire of 1906*, vol. V in *History of San Francisco Journalism* (San Francisco, 1940), pp. i–ii.
16. "Autolycus," *Stockton Evening Mail*, June 2, 1906.
17. *Bulletin*, May 22, 1906.
18. San Francisco. Board of Supervisors, *Charter of the City and County of San Francisco in effect January 8, 1900* (San Francisco: Bender-Chaquette, 1907), Article II, Chapter II, Section 34, p. 44.
19. *Chronicle*, April 28, 1906; for the final report of the subcommittee, see San Francisco. Board of Supervisors, *San Francisco Municipal Reports, 1906–7* (San Francisco, 1908), pp. 770–75; for the governor's proclamation, George C. Pardee, *Proclamation by the Governor Convening the Legislature in Extraordinary Session* (Sacramento, 1906). Pardee attended some of the sessions of the subcommittee.
20. *Municipal Reports*, p. 767.
21. Ibid., pp. 770–75.
22. Committee of Forty, "Transcript of Joint Proceedings of Subcommittee on Municipal Departments, Special Session of the Legislature

and State Legislation, Charter Amendments, Judiciary," May 8, 1906, typescript, San Francisco Public Library. This transcript, which does not have notes of meetings before May 8 and after May 23, is one of the few I have been able to locate for all the subcommittees of the Committee of Forty.

23. Ibid., May 8, 18, 1906.
24. Ibid., May 21, 1906.
25. Ibid.
26. Ibid., May 21, 22, 23, 1906; *Chronicle*, May 26, 1906.
27. Ruef's original amendment in the Committee of Forty, "Transcript," May 22, 1906, and in the *Bulletin*, May 24, 1906. I have found no minutes for meetings after May 23. The official proclamation of the governor does not spell out the contents of the proposed amendment, nor have I found in the newspapers any version of the amendment as finally adopted by the Committee of Forty. There is a text of the amendment as first introduced in the special session of the legislature, containing both Ruef's draft and the provisions subjecting sales or exchanges of property to a referendum and preventing the supervisors from extending the terms or conditions of franchises. I am assuming that this version was the one which was approved by the Committee of Forty. For the text, see California. Legislature, *Original, Amended, and Enrolled Bills*, 36th California Legislature, Extra Session, 1906 (Sacramento, 1906), Assembly Constitutional Amendment No. 2, proposed by the San Francisco Delegation, June 2, 1906, n.p.
28. *Chronicle*, May 27, 1906.
29. Ibid., June 6, 1906; "Autolycus," *Evening Mail*, June 2, 1906.
30. Committee of Forty, "Transcript," May 22, 1906; "Autolycus," *Evening Mail*, June 2, 1906.
31. *Sacramento Evening Bee*, June 4, 1906.
32. Ibid., June 5, 1906. On June 5, Johnson argued against the Ruef amendment in the Assembly Committee on Constitutional Amendments. *Sacramento Union*, June 6, 1906. Troy enumerated his objections in an article in the *Evening Bee*, June 6, 1906.
33. *Bulletin*, June 7, 1906.
34. Ibid.
35. Ibid.
36. Ruef tried to introduce this provision as a separate amendment but failed. *Union*, June 10, 1906.
37. For the text of the amendment at various stages, see California. Legislature, *Original, Amended, and Enrolled Bills*, Assembly Constitutional Amendment No. 2, June 2, 1906, and as amended, June 8 and June 11.
38. *Union*, June 12, 1906.
39. *Bulletin*, June 8, 14, 1906.
40. "Autolycus," *Evening Mail*, June 16, 1906.
41. See Phelan's letter to Andrew Crawford of the American Civic Association, July 7, 1906. Phelan Papers, Bancroft Library, University of California, Berkeley.
42. *Argonaut*, May 5, 1906; *Bulletin*, July 26, 1906.
43. Marsden Manson to Walter Bartnett, July 31, 1906, in Bartnett folder, Phelan Papers; Marsden Manson, "The Builders," *Overland Monthly*, 2nd ser. 48 (August 1906): 18–20.

44. Marsden Manson, *Report of Marsden Manson to the Mayor and the Committee on Reconstruction on Those Portions of the Burnham Plans Which Meet Our Commercial Necessities and an Estimate of the Cost of the Same* ([San Francisco] October 1906), pp. 12, 23.
45. Ibid., p. 29.
46. Ibid., pp. 24–26.
47. Walter Bartnett to James D. Phelan, October 22, 1906, Phelan Papers.
48. James D. Phelan to Herbert E. Law, October 22, 1906, Phelan Papers.
49. Herbert E. Law to James D. Phelan, October 23, 1906, Phelan Papers.
50. Walton Bean, *Boss Ruef's San Francisco: The Story of the Union Labor Party, Big Business, and the Graft Prosecution* (Berkeley and Los Angeles: University of California Press, 1952), p. 162.
51. *San Francisco Real Estate Circular* 40 (October 1906).
52. *Evening Mail*, November 3, 1906. Phelan's name does not appear. The advertisement was signed not by individuals but companies, and the two banks of which he was either president or executive officer, the Mutual Savings Bank and the First National Bank, were both listed. Phelan did write an article, "Rise of the New San Francisco," which appeared in *Cosmopolitan* 41 (October 1906): 579–81, in which he seemed to endorse the street amendment. But it is possible that he changed his mind after the article was written, when the Manson plan had appeared and the graft prosecution was announced.
53. Because of the dislocations brought about by the earthquake and fire, the voting districts in the November election bear little relation to those of prefire San Francisco. Hence no socioeconomic analysis of the returns is possible.
54. C. F. Curry [Secretary of State], *Statement of the Vote of California at the General Election, Held November 6, 1906* (Sacramento: State Printing Office, n.d.), p. 29; *Chronicle*, November 8, 1906.
55. See editorial, *Chronicle*, October 22, 1906, and other editorials down to election day.
56. *Merchants' Association Review* 11 (December 1906): 2.
57. Willis Polk, "The City Beautiful," *Town Talk*, December 22, 1906, pp. 43–44.
58. Committee on the Reconstruction of San Francisco, Finance Committee, "Minutes of Meeting #8," December 28, 1906, in Phelan Papers, carton 23.
59. Walter Bartnett to James D. Phelan, June 28, August 6, 1907, Phelan Papers. This effort was in part an attempt to increase the confidence of Eastern investors in the fireproof nature of the new San Francisco.
60. For a full account of the London experience, see T. F. Reddaway, *The Rebuilding of London after the Great Fire* (London: Jonathan Cape, 1940). A shorter version, with a strong negative judgment of Wren's plan and the other proposals, appears in Stein Eiler Rasmussen, *London: The Unique City* (Cambridge: M.I.T. Press, 1967), pp. 99–122.
61. According to Sigfried Giedion, "in the Netherlands, members of CIAM [*Congrès Internationaux d'Architecture Moderne*] met secretly through-

out the Occupation to prepare for the rebuilding of Rotterdam, which later proceeded according to their recommendation" (*Space, Time and Architecture: The Growth of a New Tradition*, 5th ed. [Cambridge: Harvard University Press, 1967], p. 700).

62. Leo Grebler, "Continuity in the Rebuilding of Bombed Cities in Western Europe," *American Journal of Sociology* 61 (March 1956): 469.

63. For reconstruction of cities in Western Europe, I have relied on three articles by Leo Grebler: "Continuity in the Rebuilding," pp. 463–69; "Street Changes in the Rebuilding of European Cities," *The American City* 70 (August 1955): 120–21, 179–80, and "New City Centers in Europe," *Urban Land* (April 1955): 3–7. Much of the information in these articles is included in his monograph, *Europe's Reborn Cities*, published as Urban Land Institute, *Technical Bulletin No. 28* (Washington, March 1956), which is by far the most thorough discussion of the question I have been able to locate. For Japan, see Amos Hawley, "Land Value Patterns in Okayama, Japan, 1940 and 1952," *American Journal of Sociology* 60 (March 1955): 487–92. Of general interest is Fred C. Ikle, *The Social Impact of Bomb Destruction* (Norman: University of Oklahoma Press, 1958), pp. 211–24. I have been less successful in locating sources on urban rebuilding in Eastern Europe. One interesting if not authoritative source is a special issue of the Polish picture magazine *Stolica* (Warsaw, 1955), published in English, with pictures and text on the rebuilding of eight Polish cities, including Warsaw. On Stalingrad (Volgograd) see *Great Soviet Encyclopedia*, translation of the 3rd ed. (New York: Macmillan, 1974) 5:567. The other examples come from Grebler, *Europe's Reborn Cities*.

64. See Stephen Thernstrom, *The Other Bostonians: Poverty and Progress in the American Metropolis, 1880–1970* (Cambridge: Harvard University Press, 1973), chs. 2, 9.

65. Phelan, "Rise of the New San Francisco," p. 580.

66. Mel Scott, *The San Francisco Bay Area: A Metropolis in Perspective* (Berkeley and Los Angeles: University of California Press, 1959), p. 76.

67. See as an example the almost morbid interest of a Methodist minister, Joseph Carey, *By the Golden Gate* (Albany, N.Y.: Albany Diocesan Press, 1902), ch. 7.

68. The *Argonaut* is a good source for anti-Chinese sentiment. Ironically, zoning as a legal means for controlling land use was first used in the United States in San Francisco, against Chinese laundries, on the grounds that they were a public nuisance and a fire risk. They were banned from residential sections by an ordinance passed in 1885, which was later upheld by courts in California and the U.S. Supreme Court. See Scott, *San Francisco*, pp. 78–79, and John Delafons, *Land-Use Controls in the United States*, 2nd ed. (Cambridge: M.I.T. Press, 1969), pp. 19–20.

69. John Francis Dyer, "Rebuilding Chinatown," *The World Today* 8 (May 1905): 553–54; Charles Keeler, "Municipal Art in American Cities: San Francisco," *The Craftsman* 8 (August 1905): 597.

70. *Chronicle*, April 27, 28, 29, 1906.

71. Ibid., May 3, 11, 17, 1906; *Bulletin*, May 8, 11, 17, 1906.

72. *Chronicle*, June 16, 1906.

73. Ibid., May 14, 1906. See also an editorial, May 10, 1906, which

hoped that the changes in the streets and the building regulations would convince the Chinese to leave the area.

74. Ibid., August 4, September 30, 1906.
75. *Bulletin*, October 17, 1906; *Journal of Progress*, October 20, 1906.
76. *Bulletin*, May 12, 18, 1906; *Chronicle*, May 16, 1906.
77. *Bulletin*, May 28, 1906.
78. Ibid., May 29, 1906; San Francisco. Board of Supervisors, *Journal of Proceedings of the Board of Supervisors of the City and County of San Francisco* 1 (New Series), Number 5, May 28, 1906, pp. 53–54, 60–61.
79. *Chronicle*, August 5, May 30, 1906.
80. *Argonaut*, June 9, 1906.
81. *Chronicle*, April 28, 1906; I. W. Hellman to Directors of Wells-Fargo Nevada National Bank, May 8, 1906, Hellman Papers; *Town Talk*, June 2, 1906; *Chronicle*, May 18, 1906.
82. *Chronicle*, August 8–9, 1906.
83. Ibid., October 26, 1906; *Journal of Progress*, November 3, 1906; *Merchants' Association Review* 11 (June 1907): 4.

Conclusion

1. *San Francisco Call*, January 8, 1908.
2. See, for example, San Francisco Chamber of Commerce, *Fiftieth Annual Report* (San Francisco, 1909), p. 18.
3. Ray Stannard Baker, "A Test of Men: The San Francisco Disaster as a Barometer of Human Nature," *The American Magazine* 63 (November 1906): 90–96.
4. William A. Magee, "San Francisco Four Years After," *Sunset Magazine* 24 (April 1910): 457, wrote that Eastern money accounted for $10.82 million of the $163 million that had been loaned on San Francisco real estate in the four years after the fire. He was referring to loans secured by mortgages, and although it seems unlikely, it is possible that other forms of loans were made.
5. Mel Scott, *The San Francisco Bay Area: A Metropolis in Perspective* (Berkeley and Los Angeles: University of California Press, 1959), pp. 120–22, 154–58.
6. U.S., Bureau of the Census, *Thirteenth Census of the United States: 1910. Reports. 9. Manufactures, 1909* (Washington: Government Printing Office, 1912), pp. 78–79. The most comprehensive and schematic treatment of rebuilding along laissez-faire lines is in J. Eugene Haas, Robert W. Kates, and Martyn Bowden, eds., *Reconstruction Following Disaster* (Cambridge: M.I.T. Press, 1977), esp. pp. 71–96. The book also includes material on other cities facing the task of rebuilding.
7. John Carrère to Senator Francis G. Newlands, May 3, 1906, Francis G. Newlands Papers, Yale University Library.
8. Burnham's plans for Manila and Baguio "unhampered, under colonial circumstances, by cumbersome democratic processes," fared much better than his San Francisco work. Thomas C. Hines, *Burnham of Chicago: Architect and Planner* (New York: Oxford University Press, 1974), p. 213.
9. *American Monthly Review of Reviews* 33 (June 1906): 647.

10. "Autolycus," *Stockton Evening Mail*, January 26, 1907.

11. *Argonaut*, June 23, 1906, p. 2.

12. Joseph D. Redding, *The Practical Benefits of Municipal Adornment* (San Francisco: Downtown Association, 1911).

13. The Permanent Down Town Association was organized on the last day of 1907. Although it was probably not a direct descendant of the organization founded by de Young, its membership was restricted to owners of property in the retail district; therefore it comprised the same interests, if not the same individuals, which de Young had mobilized. See *San Francisco Real Estate Circular* 43 (January 1908), and *Merchants' Association Review* 12 (February 1908): 5.

14. See Walton Bean, *Boss Ruef's San Francisco: The Story of the Union Labor Party, Big Business and the Graft Prosecution* (Berkeley and Los Angeles: University of California Press, 1952), ch. 11.

15. Charles Tilly, *An Urban World* (Boston: Little, Brown, 1974), p. 2.

16. Charles E. Lindblom, *Politics and Markets: The World's Political-Economic Systems* (New York: Basic Books, 1977), p. 34.

17. Robert M. Fogelson, *Los Angeles: The Fragmented Metropolis* (Cambridge: Harvard University Press, 1967).

Index

Adams, Henry, 155
AIASF. *See* Association for the Improvement and Adornment of San Francisco
Alaska, 30
Allen, Father, 105
Alphand, Adolphe, 63
American Civic Association, 75
American Contracting and Dredging Company, 60
American Monthly Review of Reviews, 211
American National Red Cross, 136, 142
Archbishop of San Francisco, 206
Argonaut, 183, 207, 211–12
Ashbury Heights, 82
Associated Charities of San Francisco, 137, 145, 152
Association for the Improvement and Adornment of San Francisco, 72, 84–86, 105, 108, 111, 113, 119–20, 123–24, 159, 189, 203; banquet; 87; founded, 82; founding members, 83
Athens, 3, 58, 62–63, 71, 76, 78, 102, 211
Aurelian, 212
"Autolycus," 51, 138, 141, 144–45, 171, 183, 189–90, 194

Baker, Ray Stannard, 156
Balboa, Vasco Nunez, 64
Baltimore, fire, 130
Bartnett, Walter J., 141, 160, 162, 195–97
Bay Bridge, 95
Bay City Water Company, 52, 212
Bennett, Edward H., 86, 106, 114
Berlin, 87, 211
Bismarck, Otto von, 211
Black, H. S., 166
Board of Manufacturers and Employers, 34
Board of Supervisors, *See* San Francisco, Board of Supervisors

Bohemian Club, 81, 83
Boston, 9, 12
Bristol, 200
Broadway, 202
Brooman Act, 208
Brunner, Arnold, 73
Bryce, James, 5–7, 23
Building Trades Council, 32, 40, 45, 169
Burchard, John, 78
Burke, W. G. 122
Buckley, Christopher Augustine, 24–25, 61
Burnham, Daniel Hudson 1–2, 72–73, 76–77, 79, 155, 178–79, 198, 209, 211; agrees to do plan, 82; arrives in San Francisco, 1904, 84; plan for Chicago, 78, 99; plans for Manila and Baguio, 85; and reconstruction of San Francisco, 159, 162, 164, 168–69, 172–73, 175
Burnham plan. *See* Burnham, *Report*.
Burnham, *Report on a Plan for San Francisco*, 1–2, 4, 87–111, 123–25, 127–28, 198, 207, 212, 214, 216; accepted, 108; civic center, 87–88, 105, 107, 110; financial center, 88; Fort Mason, 96; "general theory of the city," 87; hills, 92–93; idea of order, 100–102; imperial vision, 102; Panhandle, 93–94; perimeter of distribution, 88; *places*, 90; Potrero Heights, 96; Presidio, 96–97; residential districts, 88–89; streets, 89–94; subways, 98; Twin Peaks–Merced parks, 97–98; Telegraph Hill, 96; and reconstruction, 155, 159–62, 170–79, 189–92
Burns, William J., 126
Bush-Brown, Albert, 78
Byrne, J. W., 81

Cable cars, 21, 90, 111
Cabrillo, Juan Rodriguez, 64

257

Cahill, B. J. S., 105–7
Calhoun, Patrick, 42, 112, 114, 117, 119–27, 172
California: American conquest of, 5; constitution, 167; economy of, 14; government, 160; legislature, 177, 184, 190–94; manufacturing in, 30; population of, 7,12; supreme court of, 184
California Promotion Committee, 120
California Street, 202
Carrère, John, 73, 164, 211
Carriage Makers' Association, 34
Charles II, king of England, 199
Chicago, 5, 130
Chicago Exposition. *See* World's Columbian Exposition
China, 204
Chinatown, 202–5
Chinese: in Oakland, 203; in San Francisco, 202–5
Chinese Consulate, 204
Chinese Merchants' Association, 205
Chinese Six Companies, 204
Cincinnati, 14, 16
Cisterns, 208
Cities: on Atlantic Coast, 12–13, 16; destruction and rebuilding, 178, 199–201; diseconomies in, 19–20; in Eastern Europe, 200; growth of, 12, 14, 16; in Japan, 200; network of, 12–13,17; of Old Northwest, 13; and suburbs, 21; transportation in, 21; in USSR, 200; in Western Europe, 200. *See also* Urbanization
Citizens' Alliance, 37, 47–49, 54
Citizen's Committee of Fifty, 133–35, 167–69, 202; Transportation subcommittee, 135–36
Citizens' Defense Association, 61
City Beautiful, 70, 104, 158, 162, 199; movement, 57, 72–79, 83; and reconstruction of San Francisco, 171; in San Francisco, 210
City Front Federation, 36
City government: American, 3; boss and machine type, 3, 23, 53; and efficiency, 23–24
City planning, 1, 2, 4, 177
Cleveland, 73, 80–81
Cliff House, 132
Collier's Magazine, 167
Columbian Exposition. *See* World's Columbian Exposition

Committee of Fifty. *See* Citizens' Committee of Fifty
Committee of Forty. *See* Committee on Reconstruction
Committee of Friends of Refugees, 139
Committee of One Hundred, 64
Committee on Reconstruction, 136, 155, 167–69, 177–82, 188–89, 191–92, 195–96, 198–99, 205; (Sub) Committee on Extending, Widening, and Grading the Streets, 171–75, 179, 183–84; (Sub)Committee on Parks, Reservoirs, and General Beautification, 171, 175–76; (Sub)Committee on the Burnham Plan,171; (Sub)Committee on the Special Session of the Legislature and State Legislation, 184–85
Commonwealth Club of California, 33, 109, 123
Community, 214
Cornelius, Richard, 42
Countryman, R. H., 186
Crocker, Henry J., 45, 83
Croly, Herbert, 75, 77, 99, 109–11

Davis, Horace, 143
Davis, Willis, 81
Deneen, Jeremiah, 203
Devine, Dr. Edward, 134–35, 138–40; and housing rehabilitation, 147–52
Dewey, Admiral George, 30, 65
De Young, M. H., 139, 147, 170; opposes replanning, 177, 180–84, 190–91; 198
Dingee, William J., 51–52
Down Town Association, 212
Down Town Property Owners' Association, 181–83, 193
Draymen's Association, 35–37
Dupont Street, 186
Dupont Street Improvement Club, 204
Duryea, Edwin, 171

Earthquake. *See* San Francisco, earthquake and fire
"Earthquake love," 156
Eastern capital, 162, 166–67, 210
Emmet, Robert, 65
Employers' associations, 34–37
Evelyn, Jon, 199

Fair, James G., 60
Fairmont Hotel, 55, 124, 132
Filben, Reverend Thomas, 203
Fillmore Street, 180

Finance Committee of the Relief and Red Cross Funds, 134, 136–37, 139–45, 153, 166
First National Gold Bank of San Francisco, 60
Flint, Frank, 164–65
Ford, Tirey L., 43–44, 122, 184
Fort Mason, 203
Fort Point, 203
Fusionists, 48–49

Gage, Henry, 37
Gallagher, James, 50–51, 206
Gaskell, Charles Milnes, 155
Geary Street, 182–83, 191
Geary Street, Park and Ocean Railway, 112, 122
Geddes, Patrick, 77
George, Herbert, 37–38, 47
Glasgow, 67
Gold, 13–14
Golden Gate Bridge, 95
Golden Gate Park, 65, 82, 94, 104–5
Gold Rush (1849), 2, 11–12, 62
Graft Prosecution, 52
Greely, General A. W., 137, 139, 147

Halsey, Theodore V., 44
Harper's Weekly, 155
Harriman, E. H., 157, 166, 169, 211
Harrison, William Greer, 86
Harvey, J. Downey, 51–52
Hastings Law College, 60
Haussmann, Georges, 3, 63, 78, 102, 111, 209, 211
Hearst, Mrs. Phoebe Apperson, 66
Hearst, William Randolph, 45
Heller, E. S., 184
Hellman, I. W., 132, 156, 158, 208
Heney, Francis J., 49, 126–27, 133, 170, 197
Herrin, William F., 40, 43, 48, 149–50, 156, 166, 184
Hibernia Savings and Loan Company, 106
Hilbert, F. H., 171
Hittell, John S., 13
Holland, Arthur, 43
Home Telephone Company, 55, 212
Hooke, Robert, 199
Hopkins, Alfred, 164
Hopkins, Edward W., 84
Howard, John Galen, 168, 170–71
Howell, Josiah, 109, 186

Hunter's Point, 203–4

Imperial architectural planning, 77–79
Insurance, 162
Irish-Americans, 206
Italian-American Bank, 209

James, William, 156
Jefferson, Thomas, 61
Jennings, Rufus, 120
Johnson, Albert, 191–93
Johnson, Tom, 46
Jones, Samuel, 116
Jusserand, Jean Jules, 156

Kahn, Julius, 161
Kearney Street, 202
Keeler, Charles A., 109
Kelly Martin, 111
Kiel, 200
Knight, Valentine, 199
Kohl Building, 172

Labor unions, in San Francisco, 22, 30–38
Lane, Franklin K., 45, 165–66
Langdon, William H., 197
Law, Hartland, 119
Law, Herbert, 109, 119–20, 124; and reconstruction, 165, 171, 173, 197
Le Havre, 201
L'Enfant, Pierre Charles, 78
Leningrad, 200
Lindblom, Charles, 215
London, 87; fire and rebuilding, 130, 176, 199, 212
Los Angeles, 114; Chinese and, 204; growth of, 2, 10, 17, 216; labor unions in, 22; manufacturing in, 8; population of, 5, 7; real estate speculation in, 18; as rival to San Francisco, 69, 71–72, 83; wholesaling in, 16
Louisville, 14

Macarthur, Walter, 49, 191–92
McCarthy, P. H., 31, 39, 48
McCreery, Andrew, 208
McEnerney, Garrett, 184, 206
McKim, Charles Follen, 86, 164
McKinley, William, 65
McNab, Gavin, 157, 184, 187–88
McNear, S. B., 143
Magee brothers, 106
Magee, Thomas, 135, 165–67, 197

Manson, Marsden, 195–96, 198, 210
Market Street, 89, 173, 181, 192, 205
Market Street Railway Company, 112
Marshall, James, 11
Martin, Mrs. Eleanor, 51, 106
Massachusetts Association for Relief of California, 136
Merchants' Association, 83, 114–18, 123–24, 198, 205, 209
Merchants' Association Review, 108, 114
Merchant's' Exchange, 81, 83
Metson, William H., 171, 185
Mid-Winter Fair (1894), 61
Mills, D. O., 208
Mills Building, 132, 172, 208
Minneapolis, 138
Minnesota Committee for California Relief, 144
Mission district, 193
Mission Dolores, 89
Montgomery, John B., 64
Montgomery Street, 172, 186, 208–9
Montgomery Street Property Owners' Association, 208–9
Moscow, 87
Mulligan, Reverend T. P., 206
Mumford, Lewis, 78
Municipal ownership, 67
Municipal Street Railways Company of San Francisco, 121, 123
Mutual Savings Banks, 60

Napoleon III, 78, 102, 197, 209, 211–12
National Association of Manufacturers, 33
National Municipal League, 74
Native Sons of the Golden West, 65
Newlands, Francis, 155, 160, 162–67, 211
New Orleans, 9
New York Chamber of Commerce, 136
New York City, 7, 9, 12, 77
New York Times, 155, 161
Nob Hill, 173, 205

Oakland, 7, 21, 203–4
Ocean Shore Railway, 51–52, 55
O'Farrell, Jasper, 89
Ohio River, 13
Older, Fremont, 49, 119–20, 123, 126, 197
Olympic Club, 86
Oregon, 7
Outdoor Art League, 123

Pacific Coast region, 5–6, 16, 18
Pacific Mutual Life Insurance Company, 209
Pacific Union Club, 81, 83
Painter, Edgar, 175
Palace Hotel, 85, 163
Palmer, Thomas W., 72
Panama Canal, 60, 115
Panhandle, the, 65–67, 70, 107, 109, 120, 185; extention of, 81, 86, 106–7
Pardee, George, 43, 165, 184, 191–92
Paris, 3, 58, 62–63, 65, 71, 74, 77–78, 87, 102, 211–12
Parsons, William Barclay, 114–18, 125
Partridge, John S., 48
Pauperization, 140
Pericles, 212
Perkins, George, 164–65
Phelan, James (father), 59–60
Phelan, James Duval: and the Association for the Improvement and Adornment of San Francisco, 82–83; and Burnham, 80, 82, 84–86; and Burnham *Report*, 100, 102–3, 108–9; and the Chinese, 203; and the Citizens' Committee of Fifty, 133; "civicism," 71; early career of, 59–61; and the Finance Committee, 128, 134–37; and housing rehabilitation, 148, 151; and the library site, 105–8; as mayor, 38, 46, 62, 64; and municipal bonds, 46–47; and municipal improvements, 67; and the New San Francisco, 57–59, 61–72, 74–75, 103–4, 216; and reconstruction of San Francisco, 154, 158, 160–73; and replanning, 178, 189, 197, 202; response to planning, 212–16; and Ruef, 53; and sale of flour, 143; and San Francisco, 81, 201; and the San Francisco Relief and Red Cross Funds, 137; and the street car controversy, 113, 116, 119, 120, 123; and the strike of 1901, 36
Phelan, John (uncle), 60
Phelan, Michael (uncle), 59
Planning, 214–15
Plan of 1904, 107
Polk, Willis, 82, 171–73, 198–99
Pollok Allan, 81, 143
Port Costa Milling Company, 143
Portland, Oregon, 2, 5, 7–8, 16–17
Portrero Commercial and Manufacturers' Association, 196
Powell Street, 182

Index

Presidio, the, 67, 82, 203
Property, rights of, 201-9, 215
Property Holders' Protective Association, 206

Quincy Street, 186

Railroads, 16, 18, 30
Ralston, William, 163
Real estate speculators, 110
Real Property Investment Company, 113
Redding, Joseph, 212
Reform, in cities, 27-28
Rehabilitation Committee, 145
Reinstein, J. B., 167-68
Relief Commission, 137-38
Rincon Hill, 20
Robinson, Charles Mulford, 73, 76-77
Rome, 3, 76, 78, 102, 212
Roosevelt, Theodore, 134, 165
Rotterdam, 201
Ruef, Abraham, 47, 55-56, 133, 215; and the amendment, 187-95, 197-98, 208-9, 214; appoints commissioners, 42; and the Chinese, 203-4; early political career, 38-39; election of 1901, 41; of 1903, 45; of 1905, 47-48; graft, 52-53, 197; and labor politicians, 45; as machine politician, 54; moderate on labor issues, 40, 43, 54; and municipal bonds, 47; on municipal ownership, 46; and Pacific State Telephone Company, 44; political ambitions, 41; and reconstruction, 155, 168-72, 174-75; and replanning, 177-78, 184-87, 212; and Republican Primary League, 39; and strike of 1902, 43; and trolley franchises, 122, 124; and Union Labor Party, 29, 39-40, 44-45, 50-51; and United Railroads, 44, 121
Russian Hill, 205

Sacramento, 7, 190
Sacramento Evening Bee, 191
Sacramento River, 13
St. Francis Hotel, 55, 81, 84, 132, 192
St. Ignatius College, 60
San Andreas Fault, 128-29
San Francisco: Board of Public Works, 111; Board of Supervisors, 52, 105, 108, 120, 124-25, 127, 133, 151, 168, 173-75, 183-84, 187-89, 193-94, 205-9, 212; bond issues, 46, 55, 69; bossism in, 24-25; Burnham plan, *See* Burnham *Report*; business and labor, 33-34; as City Beautiful, 82; city charters, 61, 64-65, 69-70, 122, 168, 177; city hall, 68, 129; city hospital, 68; city planning movement in, 209; civic center, 210; civil service in, 70; commerce, 8, 12, 14; cosmopolitan, 26; decline, relative, of, 6, 17-18, 20, 26-27, 210; depression, 27; dollar limit, 69; earthquake (1868), 129; earthquake and fire (1906), 1, 128-33, 154-58; earthquakes, 162, election of 1901, 41; of 1905, 47-50, 87; finance in, 5; fire (1906), 129-30; fire limits, 205-8; foreign commerce in, 5; future growth of, 109-10; geography of, 13, 90; government reform, 61; graft in, 105, 108; graft prosecution, 56, growth of, 5-7, 13-15, 17; growth, efforts to stimulate, 27; as hamlet, 5; harbor, 13, 58; harmony in, 156; hills, 94-95; history of, 104, 213-14; immigrants in, 25-26; as imperial city, 2-3, 62, 79, 216; instant city, 12; labor unions in, 22, 29-34; land area, 20; library site controversy, 103-8, looting in, 132-33, manufacturing in, 5, 7-8, 16-17, 30; as metropolis, 2, 5, 7, 10, 14, 17, 132; migrants in, 13; migration to, 25; municipal ownership, 41, 46, 70; natural advantages, 155; parks in, 94-98; politics, 104; population, 6-7; as port, 13; press, 183; rebuilt, 210-11, reconstruction, 2, 129, 154-76; reform in, 27; refugees, 135-36; rehabilitation, 144-53; relief, 133-45, 153, 215; replanning, failure of, 201; retail district; 180-81; sewer system, 68; street railways, 103, 111-27; street system, 89-90, 195-96; strikes in, 34-37, 42-43, 57; transportation in, 21-22; utilities in, 187; "Venetian phase," 21; waterfront, 68; water supply, 98; wholesale district, 195; wholesaling in, 15-16; as Yerba Buena, 15
San Francisco Art Association, 61, 66, 81
San Francisco Bay, 13, 15, 21
San Francisco Building Trades Council, 31
San Francisco Bulletin, 40, 49, 80-81, 109, 118-19, 121, 123-25, 157, 161, 193-95; on new San Francisco, 158; op-

poses replanning, 170, 179
San Francisco Call, 40, 48, 139, 179
San Francisco Chamber of Commerce, 27
San Francisco Chronicle, 40, 48, 109, 118, 120, 139; and Chinatown, 204–5; and fire limits, 207; on new San Francisco, 158–60; opposes replanning, 170, 177–83; opposes Ruef's amendment, 188–89
San Francisco Clearing House, 161
San Francisco Examiner, 48, 139
San Francisco Gas and Electric Company, 191
San Francisco Labor Council, 32, 35, 39, 169
San Francisco Produce Exchange, 83
San Francisco Real Estate Board, 108, 119, 123–24, 159–60, 196
San Francisco Real Estate Circular, 197
San Francisco Relief and Red Cross Funds, 137, 141
San Francisco Relief Survey, 135, 140, 142–46, 149–53
San Joaquin River, 13
San Jose, 60
Santa Cruz, 51
Schmitz, Eugene E., 55, 108, 132, 157, 162; and Burnham *Report*, 87; and Citizens' Committee of Fifty, 133, 135; and Committee on Reconstruction, 155; and election of 1901, 40–41; of 1903, 45; of 1905, 49–50; and fire limits, 207; first administration of, 41–56; graft, accused of, 46, 49, 197; and labor, 41, 54; as machine politician, 54; and Manson plan, 196; and reconstruction, 167–72; and relief, 137–38; social attention, 51–52; and strike of 1902, 42–43
Seattle, 5, 7–9, 18, 204; growth of, 2, 3, 17
Serra, Father Junipero, 65
Servius Tullius, 212
Sharon, William, 163
Shaw, Leslie, 166
Sloat, John D., 64
Social Darwinism, 158
Southern Pacific Railroad, 39, 132, 157–58, 169, 191–92, 195, 211
South Park, 20
Spanish-American War, 30, 65
Sperry Flour Company, 143
Spreckels Building, 129, 132, 159
Spreckels, Claus, 121, 123, 125

Spreckels, Rudolph, 113, 119–26, 133, 170
Spring Valley Water Company, 191
Stalingrad, 201
Statue of Liberty, 74
Stockton Street, 202
Stockton Milling Company, 143
Strike, Teamsters (1901), 57
Suburbs, 21
Sullivan, Mrs. Alice Phelan, 113
Sullivan, Dennis, 129
Sullivan, Frank J., 113, 116–17, 123, 125
Sullivan, Louis, 77
Sullivan, Matt I., 192–93
Sutter Street Improvement Club, 113–14, 119–20
Symmes, Frank, 114

Taylor, Edward R., 83
Teamsters, Brotherhood of, 29, 32, 35–37
Telegraph Hill, 82, 204
Tilden, Douglas, 65
Tilly, Charles, 213
Town Talk, 41, 105–8, 123, 139
Trinity Street, 186
Trolley, electric, 21
Troy, E. P. E., 191–92
Twin Peaks, 85, 96. *See also* Burnham *Report*

Umbsen and Company Realtors, 209
Union Labor Party, 29, 38, 50, 55, 123, 190, 206, 215
United Railroads of San Francisco, 42, 52, 55, 112–13, 116–27, 169, 191, 212
United Railways Investment Company of San Francisco, 112
Union Square, 182, 191
Union-Square Property Owners' Association, 182
Union Trust Company, 209
United States Army, 135
United States Congress, 155, 163–65
United States Government, 160–65
United States Senate Park Commission, 73
Urban growth, 6
Urbanization: on Pacific Coast, 7, 18; primate city form, 18; process of, 18–20; theories of, 6

Van Ness Avenue, 180–81, 203
Vienna, 87, 211
Vining, E. P. 42–43

Vioget, Jean, 89

Walhalla, 77
Ward, Dr. James, 203
Warsaw, 200
Washington (state), 7, 18
Washington Arch, 74
Washington, D.C., 64, 71, 77–78, 80–81
Washington Monument, 74
Webb, Beatrice, 26
Weinstock, Harris, 109
Wells, Asa, 39, 41
Wells-Fargo Nevada National Bank, 208–9
Western Fire and Marine Insurance Company, 60
Western Pacific Railroad, 169, 172
Wheeler, Benjamin Ide, 168, 173
Wheeler, Charles S., 121
White House Department Store, 113
Whitell, George, 121
Wilson, W., 209
Woodward, Thomas, 172
World's Columbian Exposition (1893), 57, 72–74, 77–78, 80, 111, 162, 164
Wren, Christopher, 176, 199

Young, John, 132–33

Zant, T. E., 191–92